A Journey into the

Transcendentalists' New England

R. Todd Felton

ArtPlace Series

Roaring Forties Press
Berkeley, California

Roaring Forties Press
1053 Santa Fe Avenue
Berkeley, California 94706

Printed in Korea

ISBN 0-9766706-4-X

Library of Congress Cataloging-in-Publication Data
Felton, R. Todd, 1969-
A Journey into the Transcendentalists' New England / R. Todd Felton.
p. cm.—(ArtPlace series)
Includes bibliographical references and index.
ISBN 0-9766706-4-X (alk. paper)
1. Transcendentalists (New England). 2. Transcendentalism. 3. New England—
Description and travel. I. Title. II. Series.
B905.F45 2006
141'.30974—dc22

PS3537.T3234Z86646 2006
823'.912—dc22

2006001093

To my Grandparents Felton,
whose love of knowledge has inspired a lifetime of learning

Contents

Foreword, *by Jeffrey S. Cramer* vii

Preface and Acknowledgments ix

1. Transcendentalism: An Introduction 2

2. Boston: Public Face 12

3. Cambridge: Training Ground 38

4. Concord: Heart and Soul 52

5. Walden: Secular and Sacred 80

6. Salem: Sins of the Past 102

7. Utopian Societies: Transcendent Communities 120

8. Amherst: "Paradise" 134

Timeline 149

Notes 153

For Further Reading 159

Museums of Interest 161

Index 163

Credits 175

About the Author 178

About the ArtPlace Series 179

Foreword

A book of travel can unseat the most armchair-bound reader. "A traveler. I love his title," Thoreau wrote. "Going from—toward—; it is the history of every one of us." For a Transcendentalist, a journey was not just an opportunity to place a label on one's trunk. It was a progression, not merely from one place to another, but from one experience to another. "The question is not where did the traveler go, what places did he see?" Thoreau asked, ". . . but who was the traveler? how did he travel? how genuine an experience did he get?"

A Journey into the Transcendentalists' New England gives us an introduction to the landscapes and locations connected with the some of the greatest of American writers, when the American renaissance gave voice to a literature that was unmistakably our own, a literature that could have been written only in America. To travel in Concord, in Salem, in Boston and Cambridge, in Amherst, is to visit with Emerson, Thoreau, Hawthorne, Alcott, Dickinson, and Frost, and to know them as living, breathing human beings, whose ideas and writings resonate today in significant and vital ways.

Unlike the guide in Frost's "Directive" who "only has at heart your getting lost," R. Todd Felton has at the heart of his book our finding ourselves. Perhaps that is why he chooses to make Concord and Walden the two central chapters of this book. No other places are more closely identified with the Transcendental world than that town and that pond.

This book leads us through the Transcendental landscape, both the literal land and the land as found in the literature, but it is much more than a roadmap to famous sites. It is a roadmap to the thoughts that established what were called "new views" but which Emerson reminded us were not new at all but just "idealism as it appears in 1842." Certainly, a book that introduces contemporary readers to a sense of idealism cannot be unwelcome in a time when so many seem to have lost their way.

Whether we visit one or all the places in this book, or simply enjoy reading about them as an armchair traveler, there is—to borrow from one of our New England poets—no frigate like a book, there is no frigate like this book, to take us lands away.

JEFFREY S. CRAMER
Curator of Collections
The Thoreau Institute at Walden Woods

Preface and Acknowledgments

Some of us can remember the first time we came into contact with the Transcendentalists. For me, Thoreau's *Walden* was one of the hurdles that stood between me and high school graduation. I'd like to say reading Thoreau in my senior English course changed my life, but it didn't. For years, all I remembered was a passage about the warring ants, because our house, like many houses in California, was occasionally infested by ants, and I thought the idea of them fighting each other was cool.

However, after years of teaching writing and running a writing center, I began to be interested in how groups of writers fed off each other's ideas and energies. In my literature courses, my students explored various groups of writers and how they interacted with each other—the Beat poets, the British Romantics, the members of the Irish literary revival—so when I saw an opportunity to delve into another group of artists and thinkers, I jumped at the chance.

My initial emphasis in researching this book was on the connections among the Transcendentalists—the ways they spurred each other on through one-on-one conversations and group discussions. However, as I quickly came to appreciate, Transcendentalism is first and foremost about forging one's own relationship with the universe, whether that is a spiritual, philosophic, aesthetic, moral, or practical bond. This individuality makes it hard to convey a unified vision of Transcendentalism, or even of its practitioners.

There is a danger inherent in any study of a literary group that someone of merit will be left out. Given the loose, shifting coterie that made up the Transcendentalists, that danger is manifold. I chose to limit myself to New England Transcendentalist artists and thinkers who, through written word or deed, had made a substantial impact on the culture of the nineteenth century.

Because of that filter, some worthy writers receive scant attention in these pages. Walt Whitman, while a major voice in American literature, was neither a New Englander nor a Transcendentalist, although he greatly admired Emerson and met with him as well as with Alcott and Thoreau. The poet Ellery Channing receives only passing mention because his writing has not had a lasting impact on the American canon. These are just two of the figures who would be discussed at length if this book were much larger.

Other names, too, deserve mention, not necessarily for their gifts to literature but for their gifts to me. My wife, Chris, has long been my best editor as well as my best friend. To her I give my heartfelt thanks and gratitude for sharing all of my projects with me. My two boys, Tim and Liam, have shared with me their curiosity and joy. Throughout my many months of research and writing, they were emissaries from a world I might otherwise have forgotten. Meg Lenihan has provided invaluable advice and support throughout the project. Some of the many intelligent and thoughtful readers who helped shape the manuscript were David Eisenthal, Karen O'Meara Pullen, and Nancy Rosenwald. Sherri Schultz did a fantastic job of catching errors and improving the prose.

In addition, everywhere I went, I met tremendously helpful people eager to share their considerable knowledge, including Jeffrey Cramer, curator of the Henley Library at the Thoreau Institute; Leslie Perrin Wilson of the Concord Free Public Library; Bob Derry of the Minute Man National Historical Park; Deborah Kreiser-Francis at the Old Manse; and Mike Volmar at the Fruitlands Museum. And not least on my list are Deirdre Greene and Nigel Quinney, whose faith and support have made this project a particular joy.

A Journey into the

Transcendentalists' New England

Chapter I

Transcendentalism

An Introduction

The idyllic town of Concord drew many of the Transcendentalists, who were a marked contrast to the staid farmers of this market village

Ralph Waldo Emerson.

"[Transcendentalism is] the very oldest of thoughts cast into the mould of these new times."
—Ralph Waldo Emerson

It is a delightful irony that the central figure of the Transcendentalist movement—the minister, poet, and lecturer Ralph Waldo Emerson—did not particularly like the word "Transcendentalism." The term wasn't even his; it originally came from German philosopher Immanuel Kant's 1781 *Critique of Pure Reason*. In *Critique*, Kant uses the term to refer to a class of ideas that "transcend" experience, but Emerson preferred to think of the Transcendentalist movement as one that looked toward a bright future: "What is popularly called Transcendentalism among us, is Idealism; Idealism as it appears in 1842."

While some considered Transcendentalism alarmingly radical and new, Emerson felt quite the opposite: "The first thing we have to say respecting what are called new views here in New England, at the present time, is, that they are not new, but the very oldest of thoughts cast into the mould of these new times."

The New Times

When the nineteenth century dawned across the sixteen United States of America, the nation was only twenty-four years old. Although European settlers had been living in the "New World" for hundreds of years, the fledgling country had not yet made its mark on Western culture and art.

By the end of the nineteenth century, however, the situation was quite different. In the intervening hundred years, the United States had produced important figures in every field of the arts and social sciences whose international reputations remain strong today. Because so many of these artists and thinkers were influenced by ideas and theories connected with Transcendentalism, understanding the movement's central tenets can shed new light on works in the fields of literature, philosophy, theology, and social activism created during this time.

It was also the unique combination of the "new times" with the particular ethos of New England that allowed the Transcendentalism of Emerson and other New England writers to play its central role in the "American Renaissance"—the flowering of arts and literature that took place in the 1800s. Exploring the interaction between place and idea can give us a deeper appreciation of the role of Transcendentalism as a defining cultural force in America.

Transcendentalism Defined: An Original Relation to the Universe

In his efforts to explain how Transcendentalism fit into the "new times," Emerson identified two types of thinkers, Materialists and Idealists. The Materialists were rationalists, absorbing data from their senses and constructing the truth of the world from what they could hear, see, taste, smell, and touch. Rationalism, exemplified by the theories of British philosopher John Locke, was the bread and butter of the Unitarianism that had begun to dominate the theological landscape in the states that make up New England: Massachusetts, Connecticut, New Hampshire, Maine, Vermont, and Rhode Island.

The Idealists (or Transcendentalists) believed, with Kant and Plato before them, that there are truths that come primarily from intuition rather than sensory experience. In his *Critique of Pure Reason*, Kant maintained that humans' understanding of God came from an intuitive recognition of the inherent truth of his existence, not from external proof. This assertion, along with supporting ideas from philosophers such as Viktor Cousin, Madame de Staël, and Jean-Jacques Rousseau, as well as the British Romantic poet Samuel Taylor Coleridge, provided a theoretical basis for the literature, theology, and social activism that would define Transcendentalism.

Although many literary critics view Emerson's 1836 work *Nature* as the founding document of Transcendentalism, it is clear that the Reverend William Ellery Channing's 1828 Unitarian sermon "Likeness to God" is the urtext of the canon. In it, Channing posited that there is a single spiritual entity present in all of us, which we are also all a part of (what Emerson later called the Oversoul). Moreover, Channing said that the best place to study and observe this spiritual unity was in nature.

Mirroring such British Romantic poets as William Wordsworth, many Transcendentalist writers looked to nature for inspiration and signs of a divinity. Because they believed that Nature (now with a capital N) represented all of humankind as well as God, they felt that much could be learned by closely examining the minute elements of nature as microcosms of the larger world. In addition, much Transcendentalist literature encouraged and valued the creative individual who, spurred on by the muse of Nature, used prose and poetry to pose new ideas and new connections. There was also a concurrent turning away from the neoclassical values of order, abstraction, and symmetry toward a more organic, free-flowing art.

The first widely distributed example of this more organic art came in 1836 with Emerson's thin volume, *Nature*. This ninety-five-page extended essay provided in its first paragraph a central tenet of Transcendentalism: "The foregoing generations beheld God and nature face to face. . . . Why should not we also enjoy an original relation to the universe?" Indeed, much of

Transcendentalism can be summed up as the individual's quest for an "original relation to the universe." This is much of what drove Emerson from the pulpit into his study to become a writer and thinker. It is why Henry David Thoreau went to Walden Pond and why George Ripley founded the Brook Farm utopian community. It is also what inspired the lyricism of Emily Dickinson's poetry and Nathaniel Hawthorne's dark glimpses into America's past.

This quest took place in both individual actions and group meetings, in specific written lines as well as large-scale social reform programs, and in the secular arena as well as the religious. As the Transcendentalist literary critic Elizabeth Palmer Peabody pointed out, the Transcendentalists were hard to pigeonhole: "Transcendentalism belongs to no sect of religion, and no social party. It is the common ground to which all sects may rise, and be purified of their narrowness; for it

Transcendentalism—Whatever Is Unintelligible

Transcendentalism is a loose affiliation of highly abstract, often vague, occasionally contradictory ideas. It is therefore not surprising that there are as many definitions of Transcendentalism as there are critics to write them. Many of these are intelligent and insightful attempts at defining the movement; some, however, border on nonsense.

For example, one of Emerson's favorite ministers, Father Edward Thompson Taylor of the Seaman's Bethel in Boston's North End, dubbed Transcendentalism a "seagull with long wings, lean body, poor feathers, and miserable meat." Rebecca Harding Davis, a young contemporary of the Transcendentalists, offered this account of how the eager philosophers of the movement were initiated: "The new dialect of the Transcendentalist was easily learned. They talked it as correctly as the Chinaman does his pigeon [sic] English. Up to the [Emerson's] old gray house among the pines in Concord they went—hordes of wild-eyed Harvard undergraduates and lean, underpaid working-women, each with a disease of the soul to be cured by the new Healer."

Christopher Cranch's caricature of the "transparent eyeball" pokes good-natured fun at Emerson's occasionally overblown figurative language.

One of the least helpful but most humorous definitions was rendered in the wry wit of Victorian novelist Charles Dickens:

> *The fruits of the earth have their growth in corruption. Out of the rottenness of these things, there has sprung up in Boston a sect of philosophers known as Transcendentalists. On inquiring what this appellation might be supposed to signify, I was given to understand that whatever was unintelligible would be certainly transcendental. Not deriving much comfort from this elucidation, I pursued the inquiry still further, and found that the Transcendentalists are followers of my friend Mr. Carlyle, or I should rather say, of a follower of his, Mr. Ralph Waldo Emerson. . . . Transcendentalism has its occasional vagaries (what school has not?), but it has good healthful qualities in spite of them; not least among the number a hearty disgust of Cant, and an aptitude to detect her in all the million varieties of her everlasting wardrobe. And therefore if I were a Bostonian, I think I would be a Transcendentalist.*

The Leading Lights of Transcendentalism

The holistic quality of Transcendentalist philosophy was reflected in the breadth of interests of its leading figures and in the multiplicity of connections that bound them together. This list of the movement's best-known members is divided into three vocations—ministers, writers, and educators—but few of these energetic ladies and gentlemen actually restricted themselves to just one vocation.

MINISTERS

William Ellery Channing, 1780–1842
Best known as: Unitarian minister
Connections: uncle to Ellery Channing; mentor to Elizabeth Peabody

Ralph Waldo Emerson, 1803–82
Best known as: minister and writer and central figure of the Transcendentalists
Connections: founding member of the Transcendental Club; cousin to George Ripley; mentor of and advocate for Thoreau and Alcott; provided land for Thoreau to live at Walden

Frederic Henry Hedge, 1805–90
Best known as: minister
Connections: founding member of the Transcendental Club

Thomas Wentworth Higginson, 1823–1911
Best known as: minister, abolitionist, writer, and Emily Dickinson's editor
Connections: edited and mentored Emily Dickinson; worked with Alcott, Parker, and Channing on abolition

Theodore Parker, 1810–62
Best known as: radical Unitarian minister
Connections: supported Ralph Waldo Emerson in controversy over "Divinity School Address"

George Ripley, 1802–80
Best known as: minister, founder of Brook Farm, editor of the *Harbinger*
Connections: founding member of the Transcendental Club; friends with Ralph Waldo Emerson and Elizabeth Peabody; brought Nathaniel Hawthorne to Brook Farm; coedited the *Dial* with Margaret Fuller

WRITERS

Ellery Channing, 1817–1901
Best known as: poet
Connections: friend of Henry David Thoreau; nephew of William Ellery Channing; lived with Franklin Sanborn

Emily Dickinson, 1830–86
Best known as: poet
Connections: idolized Ralph Waldo Emerson; submitted her poetry to and corresponded with Thomas Wentworth Higginson

Margaret Fuller, 1810–50
Best known as: writer, editor
Connections: edited the *Dial* with George Ripley; worked with Bronson Alcott; close friend of Ralph Waldo Emerson

Nathaniel Hawthorne, 1804–64
Best known as: writer
Connections: lived in the Old Manse (Ralph Waldo Emerson had lived there eight years earlier), and the Wayside (which he bought from Bronson Alcott); married Sophia Peabody, sister of Elizabeth Peabody

Henry David Thoreau, 1817–62
Best known as: writer
Connections: lived with the Emersons for a time; close friends with Ellery Channing; sold his boat to Nathaniel Hawthorne

Jones Very, 1813–80
Best known as: poet, mystic
Connections: knew Nathaniel Hawthorne and Elizabeth Peabody; attended the Transcendental Club

EDUCATORS

Bronson Alcott, 1799–1888
Best known as: writer, educator
Connections: worked with Elizabeth Peabody and Margaret Fuller; close friend of Emerson; opened Concord School of Philosophy with Franklin Sanborn

Elizabeth Peabody, 1804–94
Best known as: writer, publisher, educator, organizer
Connections: Brook Farm was planned in her bookstore; hosted Margaret Fuller's "conversations;" published the *Dial*; "discovered" Jones Very

Franklin Sanborn, 1831–1917
Best known as: educator, writer
Connections: taught the Emersons' children; friend of Bronson Alcott

consists in seeking the spiritual ground of all manifestations."

While the writings of these seekers could and would be appreciated as far away as India and Russia, most were penned within a fifty-mile half-circle radiating out from Boston, Massachusetts, between 1828 and 1854. Transcendentalism's trajectory began in that former Puritan city with the rise of Unitarianism, continued in Cambridge with Emerson's major orations, and settled in Concord, where Emerson and his circle made their homes. Walden Pond, in a sense, gave the world Thoreau, just as Hawthorne could never really leave Salem. The Transcendentalist utopian societies, and Emily Dickinson in her western Massachusetts paradise of Amherst, built their new worlds upon the old ideas "cast into the mould of these new times."

Inspiration from the Land: Transcendentalist Geography

Transcendentalism so fitted New England that it could be said to have sprung from the rocky soil itself. The region's heritage of religious orthodoxy, its belief in education, and the ruggedness of its landscapes make the New Englander a breed apart. Raised on lengthy orations from the pulpit and indoctrinated with the ideals of independence, the men and women of nineteenth-century New England were practical, well educated, and imbued with a belief in individual conscience. They wanted to know how to improve their lives but were leery of overbearing authority. They listened to their local ministers, joined social movements, and attended lyceums.

Boston's centrality to both the commerce and the culture of early-nineteenth-century America made it the crossroads of Transcendentalism. The Transcendental Club met here, as did the founders of the Brook Farm utopian community. The publishers responsible for introducing the world outside of Boston to the ideas of the Transcendentalists were here. Innumerable lectures, "conversations" (discussion groups led by a paid moderator), and educational ventures allowed Bostonians to witness firsthand the quest of the Transcendentalist seekers and to draw inspiration from their journeys.

Just across the river from Boston, Cambridge provided a training ground and launching pad for Transcendentalism. Home to Harvard College, this city and the college helped develop the young minds of the seekers before sending them out, frequently to the Unitarian pulpits of Boston and beyond. The college also hosted two Emersonian orations that set the direction for the Transcendentalist movement, "The American Scholar" in 1837 and the "Divinity School Address" in 1838.

Once the movement started, the small village west of Boston called Concord became its heart and soul. Although only Henry David Thoreau among the Transcendentalists was born in Concord, Emerson's return in 1834 to the town of his ancestors created a center of gravity there that drew in almost all of the Transcendentalists at one point or another. In addition to Emerson and Thoreau, the mystic and educational reformer Bronson Alcott, the reclusive novelist Nathaniel Hawthorne, the social reformer Franklin Sanborn, and the poet Ellery Channing (nephew of the minister) all made their homes in Concord. The list of frequent Transcendentalist visitors is equally as impressive: the feminist and Transcendental critic Margaret Fuller; Salem's mystic poet Jones Very; Brook Farm founder George Ripley; the impassioned Boston preacher Theodore Parker; Transcendental publisher and educator Elizabeth Palmer Peabody; and even Walt Whitman ventured out to Concord.

The environs of Concord also provided an ideal location for the best-known example of Transcendentalist living, Walden Pond. This popular swimming and fishing hole hosted Thoreau's two-year experiment in living "deliberately," and has since become a shrine that is both secular and sacred. While it was his day-to-day living at the pond from 1845 to 1847 that brought Thoreau closer to an "original relation to the universe" than any of his fellow seekers, that experience cannot be separated from the account he chose to give the world in 1854: *Walden; or, Life in the Woods*.

While most of the Transcendentalists were turning their backs on the rigid orthodoxy of their Calvinist past, one writer chose to pick through the ruins of his Puritan ancestry in order to develop his own relation to the universe. Salem, a seafaring port just north of Boston, provided Nathaniel Hawthorne with ample sins of the past to grapple with in his fiction. The city of the famous witch trials, fallen on hard times in the nineteenth century, was a perfect place for the writer of *The Scarlet Letter* to develop his mind and ideas. The town's proximity to Boston also allowed two other natives—Elizabeth Palmer Peabody and Jones Very—to embark on their own Transcendentalist quests.

It was precisely the flawed societal structures of their predecessors that many of the Transcendentalists felt held them and others back from their quest. Two of the largest and best-known attempts at forming transcendent communities

CONCORD LYCEUM.

GRAND ENTERTAINMENT

CONSISTING OF

Readings from Popular Authors,

BY

Miss Emily Shaw,

At Town Hall, Concord, Wednesday Evening, Jan. 7th, 1863.

PROGRAMME:

I. Scenes from Twelfth Night, . *Shakspeare.*
Act I, Scene 5, and Act II, Scenes 2 and 4.
II. The Bridge of Sighs, ... *Hood.*
III. Charlie Machree, ... *Hoppin.*
IV. The Soldiers' Rally, ... *Cutler.*

INTERMISSION OF FIVE MINUTES.

V. Jonathan to John, ... *Lowell.*
VI. Romance of Swan's Nest, . *Mrs. Browning.*
VII. Scenes from King Henry V, . *Shakspeare.*
Act III, Scene 4.
VIII. More Hullahbaloo, ... *Hood.*
IX. The Day of the Lord, ... *Kingsley.*

Single Tickets 25 cts. each, for sale at the door. Postage stamps will not be taken.

LOUIS A. SURETTE, President.

B. Tolman, Printer.

Lyceums were often the only form of higher education available to adults. Thoreau and Hawthorne, both notoriously withdrawn, served as secretaries of their local lyceums.

The Lyceum Movement

The lyceum movement in America began in 1828 in Millbury, Massachusetts, when a man named Josiah Holbrook began to organize a series of lectures for adults. The lectures were so popular that the idea spread, and by the mid-1830s there were several thousand lyceum programs across the nation. Many were in small towns, although New York and Boston also had active lyceum movements.

The audiences were usually mostly young and from the laboring and merchant classes. The lectures were hour-long expositions or demonstrations given by ministers, professors, scientists, reformers, or writers. Successful lecturers offered highly informative programs or a good laugh; the best were able to do both.

Nearly all the major Transcendentalist thinkers presented at lyceums. Emerson was the busiest on the circuit, giving some fifteen hundred speeches during his lifetime and one hundred in Concord alone. Thoreau delivered twenty orations in Concord and served as the curator and secretary of the Concord Lyceum in 1839, the only position in society he ever held. The novelist Nathaniel Hawthorne also served as the secretary of the Salem Lyceum for a season.

were George Ripley's Brook Farm Institute of Agriculture and Education, in the Boston suburb of West Roxbury, and Bronson Alcott and Charles Lane's Fruitlands, just west of Concord. Although neither of these communities lasted long enough to be deemed truly successful, their attempts to bring society into better alignment with Transcendentalist philosophies were admirable for their optimism, if not for their practicality.

Unbeknownst to these communities, for her work would not appear in print until the end of the century, the western Massachusetts town of Amherst was home to a writer whose poetry would, in many ways, explicate the dreams of the Transcendentalists more clearly than any other. Secluded in her tiny paradise, Emily Dickinson spent the mid-nineteenth century quietly developing her own highly original relation to the universe. While she never visited Emerson in Concord nor rubbed elbows with the intelligentsia who frequented Elizabeth Peabody's West Street bookstore in Boston, Dickinson is perhaps the ultimate example of the individualism that both inspired and limited the Transcendentalist movement.

The Right Time: The Historical Context

Although Emerson warned against endlessly searching "among the dry bones of the past" for humanity's place in the universe, it is impossible to come to an understanding of Transcendentalism without taking into account its historical context. The chaotic changes during the first half of the nineteenth century greatly influenced the ideas of the Transcendentalists. The population of the United States was approaching twenty million by the middle of the century, and, with the exception of the financial panic of 1837, which closed the stock market for ten days, the economy continued to grow right up to the Civil War.

Inspired in many ways by the preaching of the Reverend William Ellery Channing, Boston—and indeed all of New England—was abandoning the orthodoxy of Calvinism in favor of the more rational and liberal Unitarianism. This dramatic shift confused and discomfited many New Englanders. Combined with economic prosperity, however, it fostered a social and cultural awareness that bolstered liberal causes such as abolition, education, and women's suffrage, as well as such innovations as athenaeums and lyceums, which were important cultural institutions in early-nineteenth-century America. It was due in large part to the prevalence of these social organizations that the Transcendentalists enjoyed the modest financial successes they did (Emerson, for instance, made much of his money on the lecture circuit), and it was due in large part to the fresh perspectives of the Transcendentalists that these social organizations flourished in nineteenth-century America.

The success of the movement also owed a great deal to the increasing financial stability of antebellum New England. Boston was coming into its own as a shipping port, and the industrial revolution was bringing manufacturing to New England. Great wealth was flowing into the port cities of Boston, Salem, and New York. With the 1826 opening of the first railroad in Quincy, just south of Boston, and the doubling of the industrial output of the United States between 1840 and 1850, the sleepy market villages of New England became suburbs and mill towns.

The untamed wilderness frontiers moved farther west, and the undeveloped lands of New England were no longer the dark, dangerous places they had been for the Puritans eking out their existence in the hills of Massachusetts. Instead, the wild lands were now viewed increasingly as sources of inspiration and proof of the unity of the Spiritual with the Natural.

The years between the War of 1812 and the Civil War, while a time of great economic prosperity for New England, were also turbulent and occasionally violent. The issue of slavery and its expansion into the newly settled territories was never far from many people's minds as they struggled to reconcile their understanding of the past with an unclear American future. For many, the use of slaves underscored the

The Hudson River School

As Emerson urged the American scholar, in a famous 1837 address at Harvard, to turn his back on the "courtly muses of Europe" in order to create a truly American tradition, the visual artists of the Hudson River School were doing just that. Following the lead of Thomas Cole, a group of painters, mostly living in the Hudson River valley of New York State, were painting sweeping landscapes filled with light and color. Essentially concurrent with Transcendentalism, the Hudson River School, active from 1835 to 1870, was the first native school of American art.

Artists such as Thomas Cole, Thomas Doughty, Asher Durand, Frederic Church, and George Gatlin sought to display a vast wilderness filled with promise for the small yet uplifted human figures shown communing with it. Many key Transcendentalist themes—inspiration from the natural world, the spiritual unity found in nature, friendship among men of ideas—can be found in the works of the Hudson River School. For example, in James Hamilton's painting *Scene on the Hudson* the human figure is dwarfed by the scale of the natural world.

***Scene on the Hudson* by James Hamilton (1845).**

Walden Pond continues to be enjoyed by fishermen and literary pilgrims alike.

differences between the agrarian South and the more industrial North.

In 1836, the Massachusetts Supreme Court ruled that any slave brought within the state's borders by a master would be a free person. The next twenty-seven years, leading to the 1863 Emancipation Proclamation, brought further successes for the antislavery movement, such as the organization of the Underground Railroad in 1838, as well as losses, such as the 1857 Dred Scott decision, in which the U.S. Supreme Court ruled that Scott, born a slave, could never be a free man because slaves were property, not citizens. By the time John Brown led twenty-one armed men in an assault against the federal arsenal at Harpers Ferry, Virginia, in 1859, the nation was already beginning to break apart over the issue of slavery.

These events were being reported to the country's citizens at an increasingly rapid pace. With the proliferation of newspapers in the early part of the nineteenth century, and basic literacy for white adults near 90 percent by midcentury, people had unprecedented access to news and ideas filtered through a variety of perspectives (temperance, abolitionist, Christian, suffragist, and so on). Newspapers, magazines, and cultural figures were beginning to rival the clergy as influences on the ideas and values of the lay public.

The Transcendentalists, for their part, succeeded as a philosophical and literary movement because they did not demand adherence to a doctrine or prescribe a set of rules. Transcendentalism valued each individual as a spirit equal to and intimately connected to another. It encouraged each soul to develop its own original relationship with the universe, based on its particular situation.

That is why the Transcendentalism that Emerson spoke about to Harvard Divinity School students in 1838 could be felt and explored by Emily Dickinson twenty years later, some ninety miles to the west. What Thoreau accomplished by living at Walden Pond exemplified the same values and ideals that brought hordes of people to Boston's Music Hall to hear Theodore Parker preach. Transcendentalism provided New Englanders with a uniquely American philosophy, one of individuality and idealism, intimately tied to place . . . their place.

Chapter 2

Boston

Public Face

Boston, 1873.

Boston, New England's only real metropolis, was the center of the American literary landscape for most of the nineteenth century. Oliver Wendell Holmes dubbed Boston's State House "the hub of the solar system," and the phrase was quickly applied to the city as a whole by proud Bostonians, who had no doubt that their city was the center of the country. Situated on a peninsula jutting out into Boston Harbor, this growing city proved an ideal location for the publishing and distribution of many of America's first and finest literary works.

After the War of 1812, the city surpassed its neighbor to the north, Salem, as the leading port and shipping center of New England. By midcentury, the industrial revolution had brought both unbelievable wealth and an influx of poverty-stricken immigrants, which helped fuel the enormous changes taking place in the city. The well-ordered society of the Puritans and Calvinists soon became a hotbed for radical thought and theology, a fertile ground for social movements defending the oppressed and enslaved, and a bustling publishing center that gave the young nation much of its literature. Lectures, formal discussion groups, clubs, and planning societies debated and developed many of the ideas that were to make an indelible mark on American society. This was the Boston of the nineteenth century that helped introduce Transcendentalism to the world.

A Heritage of Rebellion

Ever since its founding on September 7, 1630, Boston has had a rich history of rebellion and conformity, radicalism and conventionalism. As a chartered English colony in the seventeenth century, the Massachusetts Bay Colony and its capital, Boston, were steeped in the Puritan values of hard work, moral uprightness, and education. These helped give the fledgling community stability as well as a sense of purpose and mission. John Winthrop, the colony's first leader, declared Boston to be "the City on a Hill," a beacon of Christianity whose success was a clear indication of God's approval.

This "blessed" city, as one of the major cultural and political centers of the thirteen colonies, played a pivotal role in the years leading up to the Revolutionary War. The Boston Massacre, the Boston Tea Party, the Battle of Bunker Hill, and Paul Revere's famous ride are all a part of Boston's historical pedigree. All are duly commemorated in the city's two-and-a-half-mile Freedom Trail, a red-painted path that leads visitors from its starting point on Boston Common to the major historical sites around the city connected with the birth of the nation.

Like the American Revolution, the literary and philosophic movement that came to be known as Transcendentalism found much in Boston to aid its growth. From the pulpits of the newly established Unitarian churches across the city, Harvard-educated ministers clarified and expanded upon the theological underpinnings of many of the movement's central tenets. The various Transcendentalist clubs and societies that formed to share observations and readings met most often in Boston. Schools and discussion groups formed here, too, and allowed the Transcendentalists to introduce their ideas to a receptive audience of inquiring minds.

Boston was the preeminent U.S. city in the mid-nineteenth century.

And, not least in importance, Boston housed the publishers who gave the Transcendentalists access to wider audiences throughout New England, the country, and the world. The city also provided the Transcendentalists with places to work and think, as well as a network of colleagues in related movements, such as those pressing for women's suffrage and the abolition of slavery. Although many of the movement's major figures made their homes in Concord, the world knows them largely through their activities in Boston.

Poetry of Insight: British Romanticism and American Transcendentalism

What Emerson and the Transcendentalists were trying to do for theology was in many ways a continuation of what poets such as William Wordsworth and Samuel Taylor Coleridge had done for English poetry at the beginning of the nineteenth century. In 1798, Wordsworth and Coleridge published *Lyrical Ballads*, a collection of their poems. In the preface to the book (which was republished in 1800 and 1802 with extended and revised prefaces), Wordsworth defined the main tenets of the Romantic movement: an emphasis on individual experience and imagination along with a concurrent breaking away from traditional forms and imaginative conformity. Wordsworth also strove to use the language of the common man to illustrate his unique visions.

Wordsworth's long autobiographical poem *The Prelude*, Coleridge's *The Rhyme of the Ancient Mariner*, and the shorter poems of John Keats and Percy Bysshe Shelley are among the best-known works of the Romantics.

The Reverend William Ellery Channing attracted the attention and admiration of many of the Transcendentalists for his radical sermons, just as he attracted the ire of some of Harvard College's more dogmatic leaders.

Pulpits of Change

The energy and momentum of Boston's early-nineteenth-century Unitarianism provided the foundation and the freedom for a new theology, divorced from the restricting doctrine of Calvinism. Unitarianism supplied, literally and figuratively, the forums where clergy and laypeople could hold spiritual beliefs up to the new light supplied by German philosophers such as Immanuel Kant and British Romantic writers such as Samuel Taylor Coleridge, William Wordsworth, and Percy Bysshe Shelley.

While much of the initial Transcendentalist activity took place at Harvard Divinity School in Cambridge, where the appointment of the liberal Henry Ware Sr. to the Hollis Chair of Divinity in 1805 was viewed as a landmark victory for liberal Christianity, the theological underpinnings of Transcendentalism were born across the Charles River at ❶ **the Federal Street Church, 100 Federal Street** (now the regional headquarters of Bank of America). The Reverend William Ellery Channing served as minister here from 1780 until his death in 1842.

Channing's landmark sermon "Likeness to God," delivered in 1828, contains many of the fundamental beliefs of the Transcendentalist movement. "True religion consists in proposing as our great end, a growing likeness to the Supreme Being," he proclaimed, and this likeness "belongs to man's higher or spiritual nature." For a community that had persecuted Anne Hutchinson for suggesting that the Holy Ghost could reside in a "justified" person, this was a radical position.

Channing's sermon further laid out the path for the Transcendentalists. First, it gave parishioners permission to look within for proof of a deity that the

Church had claimed could be found only in the miracles described in the Bible. In order to know that deity, Channing said, humans must know themselves: "That unbounded spiritual energy which we call God, is conceived by us only through consciousness, through the knowledge of ourselves." In order to understand what they experienced while looking inward, Channing encouraged his audience to develop "a kindred mind, which interprets the universe by itself," as opposed to an "outward eye," which perceives merely the surface of things.

Channing also brought his audience's attention literally outside, to nature, which previously had been more connected with primeval danger and the devil. In a move that anticipated Thoreau's *Walden*, Channing found God "in the structure of a single leaf" and encouraged his audience to "discern more and more of God in every thing, from the frail flower to the everlasting stars." In doing so, he said, "true religion thus blends itself with common life," and his followers could "strive to awaken in men a consciousness of the heavenly treasure within them."

These ideas brought animosity both from the established churches and from Harvard's more dogmatic leaders, but they also attracted some of the finest minds of the time to his pews. Among his acolytes was Elizabeth Palmer Peabody, a young woman from Salem eager to engage him in a discussion of ideas. Soon the future publisher and critic was helping the minister prepare his sermons and acting as a theological sounding board. She served as his unofficial secretary for ten years and did much to aid the progress of his liberal theology.

Channing was not the only progressive thinker in Boston, however. Another theologian who became an integral part of the Transcendentalist movement was George Ripley, the minister of the Purchase Street Church from 1826 to 1841. In addition to his sermons and published pamphlets promoting

Federal Street Church was the home pulpit of the Reverend William Ellery Channing, who was viewed by many of the Transcendentalists as the father of their movement.

Transcendentalism, Ripley was involved in a number of significant activities of the movement. He was a founding member of the Transcendental Club, and he carried on a lengthy published debate with Harvard professor Andrews Norton in defense of Emerson's "Divinity School Address" of 1838. But his best-known contribution to Transcendentalism was an experiment in utopian living known as the Brook Farm Institute of Agriculture and Education (see chapter 7).

Boston Common today looks much the same as it did to the members of the Transcendental Club.

Another progressive voice in Unitarianism, perhaps its most radical, was that of Theodore Parker. A native of Watertown, Massachusetts, Parker graduated from Harvard Divinity School after being mentored by fellow Transcendentalist and Unitarian minister Convers Francis. In 1837 he landed a job with the small sixty-member Spring Street Church in the Boston suburb of West Roxbury.

Parker provoked the anger of the Boston Unitarian establishment with his 1841 ordination sermon, "Discourses on the Transient and Permanent in Christianity." In examining what was inherent and true in the Christian faith, Parker tried to push his audience out from behind the metaphorical skirts of their ministers and into a firsthand relationship with God by first questioning the necessity of

Elizabeth Palmer Peabody was involved at some level with many Transcendentalist ventures. Her West Street bookstore was an important gathering place for Boston's literati. Brook Farm was conceived in its back rooms; the *Dial* was produced there. The bookstore even hosted the marriage ceremonies of Sophia Peabody to Nathaniel Hawthorne and Mary Peabody to Horace Mann.

the ministers, and even Jesus, in understanding religious truths:

> *Yet it seems difficult to conceive any reason, why moral and religious truths should rest for their support on the personal authority of their revealer, any more than the truths of science on that of him who makes them known first or most clearly. It is hard to see why the great truths of Christianity rest on the personal authority of Jesus, more than the axioms of geometry rest on the personal authority of Euclid or Archimedes. The authority of Jesus, as of all teachers, one would naturally think, must rest on the truth of his words, and not their truth on his authority.*

Parker also attempted to wrest the moral authority of religion out of the hands of the ministers and into the individual consciences of his congregation: "If Christianity were true, we should still think it was so, not because its record was written by infallible pens; nor because it was lived out by an infallible teacher, — but that it is true, like the axioms of geometry, because it is true, and is to be tried by the oracle God places in the breast." This "oracle" in the breasts of his

Theodore Parker's fiery and radical speeches brought many to his pews at the Spring Street Church in West Roxbury and, later, Boston's Music Hall.

congregation allowed them to see that "Christianity is a simple thing; very simple. It is absolute, pure Morality; absolute, pure Religion; the love of man; the love of God acting without let or hindrance. The only creed it lays down is the great truth which springs up spontaneous in the holy heart—there is a God."

Parker clearly understood that the radicalism of his statements would provoke a strong reaction. He attempted to defend himself against cries of blasphemy by pointing out that religion is always in a state of change: "The heresy of one age is the orthodox belief and 'only infallible rule' of the next."

Unfortunately for him, much of Unitarian Boston was not ready for his progressive thought. An anonymous layperson, writing in the newspapers following the sermon, made this point abundantly clear: "I would rather see every Unitarian congregation in our land dissolved and every one of our churches razed to the ground, than to assist in placing a man entertaining the sentiments of Theodore Parker in one of our pulpits."

Parker did remain in his pulpit until 1845, however, when he resigned to found his own Unitarian church in

Boston. His new Twenty-eighth Congregational Society was enormous, and he often preached to thousands of worshippers in Boston's Music Hall.

It is perhaps impossible to complete any discussion of the connections between Unitarianism and Transcendentalism without mentioning Ralph Waldo Emerson's three-year post at the Unitarian Second Church of Boston. His father had been the minister of the First Parish Church of Boston, just as his grandfather, William Emerson, had been the minister of Concord's First Church. The younger Emerson's stint, however, was perhaps as unremarkable as his passage through Harvard College and Harvard Divinity School. Although a gifted orator and a passionate examiner of theological ideas, Emerson was not a complete success as a minister; he had difficulty connecting with his parishioners and was a weak spiritual guide, partly due to his ambivalence about his position.

Parker's Twenty-eighth Congretional Society rented Boston's Music Hall and filled it with thousands who came to hear Parker preach.

In his letter of resignation and his farewell sermon of 1832, Emerson explained that he could not, in good conscience, perform the communion when he did not believe that Jesus meant for it to be a ceremony. Privately, though, he admitted to the difficulty of having to pray publicly when he was not moved to do so. He was also not confident in his ability to perform all the duties required of a minister. His departure from the church was not a clean break, though; he continued to speak from the pulpit both in and around Boston, as well as back in Concord, for many years; toward the end of his life, he returned to the Unitarian church as a member.

Like-Minded Seekers

While there would remain close ties between the two, Transcendentalism soon outgrew the confines of Unitarianism and needed forums beyond pulpits and theological debates. Although Transcendentalist ideas were discussed informally during innumerable dinners, walks, and post-lecture conversations, two meeting places played an especially important role in fashioning this new American literary and philosophical tradition: the Transcendental Club and Elizabeth Palmer Peabody's West Street bookstore and foreign language library.

The Transcendental Club officially began on September 19, 1836, as a meeting of what Frederic Francis Hedge called "like-minded seekers." Hedge, Ralph Waldo Emerson, and George Ripley had met after Harvard's bicentennial celebration the week before and created what they called a "symposium" to discuss ideas of religion, philosophy, literature, education, and culture away from the restrictive arenas of the church and Harvard. The first meeting took place at George Ripley's house in Boston. Philosopher and educator Bronson Alcott, Unitarian minister James Freeman Clarke, and a handful of Harvard Divinity School students joined Ripley, Hedge, and Emerson.

Over the next four years, the group met nearly every month when Frederic Hedge came to Boston from his home in Bangor, Maine. The meetings were held at members' houses around Boston and Concord, although never in Cambridge. The loose and rotating membership included many of the intellectual giants of the era: educator and publisher Elizabeth Peabody; the feminist critic Margaret Fuller; the poet Jones Very; Ellery Channing, the poet who was Reverend Channing's nephew; the poet and caricaturist Christopher Cranch; and many others.

The Transcendental Club was not for the faint of heart or mind; the topics set for the meetings, or "symposiums" as they preferred to call them, were as weighty as they were abstruse. Over the four years of their meetings, the group covered such philosophical topics as mysticism, genius, education, religion, pantheism, and inspiration, to name just a few.

Unitarianism vis-à-vis Transcendentalism

Although Unitarianism and Transcendentalism are clearly linked, there are some important differences between the two. First, the Unitarianism of the nineteenth century was an established religion supported by Harvard Divinity School as well as by an increasing number of churches, ministers, congregations, and associations across New England. Transcendentalism, in contrast, was expounded by a loose affiliation of philosophers, ministers, writers, and social activists who believed in many of the same ideas but differed radically in other ways.

Of the many subtle differences between Unitarianism and Transcendentalism, perhaps the most notable was one of mere degrees: the Transcendentalists felt that Unitarianism did not go far enough in embracing the passionate and intuitive communion with the Divinity they believed was an integral part of all people. They often characterized Unitarianism as too rationalistic and lacking warmth; Emerson went so far as to call it "corpse-cold." For their part, the Unitarians were uneasy with the criticism of organized religion inherent in many of the Transcendentalist stances.

In more recent times, the Unitarian establishment, especially after its merger with the Universalists in 1961, has embraced those same philosophers who were ostracized for their radical views in the nineteenth century. The Unitarian Universalist website now features biographies of ministers including Channing, Parker, Emerson, and Ripley, who in their day had contentious and rocky relationships with the church. The website also devotes space to more secular Transcendentalists such as Bronson Alcott, Nathaniel Hawthorne, and Henry David Thoreau.

The Saturday Club

Twenty years after he helped found the Transcendental Club, Emerson was happy to be a part of another social club, the Saturday Club, which met most often at ❷ the Parker House, a hotel and restaurant at 60 School Street. It was much like the Transcendental Club in that it featured dinner and conversation among brilliant and highly educated men (although the Transcendental Club had included women too) and spawned a publication—in this case, the *Atlantic Monthly.*

Saturday Club members were more eclectic than the Transcendentalists, though, and by no means philosophically similar. They included the scientist Louis Agassiz, Judge Hoar of Concord, Oliver Wendell Holmes, Henry Wadsworth Longfellow from Harvard, James Elliot Cabot, and various Transcendentalists in addition to Emerson, Alcott, and even the ever-shy novelist Nathaniel Hawthorne.

The best-known account of the club is Holmes's poem "At the Saturday Club," published in the January 1884 *Atlantic Monthly*. In it, Holmes memorializes his club friends, including Hawthorne, Alcott, and Emerson:

Hawthorne: *The great ROMANCER, hid beneath his veil*
Like the stern preacher of his sombre tale;
Virile in strength, yet bashful as a girl
Prouder than Hester, sensitive as Pearl.

Alcott: *From his mild throng of worshippers released*
Our Concord Delphi sends its chosen priest,
Prophet or poet, mystic, sage, or seer,
By every title always welcome here.

The Parker House opened in 1855; its renovated version is now part of Boston's Freedom Trail and Literary Trail.

Emerson: *Ask you what name this prisoned spirit bears*
While with ourselves this fleeting breath it shares?
Till angels greet him with a sweeter one
In Heaven, on earth we call him EMERSON.

The *Dial*

Many of the Transcendental Club members sought an outlet for their ideas, an organ for publishing their views and inviting others to join them. At the suggestion of member Frederic Francis Hedge, the club began thinking about a journal. By the time the spring of 1840 had arrived, the club was serious about the undertaking and had appointed Margaret Fuller as the editor. Bronson Alcott provided the name, "The Dial," and George Ripley agreed to be the assistant editor.

Ripley announced the journal in a prospectus published on May 4, and articles from Emerson, Thoreau, Fuller, Parker, Hedge, and Alcott were lined up for the first edition, which was published in July. Subscriptions to the quarterly cost a relatively expensive three dollars a year—close to a week's salary for a mill worker.

THE DIAL:
A
MAGAZINE
FOR
LITERATURE, PHILOSOPHY, AND RELIGION.
TO BE CONTINUED QUARTERLY.
No. I.
JULY, 1840.
BOSTON:
WEEKS, JORDAN, AND COMPANY,
LONDON:
MDCCCXL.

During its four-year stint, the *Dial* was edited first by Margaret Fuller and then by Ralph Waldo Emerson.

Over the four years of its existence, the *Dial* published a number of important and powerful essays, including Emerson's essay on Transcendentalism, Thoreau's "A Natural History of Massachusetts," and Elizabeth Peabody's explanation of Brook Farm. The most controversial were Alcott's "Orphic Sayings," a catalog of obscure and often impenetrable statements that proved all too easy to parody. These three from the first edition of the *Dial* demonstrate some of Alcott's murky prose:

> *Listen divinely to the sibyl within thee, saith the Spirit, and write thou her words. For now is thine intellect a worshipper of the Holy Ghost; now thy life is mystic—thy words marvels—and thine appeal to the total sense of man—a nature to the soul.*

> *There is neither void in nature, nor death in spirit,— all is vital, nothing Godless. Both guilt in the soul and pain in the flesh, affirm the divine ubiquity in the all of being. Shadow apes substance, privation fullness; and nature in atom and whole, in planet and firmament, is charged with the present Deity.*

> *Nature is quick with spirit. In eternal systole and diastole, the living tides course gladly along, incarnating organ and vessel in their mystic flow. Let her pulsations for a moment pause on their errands, and creation's self ebbs instantly into chaos and invisibility again. The visible world is the extremist wave of that spiritual flood, whose flux is life, whose reflux death, efflux thought, and conflux light. Organization is the confine of incarnation,— body the atomy of God.*

With only thirty subscribers for its first edition and never more than three hundred at any given time, the *Dial* was not a financial success. Neither Fuller nor Emerson earned money from editing the journal, and it finally ran out of funds and momentum in 1844.

Since then, the *Dial* has had a number of resurrections. The first was in 1880, when it was brought back as a "socially humanitarian" journal. This incarnation drifted into radicalism, however, and was on the verge of dying again when Scofield Thayer took it over in 1918. Thayer transformed it into a highly respected organ for some of the major voices of the early twentieth century including Sherwood Anderson, E. E. Cummings, Kenneth Burke, William Butler Yeats, Ezra Pound, Amy Lowell, Kahlil Gibran, Hart Crane, Marianne Moore, Carl Sandburg, and Van Wyck Brooks. Unfortunately, that version folded in 1929. No more was heard until 1961, when the publishers Russell and Russell brought out a four-volume set of the original *Dial.*

In addition to the lofty discussions, two major undertakings were planned at these meetings. The first was the creation of a quarterly magazine that would be a voice of the new progressive movement. After some searching, the members agreed on Margaret Fuller as editor, with George Ripley as assistant editor. Emerson and Thoreau also agreed to help. The *Dial* was launched in July 1840, after being conceived at a September meeting nearly a year earlier.

The club's other significant undertaking was the dream of member George Ripley. He announced at the October 1840 meeting that he was resigning his ministry to begin a community called Brook Farm. In a follow-up letter to Emerson the next month, Ripley asked for his assistance in creating this "society of liberal, intelligent, and cultivated persons, whose relations with each other would permit a more simple and wholesome life, than can be led amidst the pressure of our competitive institutions." Emerson politely declined to join but visited often and offered his encouragement.

Much of the detailed planning for the Brook Farm community took place at ❸ Elizabeth Peabody's bookstore at 15 West Street. The bookstore, which was actually the front parlor of the Peabody home, served as a perfect meeting place for Boston intelligentsia. Its shelves were stocked with the books of foreign authors not found elsewhere—Kant, Hegel, Goethe, Plato, Swedenborg, Confucius—as well as Hindu texts such as the Bhagavad Gita and the Upanishads. The walls were hung with the work of a beautiful and talented painter—Sophia

The West Street Grill and Brattle Books (one of the oldest bookstores in Boston) now occupy the building where the Peabodys lived and Elizabeth had her bookshop.

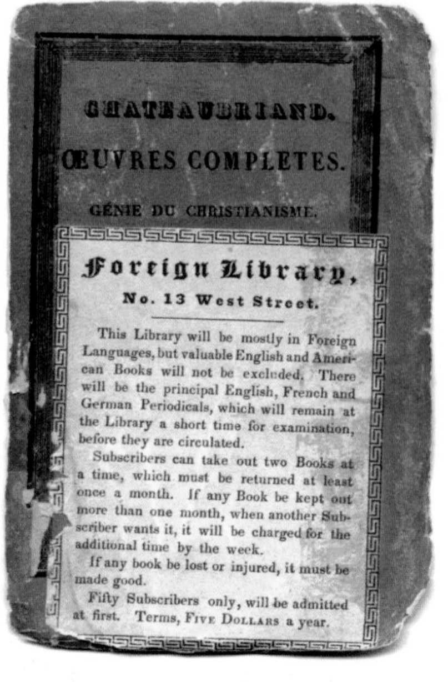
CHATEAUBRIAND.
ŒUVRES COMPLETES.
GÉNIE DU CHRISTIANISME.

Foreign Library,
No. 13 West Street.

This Library will be mostly in Foreign Languages, but valuable English and American Books will not be excluded. There will be the principal English, French and German Periodicals, which will remain at the Library a short time for examination, before they are circulated.

Subscribers can take out two Books at a time, which must be returned at least once a month. If any Book be kept out more than one month, when another Subscriber wants it, it will be charged for the additional time by the week.

If any book be lost or injured, it must be made good.

Fifty Subscribers only, will be admitted at first. Terms, Five Dollars a year.

Elizabeth Palmer Peabody's library and bookstore collection totaled nearly one thousand volumes when she gave it to the Concord Library.

Peabody, the proprietor's younger sister, who would later be known as Mrs. Nathaniel Hawthorne.

The bookstore's owner, Elizabeth Peabody, was a dominant figure in New England literary circles. The eldest daughter of a dentist, she inherited much of her strong will and determination from her mother. Before starting the bookstore, Elizabeth had already started a school for girls, worked closely with Reverend Channing, and held her own series of for-profit "conversations."

After hours, the bookstore served as a meetinghouse and gathering place. George Ripley would frequently hold forth on utopian ideals to an audience of young men such as Thomas Wentworth Higginson (later Emily Dickinson's editor and friend) and James Freeman Clarke (who would later perform the marriage of Sophia Peabody to Nathaniel Hawthorne) from Harvard Divinity School. As Peabody described it, these were busy years:

> *I had . . . a Foreign Library of new French and German books, and then I came into contact with the world as never before. The Ripleys were starting Brook Farm, and they were friends of ours. Theodore Parker was beginning his career, and all these things were discussed in my bookstore by Boston lawyers and Cambridge professors. Those were very living years for me.*

Building on Elizabeth Peabody's success offering "conversations" for profit to a women-only audience, Margaret Fuller convened a series of discussion groups tackling serious philosophical topics during the winters from 1839 to 1844. The groups would meet from noon to 2 p.m. on Wednesday afternoons, once a week for thirteen weeks. The format usually included assigned reading and a discussion moderated by Fuller.

In an era when there were few educational opportunities for women, this was an unusual chance for women to exercise their intellect. Not surprisingly, the conversations attracted many of the finest female minds in the area. The first series focused on the differences between men's and women's educational opportunities, and later series covered mythology and the arts.

Brilliant and dedicated, Margaret Fuller was one of Transcendentalism's best conversationalists.

Six Degrees of Separation

In the relatively small world of New England's intelligentsia, coincidences are bound to occur, and the Transcendentalists are no exception. Start with Emerson: His grandfather's house was home to two Transcendentalists (Emerson and Hawthorne) and ended up in the possession of the Reverend Samuel Ripley. A cousin of both Samuel Ripley and Emerson, George Ripley, founded Brook Farm and the Transcendental Club, and assisted Margaret Fuller in editing the *Dial*. The *Dial* was published by Elizabeth Palmer Peabody, whose younger sister, Sophia, married Hawthorne after he left Brook Farm, where he had lived with George Ripley, who then helped him rent the Old Manse, which had been in Emerson's family for several generations. And Elizabeth Peabody was Bronson Alcott's assistant at the Temple School in Boston, where Margaret Fuller also taught.

Transcendentalist Women

One of Transcendentalism's greatest strengths, as well as a key to its success, was its embrace of progressive social causes, specifically abolition, natives' rights, and the rights of women. Transcendentalist "feminism" (a term that would not be used until 1895), however, clearly succeeded in ways that the first two causes did not. While there were no blacks or Native Americans in the Transcendentalist circle, there were women—women whose opinions were sought and intellects were respected.

Probably the most visible of the female Transcendentalists was Margaret Fuller. Although unable to attend Harvard—its "women's annex," Radcliffe College, wasn't founded until the end of the century—Fuller did gain the right to use Harvard's library, the first woman to do so. She was one of a handful of female members of the Transcendental Club, and served as editor of its journal, the *Dial*, until she handed off the role to Emerson. Later, she became one of the only women of the nineteenth century to serve as a foreign correspondent for an American newspaper, Horace Greeley's *New York Tribune*. Her literary works, most notably a translation of Eckerman's *Conversations with Goethe* and her magnum opus, *Woman in the Nineteenth Century,* met with critical acclaim.

Another woman whose Transcendentalist activities helped her break new ground was Elizabeth Palmer Peabody. The first to hold "conversations" for women for profit, the first woman in Boston to be a publisher, the first to open a kindergarten in America, Peabody was endlessly energetic. A driving force in the Boston intellectual scene, she was responsible for hosting, supporting, or initiating many of the Transcendentalists' activities throughout New England.

Advocacy of women's rights was not limited to the Transcendentalist women. Almost all the major educational endeavors connected with the Transcendentalists sought to equalize the balance of power between the sexes. One glaring exception was Bronson Alcott's utopian community, Fruitlands. While the men sat around discussing and philosophizing, the majority of the farm work fell to Abba Alcott and her four girls. Fruitlands failed after only a few months.

In addition to these serious intellectual inquiries, the bookstore hosted romantic events as well. Two weddings took place in the back rooms, where the Peabody family lived. The first was between a relatively unknown but strikingly handsome author from Salem, Nathaniel Hawthorne, and Elizabeth's equally striking sister, Sophia. The Hawthornes were married in July 1842 by the liberal Unitarian minister James Freeman Clarke. The second marriage was between the middle Peabody sister, Mary, and the educational reformer Horace Mann. Also presided over by Clarke, this ceremony took place in May 1843.

Today the building might still be a lovely place for a small wedding. The books are gone; in 1878 Peabody donated them to the Concord Free Public Library, which still has 415 of the thousand volumes that went into the circulating collection. In their place now are wine glasses and white linen. After hosting a number of retail establishments over the years (and changing its street number from 13), 15 West Street is now home to the West Street Grille, an upscale restaurant where the young and stylish of Boston come to dine and mingle.

Elizabeth Peabody's bookstore also made its mark in a more public way when she began publishing the *Dial* there. Evidence suggests that this made her the first woman publisher in Boston, and most likely in all of North America. She also published some of Hawthorne's early work before he moved to Ticknor and Fields. In

Field's Failure

For all of James T. Fields's business acumen (he introduced the system of advances and royalties to American publishing, for instance), he made at least one notable mistake. When a young writer from Concord showed him her stories, Fields was not impressed. "Stick to your teaching," he told her. "You can't write." He did, however, acknowledge the financial stresses that had pushed the young woman into publishing and gave her forty dollars to start a school.

Undaunted by this rejection of her literary efforts, the young Louisa May Alcott kept at writing, producing more than thirty books and collections of stories during her thirty-four-year career. After *Little Women* had been published to tremendous success, Alcott mailed the forty dollars back to Fields with the note:

Dear Mr. Fields

Once upon a time you lent me forty dollars, kindly saying I might return them when I had made "a pot of gold."

As the miracle has been unexpectedly wrought I wish to fulfil my part of the bargain & herewith repay my debt with many thanks.

Very truly yours

L. M. Alcott

An otherwise impeccable judge of literature, James T. Fields told Louisa May Alcott to "stick to your teaching . . . you can't write."

1849 she began publishing a journal of her own, *Aesthetic Papers*. Although it lasted just one issue, it was particularly notable for publishing an essay by a still relatively unknown writer who had recently returned from a sojourn by a lake. The essay, "Resistance to Civil Government" by Henry David Thoreau, has become one of the best-known works of the period (under its later title, "Civil Disobedience"), and has certainly outlasted the fame of the magazine in which it first appeared.

Another publishing house and hub was just a few blocks east, on the corner of Washington and School Streets. If Elizabeth Peabody's bookstore and library introduced many American thinkers to writers from abroad, ❹ the Old Corner Bookstore at 3 School Street introduced many Americans to their country's own writers.

This building, tucked in among the larger buildings of downtown, served as the center of the America's literary world when Ticknor and Fields operated their publishing business here.

The stunning glass and steel building is the twenty-first-century version of Ticknor and Fields.

From their offices in the Old Corner Bookstore, publishers James T. Fields and William Ticknor brought out many of the major works of the nineteenth century, by authors who even now are some of the best-known names of American letters: Ralph Waldo Emerson, Oliver Wendell Holmes, Henry Wadsworth Longfellow, James Russell Lowell, and Nathaniel Hawthorne. But it was more than a catalog that made Ticknor and Fields such a powerhouse—it was the personal relationships that the men, especially Fields, developed with the writers in their stable. Author Rebecca Harding Davis called Fields "the shrewdest of publishers and kindest of men. He was the wire that conducted the lightning so that it never struck amiss."

Most of the major writers of the time stopped by the Old Corner Bookstore once or twice a week, and some came every day. As George Curtis noted, it was "the hub of the Hub," which attracted "that circle which compelled the world to acknowledge that there was an American literature." Hawthorne, in particular, felt very comfortable here and came whenever he was in town. In *Glimpses of Authors*, Caroline Ticknor, the publisher's granddaughter, describes Hawthorne's "spot":

> *In the small counting-room was "Hawthorne's Chair," in a secluded nook; there he was wont to sit dreaming in the shadow, while the senior partner was busy at his desk close by: . . . There Hawthorne would take up his positions where he could see and yet be out of sight, and in his chair, for many years it was his custom to ensconce himself, whenever he visited the "Corner"; he often spent whole hours there resting his head upon his hand apparently in happy sympathy with his environment.*

In some ways, the Old Corner Bookstore was a victim of its own success. After its heyday in the mid-nineteenth century, the publishing firm of Ticknor and Fields left (it later became Houghton Mifflin). The building then became home, successively, to a string of other bookstores, a haberdashery, a photo supply store, and a pizza joint. In 1960 it was saved from becoming a parking lot by the nonprofit group Historic Boston. Now a protected historic site, it has been home to the Globe Corner Bookstore and the Freedom Trail Foundation and is now a jewelry store. In an ironic twist, the small, two-story brick building is now dwarfed by the enormous glass-walled Borders bookstore just across the street.

Another major hub of Transcendentalist activity was ❺ **the Masonic Temple** at **88 Tremont Street.** Built in the early 1830s, this enormous Gothic structure served as a lyceum for Boston society. Emerson gave his first lectures there, a series of ten talks on English literature. The building also served as the meetinghouse for James Freeman Clarke's Church of the Disciples. In addition, an elementary school begun by Bronson Alcott operated out of room 7 from 1834 to 1839.

Given Transcendentalism's inherent optimism and belief in the pure spirituality of children, it was probably inevitable that it would spawn an educational reform movement. Although many took up this mantle over the years, including Elizabeth Palmer Peabody with her Pinckney Street kindergarten, George Ripley with Brook Farm, and Alcott and Franklin Sanborn with the Concord School of Philosophy, perhaps the best-known endeavor was Alcott's School for Human Culture, better known as the Temple School.

This enormous Gothic building, the Masonic Temple, hosted many of the Transcendentalist activities, including Bronson Alcott's famously controversial school.

This small volume documented and explained many of Alcott's progressive pedagogies and was one of Elizabeth Peabody's earliest literary efforts.

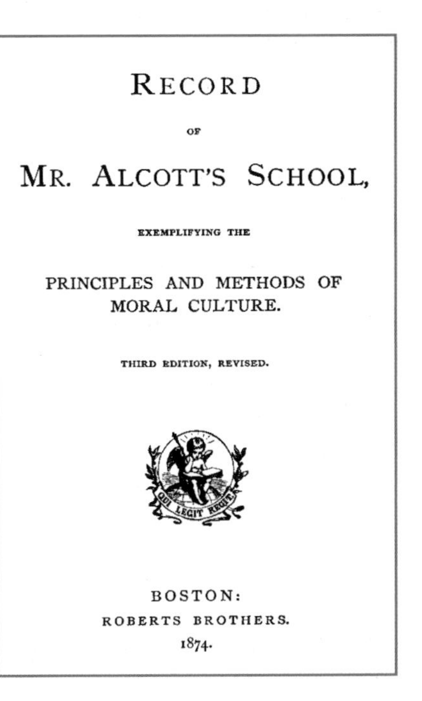

RECORD

OF

MR. ALCOTT'S SCHOOL,

EXEMPLIFYING THE

PRINCIPLES AND METHODS OF MORAL CULTURE.

THIRD EDITION, REVISED.

QUI LEGIT REGIT

BOSTON:
ROBERTS BROTHERS.
1874.

Founded in 1834 with a class of thirty boys and girls, the Temple School took a radically different approach to the teaching of children than did the public schools of the time. As described in the 1836 *Record of a School* by Elizabeth Palmer Peabody, who was serving as his assistant, Alcott believed in the inherent intelligence of his pupils. Rather than education by memorization and recitation, he taught by lecture and discussion. Lessons frequently included a reading by Alcott and then a discussion led by him. Students, whose ages ranged from six to twelve, were encouraged to voice their own ideas and opinions.

The Gospels provided the basis for the discussions and the platform from which conversation ranged across many topics. The most controversial brushed on sexuality and human reproduction, as described in Alcott's second volume describing his teaching practices, *Conversations with Children on the Gospels*:

> *Mr. Alcott. Yes; you have the thought. And a mother suffers when she has a child. When she is going to have a child, she gives up her body to God, and he works upon it, in a mysterious way, and with her aid, brings forth the Child's Spirit in a little Body of its own, and when it has come, she is blissful. But I have known some mothers who are so timid that they are not willing to bear the pain; they fight against God, and suffer much more.*

While this may not offend our modern sensibilities, any discussion of the birthing process, no matter how vague or sober, was scandalous for Victorian Boston. When *Conversations with Children on the Gospels* appeared in 1836, Alcott was scorched by the outcry. Many parents pulled their students from

Abolitionist Movement

One of the central tenets of Transcendentalism was the belief that the very essence of God runs through each person and connects the individual with what Emerson termed the Oversoul. Therefore, many Transcendentalists found it intolerable that their black brethren were being held as slaves. Antislavery activities took a variety of forms, but nearly all of the major Transcendentalists became involved with the abolitionist movement in one way or another.

Not surprisingly, Boston was central to this movement. William Lloyd Garrison, one of the city's earliest activists, made his first major antislavery speech in 1829 in **6 the Park Street Church,** at **1 Park Street** and began publishing the *Liberator* in 1831. In 1832 he started the New England Anti-Slavery Society at the African Meeting House at 8 Smith Court, in the Beacon Hill neighborhood, and he worked with the Tappan family of New York to form the American Anti-Slavery Society in Philadelphia in 1833.

Garrison's power as an orator and writer is evident in this passage from the first issue of the *Liberator*:

> *On this subject [slavery], I do not wish to think, or speak, or write with moderation. No! no! Tell a man whose house is on fire, to give a moderate alarm; tell him to moderately rescue his wife from the hands of the ravisher; tell the mother to gradually extricate her babe from the fire into which it has fallen; —but urge me not to use moderation in a cause like the present. I am in earnest—I will not equivocate—I will not excuse—I will not retreat a single inch—AND I WILL BE HEARD.*

Ministers such as Parker, Channing, and Clarke were among Transcendentalism's most visible abolitionists. All three of these men, as well as many others in churches across Massachusetts and New England, spoke out against slavery almost weekly in their sermons, while writers such as Emerson and Thoreau also took up the call.

The radical abolitionist John Brown attacked an arsenal at Harpers Ferry, Virginia, in hopes of inspiring an uprising of slaves. He was caught and hanged for treason and immortalized by writers such as Emerson and Thoreau.

Emerson was vocal on such issues as the Fugitive Slave Law and the Kansas-Nebraska Act, which established the states of Kansas and Nebraska and left the issue of slavery up to territorial settlers, or "popular sovereignty." This allowed each side of the slavery issue to exert enormous pressure on the citizens of those new states, frequently leading to unrest and bloodshed. He hosted the abolitionist John Brown twice in his home and clearly supported Brown's goals, if not his methods. Thoreau, whose lectures "Slavery in Massachusetts" and "A Plea for Captain John Brown" clearly demonstrated his position, was perhaps the most passionately vocal abolitionist writer. He first gave his lecture "Slavery in Massachusetts" at an antislavery convention in Framingham in 1854, after which William Lloyd Garrison burned the Constitution.

Park Street Church today.

Others took an even more active role against slavery. Franklin Sanborn, Concord's Transcendentalist schoolmaster, was instrumental in bringing John Brown to Concord and introducing him to the liberal thinkers there. Theodore Parker hid a fugitive in his house, agitated on behalf of escaped slave Anthony Burns, and raised money to buy weapons for John Brown. The antislavery Boston Vigilance Committee (which included Alcott, Parker, Channing, and Thomas Wentworth Higginson) tried to ensure the safety of Burns and other escaped slaves, such as Thomas Sims. The Alcott and Thoreau families were active participants in the Underground Railroad, which passed through Concord on its way to Canada.

Tremont Street, looking toward Park Street Church.

Quiet Places: Boston Common and the Boston Athenaeum

Sandwiched between Tremont Street and Beacon Hill, running from Arlington Street on the west side to Park Street on the eastern border, are the fifty acres of ❼ **the Boston Common.** Long a major feature of the city, its walks, gardens, and ponds were a major attraction for the nature-loving Transcendentalists.

Emerson, who had grazed his family's herd of cows on the Common as a child (grazing was allowed until 1830, when the area became a park), particularly enjoyed strolling the paths as an adult. In fact, it was on just such a stroll in 1860 that he gave advice to a young Walt Whitman. Whitman later described the event in his journal:

> *I walk'd for two hours, of a bright sharp February mid-day twenty-one years ago, with Emerson, then in his prime, keen, physically and morally magnetic, arm'd at every point, and when he chose, wielding the emotional just as well as the intellectual. During those two hours he was the talker and I the listener. It was an argument-statement, reconnoitering, review, attack, and pressing home . . . of all that could be said against that part (and a main part) in the construction of my poems, "Children of Adam." . . . I could*

the school, and when he endeavored to educate a mulatto girl alongside the children of his Boston patrons, the rest of the families abandoned him. The school folded in 1839, devastating Alcott, who was bedridden for a number of months due to the stress of the personal crisis.

Unfortunately, the Masonic Temple did not enjoy as enduring an existence as some of its more famous occupants. It was sold in 1858 to the U.S. government, which used it as a courthouse until it was demolished to make way for a department store. The Masons now occupy a site just down the road, at 186 Tremont Street.

never hear the points better put—and then I felt down in my soul the clear and unmistakable conviction to disobey all, and pursue my own way. . . . Whereupon we went and had a good dinner at the American House. And thenceforward I never waver'd or was touch'd with qualms.

After their walk on the Common, Emerson took Whitman over to ❽ **the Boston Athenaeum** and registered him as a guest. A private library founded in 1807 by the members of the Anthology Society, the Athenaeum began modestly but quickly became a center of Boston's intellectual universe. By 1851, the Athenaeum had moved from Tremont Street, and its home for thirty-seven years on Pearl Street, to its current location at **10½ Beacon Street.** It had also become one of the five largest libraries in the country. Coincidentally, this Beacon Street location was also the former site of Emerson's boyhood home.

The Athenaeum provided a quiet haven for working amid the bustle of the city for Emerson, Hawthorne, Longfellow, Amy Lowell, Lydia Maria Child, and, when he was in town, Walt Whitman. Hawthorne seemed particularly at home among the dusty volumes and quiet solitude of the Pearl Street location. In fact, as he recounts in "The Ghost of Dr. Harris," it was

Boston Common

Boston Common has changed little since Emerson and Whitman shared their February walk. The park, together with the Public Garden, forms a seventy-five-acre sanctuary bordered by the exclusive Beacon Hill neighborhood to the north, downtown to the east, the newly revived "Ladder District" (what used to be called Downtown Crossing) to the south, and the shopping haven of Back Bay to the west.

Although the Common's greatest attractions may still be the paths that allow for sunny midday walks (if the weather cooperates) and the playing fields that line Charles Street, it has also become famous for its Frog Pond, swan boats, and flower gardens and sculptures. It was further immortalized in *Make Way for Ducklings,* Robert McCloskey's classic children's story about a family of ducks who live in the Public Garden.

Placed on the Common in 1982, Pitynski's sculpture *The Partisans* depicts the Jewish and Polish guerilla fighters of World War II and is part of the Immigrant Heritage Trail.

The Boston Athenaeum was a favorite destination for Emerson, Thoreau, and Hawthorne. In the late nineteenth century, the Athenaeum moved to its current location on Beacon Street.

here that he met up with a ghost of one of the members and, for fear of disrupting the reigning silence, quietly ignored him:

> *Being a ghost, and amenable to ghostly laws, it was natural to conclude that he was waiting to be spoken to before delivering whatever message he wished to impart. . . . In the reading room of the Athenaeum conversation is strictly forbidden, and I could not have addressed the apparition without drawing the instant notice and indignant frowns of the slumberous old gentleman around me. I myself, too, at that time, was as shy as any ghost, and followed the ghost's rule never to speak first.*

Beyond these red doors is one of Boston's most storied institutions. Emerson, Hawthorne, and Whitman all used the Boston Athenaeum to do their research.

The Athenaeum continues to serve both living and spectral members as a wonderful resource for intellectual inquiry. It now boasts a half-million volumes spread over five galleried floors, special collections such as Confederate State imprints and books from the library of George Washington, and a variety of online resources. In addition, it hosts events ranging from lectures on Copernicus to afternoon teas, architectural tours, and literary salons. A guided tour can help the visitor better understand all that lies beyond the red doors.

Boston Today

As the northernmost city in the Boston–New York–Washington, D.C., corridor, Boston has done a wonderful job of retaining its cobblestoned heritage of rebellion and intellectual inquiry. From the much bemoaned "curse" on the Red Sox that lasted eighty-six years to the Freedom Trail wending its way through downtown, Boston is a town clearly holding on to its past as it looks to the future. One fine example of this is the famed ❾ **Quincy Market and Faneuil Hall** area, just off the waterfront.

Built in 1742 as a wholesale market and revitalized in the mid-1960s as a tourist attraction, Quincy Market offers a wondrous variety of food from around the world. Of course the seafood, especially lobster, is still king here, but one can also find fresh burritos and sushi (not at the same counter, of course). The ubiquitous McDonald's is here too, but it seems more palatable in its brick exterior. Franchises aside, Quincy Market is still, at its heart, a colonial market and gathering place.

Boston's heritage is still clearly visible elsewhere as well. The charming yet exclusive Beacon Hill neighborhood of Pinckney Street and Louisburg Square was home to Thoreau, the Alcotts, Nathaniel Hawthorne, the Fields, and the Channings. Thoreau once lived as a

The Grand Tour

A proper Transcendentalist education seemed to include at least one trip abroad. Most of the major figures in the movement made a pilgrimage across the Atlantic, whether for health, opportunity, education, or, occasionally, escape. Emerson, Alcott, Hawthorne, Fuller, Hedge, Channing, Parker, and a number of others all visited Europe at least once in their lives, and the influence of European Romanticism on the Transcendentalists is clearly discernible.

The busiest harbor in America, Boston was the primary departure point for Europe during the mid-nineteenth century.

Emerson first left for Europe on Christmas Day, 1832. On that trip he explored Malta, Italy, France, England, and Scotland, and managed to have interviews with Samuel Taylor Coleridge, William Wordsworth, and Thomas Carlyle. This trip was clearly an important influence on Emerson's development as the future Sage of Concord. He wrote often about his European experiences, made two return trips, and supported a number of trips made by others in the movement.

Bronson Alcott's 1842 trip to England is one example of Emerson's sponsorship. The trip was also a turning point in Alcott's life, although not one presaging a great success. During his time in England, Alcott visited a school based on his pedagogical methods, called Alcott House, and met a social reformer by the name of Charles Lane. The two men's spiritual idealism and asceticism merged well, and Lane returned to Massachusetts with Alcott to start an ill-fated utopian society, Fruitlands.

Margaret Fuller's trip was considerably more tragic. Although Fuller had dreamed of exploring literary Europe from an early age, she had to delay her trip until later in her career, when she had already achieved much success. Her editor at the *New York Tribune,* Horace Greeley, sent her to Europe in 1846 as one of the first female foreign correspondents for an American news organization. In Italy, she fell in love with the Marquis Ossoli and became involved with the revolution there. Two years later, as they sailed to America with their infant son, their ship broke up on the rocks near Fire Island, New York, and the whole family perished.

Built in 1742, Quincy Market is now one of Boston's most recognizable landmarks. Samuel Adams helped inspire rebellion in the upstairs meeting room.

child at ❿ 4 Pinckney Street; Elizabeth Peabody held kindergarten classes at ⓫ 15 Pinckney Street; Nathaniel Hawthorne lived at ⓬ 54 Pinckney Street; and the Alcotts rented rooms at ⓭ 20, 43, and 81 Pinckney Street. The last home of Bronson Alcott and his daughter Louisa May was just around the corner at ⓮ 10 Louisburg Square. The publisher and friend of the Transcendentalists, J.T. Fields lived at ⓯ 148 Charles Street and the Reverend William Ellery Channing lived at ⓰ 83 Mount Vernon Street. Today, the main streets in the area, Boylston and Newbury streets, are vibrant shopping areas built on what used to be salty marshlands. And across the Charles River is Boston's venerable neighbor, Cambridge.

Chapter 3

Cambridge

Training Ground

This 1840 etching depicts a procession of alumni at Harvard.

Cambridge's connection to Transcendentalism is a complex one. Home to Harvard College, where most of the major figures of the movement received their education, Cambridge was integral to the movement in many ways. Two of the defining events of Transcendentalism, Emerson's "American Scholar" speech and his address to the Divinity School, took place at Harvard. And, not least of all, Harvard's embrace of Unitarianism and liberal Christianity in the early nineteenth century made possible many of the philosophical leaps by the Transcendentalist theologians.

It was just those leaps that strained the Transcendentalists' relationship with ❶ **Harvard College,** however. Professors and administrators at the college felt the Transcendentalists took liberality far enough to be dangerous to their authority, if not the whole fabric of society. They apparently found their views confirmed in Emerson's "Divinity School Address," in which he charged that the Unitarianism of the college had grown stultified and devoid of life. For this claim, Emerson was treated to a thirty-year break from invitations to speak at Harvard. It wasn't until late in his career, when he was internationally famous, that the school and the Transcendentalist philosopher resumed diplomatic relations.

Unveiled in 1836 at the university's bicentennial celebration, the Harvard shield, containing the Latin word *veritas* ("truth") is based on a sketch presented at a Board of Overseers meeting in January 1644.

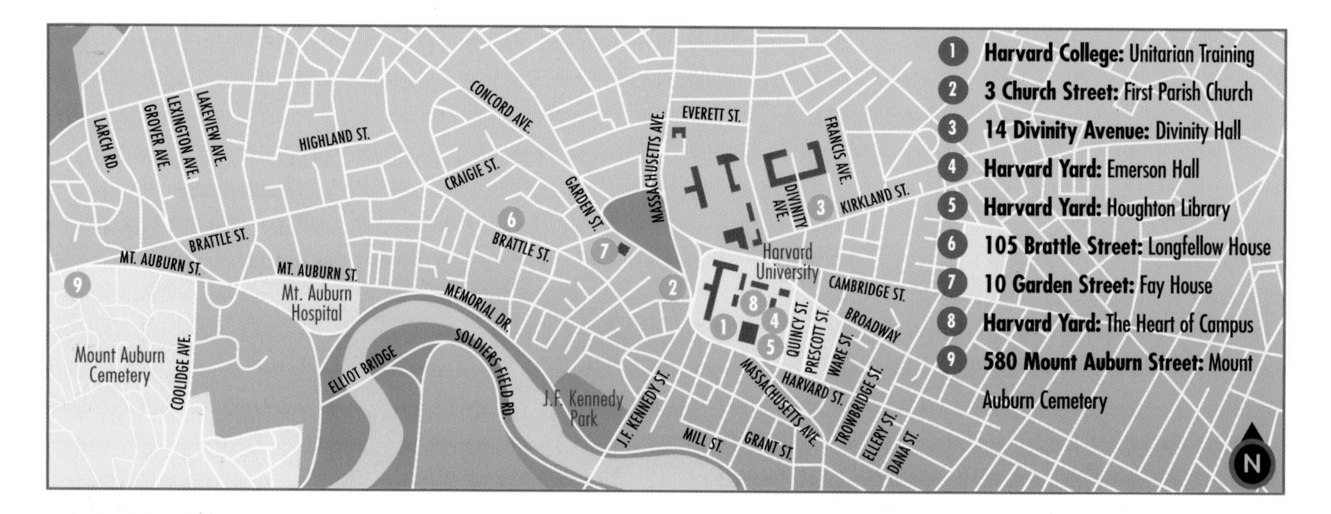

Thoreau as Alum

Not all of the Transcendentalists were as enamored of their college education as were Emerson, Higginson, and Hedge. Thoreau, who had lived in Harvard's Hollis Hall and helped found the Natural History Society, graduated in 1837, but in *Walden* he questioned the true value of his Crimson degree:

> *Those things for which the most money is demanded are never the things which the student most wants. Tuition, for instance, is an important item in the term bill, while for the far more valuable education which he gets by associating with the most cultivated of his contemporaries no charge is made. . . . To my astonishment I was informed on leaving college that I had studied navigation!—why, if I had taken one turn down the harbor I should have known more about it. Even the poor student studies and is taught only political economy, while that economy of living which is synonymous with philosophy is not even sincerely professed in our college. The consequence is, that while he is reading Adam Smith, Ricardo, and Say, he runs his father in debt irretrievably.*

In fact, Thoreau saw so little value in the degree that he never paid the five dollars to receive his actual diploma.

This crayon portrait of Thoreau was made in 1854.

Emerson, who had also lived in Hollis Hall and had graduated in the exact middle of his fifty-nine-member class, once remarked to a guest contemplating study at Harvard that the college taught all of the branches of knowledge. Quipped Thoreau, "Yes, indeed, all the branches and none of the roots." But however little respect Thoreau paid to the curriculum at Harvard, he did in many ways remain connected to his alma mater. In 1849, he applied for and received borrowing privileges at the Harvard library. He also helped Harvard scientist Louis Agassiz gather specimens, and after his death, his own collection of nearly a thousand different plant specimens greatly augmented the college's collection.

In the meantime, Harvard continued to produce young men of intellect and distinction. Some went on to lead productive lives in business, law, or politics, while others succumbed to what Harvard professor and leading Unitarian scholar Andrews Norton called "the latest form of infidelity"—the radical new ideas of Transcendentalism. The list of movement figures with ties to Harvard is certainly impressive: Emerson, Thoreau, William Ellery Channing (the minister), Ellery Channing (the poet), George Ripley, Franklin Sanborn, Theodore Parker, Frederic Henry Hedge, Thomas Wentworth Higginson, George Putnam, Jones Very, and Margaret Fuller. For most of these writers and thinkers, Harvard provided an introduction to the literature and philosophy of other cultures. George Ticknor's return from Germany in 1819, to become the Smith professor of French and Spanish languages and literatures, opened a new interest in German philosophy.

"Dreading to Leave an Illiterate Ministry"

Harvard College was established in 1636 by a vote of the Great and General Court of the Massachusetts Bay Colony, the same year "Newtowne" was rechristened "Cambridge" in recognition of Cambridge University, England. The college took on the name Harvard in 1639 to recognize the gift of John Harvard's library and half his estate when the young minister died.

Harvard University has the honor of being the oldest institution of higher education in the country as well as one of the most prestigious in the world. Although it has never formally affiliated with any denomination, from its start the college has seen its mission as educating the clergy of the New World. The words of one of the university's founders are inscribed on a panel on the Johnson Gates to Harvard Yard: "One of the next things we longed for and looked after was to advance learning and perpetuate it to posterity; dreading to leave an illiterate ministry to the churches, when our present ministers shall lie in the dust."

For much of its first two hundred years of existence, Harvard closely followed the Puritan, then Calvinist inclinations of Boston, the city across the river. In the late eighteenth century, a battle for control of the college began between the more conservative Calvinists and the more liberal Unitarians. This lasted until the 1805 appointment of the liberal Henry Ware Sr. to the Hollis Chair of Divinity. This position, long held by a strict Calvinist, set the direction for the theological curriculum of the college. The appointment of Ware was seen as a clear indication that Harvard was moving in a more progressive direction. Ultimately, the Calvinists withdrew to found the Andover Theological Seminary in 1808, leaving Harvard firmly in the control of the Unitarians.

John Harvard, a young minister, gave the fledgling college his library and half his estate when he died. In return, his statue sits in the central yard of one of the world's best-known universities—a school that also bears his name.

While the Reverend William Ellery Channing was in his Federal Street Church in Boston sowing the seeds of what would eventually grow into Transcendentalism, Harvard was further embracing its role in training ministers with the opening of Harvard Divinity School in 1816. Students had begun studying a more organized theological curriculum under the direction of Henry Ware and Unitarian scholar Andrews Norton.

In 1819 Norton became the Dexter professor of sacred literature. In that position, he sought to firmly establish the truth of Christianity in general, and Unitarianism specifically, on the basis of the miracles described in the Gospels. His stature grew so impressive that he was commonly referred to as "the Unitarian Pope."

When Divinity Hall was dedicated in 1826, Channing proposed that it be used for the "training of warm . . . generous spirits." Most of those generous spirits did in fact go on to fill the nearly 250 New England parishes that became Unitarian in the nineteenth century. A number of them became involved with the Transcendentalist movement and later left their pulpits, as in the cases of Emerson, George Ripley, and John Dwight, a Unitarian minister turned Transcendentalist music critic. Others, such as Moncure Conway, James Freeman Clarke, and Theodore Parker, remained with their churches but preached a blend of Unitarianism and Transcendentalism that often made them controversial.

"We Will Walk on Our Own Feet"

On September 8, 1836, Harvard College marked its two-hundredth anniversary. It was an enormous celebration, bringing nearly 1,300 alumni back onto campus. The day proved to be momentous in many ways. President Josiah Quincy Sr. unveiled, in the form of a large banner atop the celebration tent, the college's new seal: three open books spelling out *veritas* ("truth"), the seal that Harvard still uses today. A professional choir debuted the college's new fight song, "Fair Harvard." Meanwhile, three men in the back were busy ignoring the festivities, preferring to engage each other in a dialogue about current theology and opinions. These men, Ralph Waldo Emerson, George Ripley, and Frederic Henry Hedge, continued their conversation after adjourning to the nearby Willard's Hotel. There, they agreed to meet again on September 19 at Ripley's house in Boston to convene the symposium of "like-minded seekers" that would become the Transcendental Club.

Emerson returned to campus nearly a year later to further the cause of Transcendentalism with his oration before the Phi Beta Kappa Society on August 31, 1837. This speech, given at ❷ **the First Parish Church** at **3 Church Street,** was the second of his major speeches against mindless conformity and for the natural philosophy that would come to be known as Transcendentalism. Coming a year after Emerson had published his landmark book *Nature*, this seventy-five-minute speech, now known as "The American Scholar," took aim at the state of American education and letters,

Phi Bate

Phi Beta Kappa was founded on the Harvard campus in 1781 with a charter from the Phi Beta Kappa club of William & Mary. The William & Mary branch had been a rival to the Flat Hat Club (FHC), a secret society at that college, and had attempted to outdo the FHC with secret initiations and ceremonies. Phi Beta Kappa began to export its secrets to Yale as well in the 1780s, but because the chapters at Yale and William & Mary have disbanded and re-formed from time to time, Harvard can lay claim to having the longest-running chapter in existence.

At Harvard, the club became more of a literary club than a philosophical one, and has now evolved primarily into an academic distinction for undergraduates. The society also gives three excellence-in-teaching awards and research fellowships for work at Radcliffe. In addition, it continues the tradition of inviting poets and speakers of stature to speak during commencement week, just as Emerson did. The roster of recent guests is impressive: May Swenson, Annie Dillard, Galway Kinnell, Seamus Heaney, Nadine Gordimer, Grace Paley, John Edgar Wideman, and Madeleine Albright.

These gates serve as the traditional and ceremonial entry into Harvard. The First Parish Church, where Emerson gave his "American Scholar Address" in 1837, is just outside the gates.

dismissing most of what the young scholars had learned in their four years at Harvard and arguing in favor of a new start for American culture:

> *Our day of dependence, our long apprenticeship to the learning of other lands, draws to a close. The millions that around us are rushing into life, cannot always be fed on the sere remains of foreign harvests. Events, actions arise, that must be sung, that will sing themselves. Who can doubt that poetry will revive and lead in a new age, as the star in the constellation Harp which now flames in our zenith, astronomers announce, shall one day be the pole-star for a thousand years?*

The man to lead this charge was Emerson's "American scholar," or what he described as "Man Thinking." Having found Nature in himself and himself in Nature, inspired into action by the best books, the American scholar's duty is "to cheer, to raise, and to guide men by showing them facts amidst appearances. He plies the slow, unhonored, and unpaid task of observation."

While this might subject "Man Thinking" to poverty, scorn, and solitude, there would be benefits: "For all this loss and scorn, what offset? He is to find consolation in exercising the highest functions of human nature. . . . He is the world's eye. He is the world's heart." This position also lifts him above the "bugs and spawn" that Emerson calls "men in history, men in the world of to-day"—precisely the type of men who had invited him to speak at Harvard.

Building on this momentum, Emerson finished his address with a statement of the Transcendentalist awareness of self that would so shake up the establishment: "If there be one lesson more than another which should pierce his ear, it is, The world is nothing, the man is all; in yourself is the law of all nature . . . it is for you to know all; it is for you to dare all." Noting that the American scholar has "listened too long to the courtly muses of Europe," Emerson sounded his call to arms in the name of individual man as part of the Divinity:

> *We will walk on our own feet; we will work with our own hands; we will speak our own minds. The study of letters shall be no longer a name for pity, for doubt, and for sensual indulgence. The dread of man and the love of man shall be a wall of defence and a wreath of joy around all. A nation of men will for the first time exist, because each believes himself inspired by the Divine Soul which also inspires all men.*

Many felt elated and inspired by Emerson's boldness; Oliver Wendell Holmes called it an American "intellectual Declaration of Independence." Others were taken aback by the assertion that Harvard's curriculum was too focused on the past and on European influences. What controversy there may have been, however, was infinitesimal compared to the uproar generated by the speech he gave one year later.

If Emerson's "American Scholar" oration was the Declaration of Independence, his July 1838 address to the six graduates, the faculty, and the administration of Harvard Divinity School was the Battle of Bunker Hill. Speaking in ❸ **Divinity Hall,** at **14 Divinity Avenue,** Emerson began more poetically—"The grass grows, the buds burst, the meadow is spotted with fire and gold in the tint of flowers"—and quickly made the link between our apprehension of this "secret, sweet, and overpowering beauty" and "the sentiment of virtue." Emerson claimed this virtue comes from the realization that God is a part of us and we are a part of God: "If a man is at heart just, then in so far is he God; the safety of God, the immortality of God, the majesty of God do enter that man with justice."

This realization "awakens in the mind a sentiment which we call the religious sentiment," which is easy to come by; it just requires a leap of faith. "It is guarded by one stern condition; this, namely; It is an intuition. It cannot be received at second hand. Truly speaking, it is not instruction, but provocation, that I can receive from another soul. What he announces, I must find true in me, or wholly reject."

While Emerson was delivering these words, conservative men such as Andrews Norton were likely getting fidgety. This was not the speech they had been expecting. And what

Emerson delivered his "Divinity School Address" from this lectern.

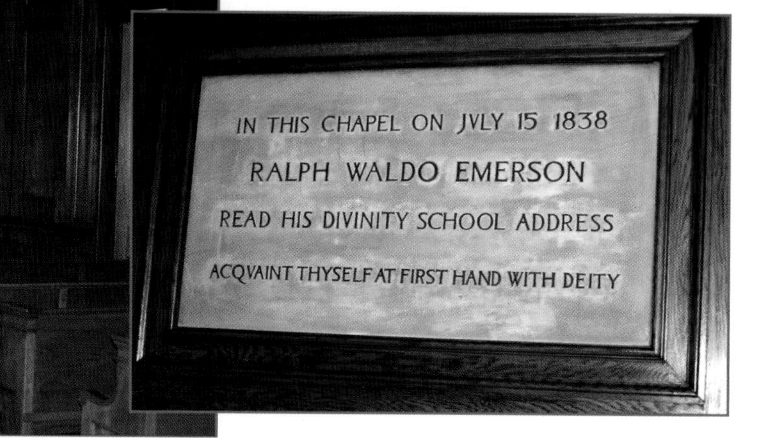

came next was a more direct attack on all they held sacred. "By his holy thoughts, Jesus serves us, and thus only. To aim to convert a man by miracles, is a profanation of the soul. A true conversion, a true Christ, is now, as always, to be made, by the reception of beautiful sentiments."

But what most likely put the Divinity School faculty over the edge was Emerson's next accusation:

> *Not any profane man, not any sensual, not any liar, not any slave can teach, but only he can give, who has; he only can create, who is. The man on whom the soul descends, through whom the soul speaks, alone can teach. Courage, piety, love, wisdom, can teach; and every man can open his door to these angels, and they shall bring him the gift of tongues. But the man who aims to speak as books enable, as synods use, as the fashion guides, and as interest commands, babbles. Let him hush.*

One can imagine the hush in the room as the tall, gaunt poet from the village of Concord, the Harvard Divinity School graduate who had left his own ministerial post some five years earlier, delivered these words to the young men who were proposing to devote themselves to the "holy office" of preaching.

It took only a little over a month for Norton to respond in print to Emerson's speech. The professor's article, "The New School in Literature and Religion," appeared on page two of the August 27 issue of the *Boston Daily Advertiser*. It leveled criticism at the Transcendentalists with all the vengeance Norton could muster:

> *The characteristics of this school are the most extraordinary assumption, united with great ignorance, and incapacity for reasoning. There is indeed a general tendency among its disciples to disavow learning and reasoning as sources of their higher knowledge. . . . There are great truths with which they are laboring, but they are unutterable in words to be understood by common minds. To such minds they seem nonsense, oracles as obscure as those of Delphi.*

In all likelihood, Norton was not at all concerned about the ideas of a few relatively unemployed philosophers scattered about Massachusetts. He was deeply concerned, however, about the effects on his students, who, along with those he called "silly women," might be "drawn away from their Christian faith, if not divorced from all that can properly be called religion."

Norton sought to combat Emerson's influence with a finger-waving admonition: "The preacher [Emerson] was invited to occupy the place he did, not by the officers of the Divinity College, but by the members of the graduating class. These gentlemen, therefore, have become accessories, perhaps innocent accessories, to the commission of a great offence." Norton finished by sounding a general cry of panic: "Should such preachers [as Transcendentalists] abound, and grow confident in their folly, we can hardly overestimate the disastrous effects upon the religious and moral state of the community."

A year later, Norton was still fuming. He delivered his rebuttal, "A Discourse on the Latest Form of Infidelity, Delivered at the Request of the Association of the Alumni of the Cambridge Theological School, on the 19th of July, 1839." This speech was given at the same event as Emerson's address had been, but this time the students were not allowed to choose their own speaker. In it, Norton attempted to firmly establish the legitimacy of Unitarianism on the basis of the miracles that Jesus performed.

His discourse prompted a reply from Unitarian minister and Harvard graduate George Ripley, precisely—and long-windedly—titled: "'The Latest Form of Infidelity' Examined. A Letter to Mr. Andrews Norton, Occasioned by His 'Discourse Before the Association of the Alumni of the Cambridge Theological School' on the 19th of July, 1839." Thereafter, both sides fired off successive lengthy retorts until some five hundred pages had been expended on a passionate debate about whether the miracles described in the Gospels were factually accurate.

The debate that ensued after the publication of this pamphlet took the form of a long, arcane theological argument between two brilliant scholars who seem to have had little sense of irony.

LETTERS

ON

THE LATEST FORM OF INFIDELITY,

INCLUDING

A VIEW OF THE OPINIONS

OF

SPINOZA, SCHLEIERMACHER, AND DE WETTE.

BY GEORGE RIPLEY.

BOSTON:
JAMES MUNROE AND COMPANY.
MDCCCXL.

Finally, Theodore Parker, a Unitarian minister in West Roxbury who had graduated from the Divinity School only a few years before, stepped into the fray under the pseudonym Levi Blodgett and brought the debate back to terms the average person could understand. Claiming to be an "obscure" man, saying that "ower much o' my life has been spent at the plough, and ower little at the college or the schule," Parker as Blodgett made the following plea:

> *I beseech you, in behalf of numbers of my fellows, pious and unlearned as myself, to do one of two things, either to prove that the miraculous stories in the Bible are perfectly true, that is, that there is nothing fictitious or legendary from Genesis to Revelations . . . or leave us to ground our belief in Christianity on its truth,—which is obvious to every spiritual eye that is open.*

After this, the furor died down. Emerson, however, would not be invited back to Harvard for almost thirty years.

By 1866 Harvard had either forgiven or repented sufficiently to feel itself able to award Emerson an honorary degree, and in 1867 it appointed him to its board of overseers. From 1868 through 1870, he was

Although Emerson was for many years persona non grata at Harvard, the university has done a remarkable job of making amends by highlighting Emerson's legacy.

even allowed to give a series of lectures entitled "The Natural History of the Mind." Harvard has since placed a plaque at the back of the Divinity Hall chapel that commemorates his historic address. His triumph was complete when ❹ Emerson Hall opened in 1900, featuring in the lobby a bronze statue of the writer by Frank Duveneck.

The Harvard of Today

Although Harvard is not the dominating force that it was in its first three hundred years, it is still the premier university in the nation. It consistently ranks first, second, or third in national higher education surveys, and its name recognition is unparalleled. It boasts the largest endowment of any academic institution in the world. The nearly twenty thousand undergraduate and graduate students have access to more than ninety individual libraries and almost fifteen million volumes, making the Harvard University library

Harvard Yard is bordered on one end by the Widener Library and by Memorial Church on the other.

system the largest university library in the world, and second in the nation only to the Library of Congress.

In the late 1930s, Harvard's librarian, Keyes Metcalf, suggested that the university build a separate facility for the rare books and manuscripts accumulating on the first floor of the Widener Library. In 1942, ❺ **the Houghton Library** opened its doors as the first American university library for rare books and manuscripts. It incorporated such then cutting-edge technologies as climate control, air filtration, and security.

The Houghton Library now holds some fifty thousand books and ten million manuscripts, including the Hyde Collection of Dr. Samuel Johnson, the Theodore Roosevelt Collection, and the bulk of Ralph Waldo Emerson's collection of books and manuscripts. Emerson's journals, correspondence, and even his account books fill whole aisles of this fascinating library.

Harvard Divinity School continues to be one of the finest nonsectarian theological training grounds in the world, with faculty and students representing more than fifty denominations from around the world. The curriculum focuses on the interpretation of scripture with an emphasis on Christian traditions but within the context of religion worldwide.

Women and Harvard

When Margaret Fuller became the first woman to gain admittance to Harvard's library in the early 1830s, it was as close to studying at the college as she could get. Although men such as the Reverend William Ellery Channing advocated the inclusion of women on campus, it wasn't until the late nineteenth century that Harvard took them up on the challenge. In 1879, the college opened an "annex" that offered "private tuition to properly qualified young women who desire to pursue advanced studies in Cambridge." This "Society for the Collegiate Instruction of Women" enrolled twenty-seven women the first year.

By 1894, the program had gained enough momentum to be incorporated by the Massachusetts legislature. As a corporation, the school, now named Radcliffe College, could offer bachelor's degrees provided and approved by Harvard. Elizabeth Cary Agassiz, the wife of noted Harvard scientist Louis Agassiz and a friend of Thoreau and Emerson, was appointed the first president of the college, making her one of the first female college presidents in the United States.

From that point on, it was simply a matter of time and circumstances before the two ventures merged. In 1943, war-depleted Harvard found that it was more efficient to include women in classes on campus rather than teach separate classes for them. The year 1963 marked the first time women received Harvard degrees. In 1999, the college assumed all duties for Harvard's undergraduate women, while Radcliffe moved toward research and advanced study. Now women make up about half of Harvard's student body, and the college has the most extensive women's Division I athletic program in the country.

Among the early graduates of Radcliffe College was Helen Keller, who earned her degree (cum laude) in 1904.

Cambridge Today

As Harvard has grown, so has its host town of Cambridge. The city now lays claim to two major research universities, Harvard and the Massachusetts Institute of Technology, while a third, Boston University, lies just across the Charles River. Of the million-plus people who live in Cambridge, many are involved in education, high-tech, biotechnology, or health care. Cambridge is seen as an integral part of the Boston area's cultural prominence and a highly desirable community in which to live.

Longfellow's house on Brattle Street.

Aside from Harvard, Cambridge today features a number of important literary sites, such as 6 Henry Wadsworth Longfellow's home at 105 Brattle Street. Although not a Transcendentalist, Longfellow, one of America's greatest poets, was a close friend to Hawthorne and hosted Emerson often. 7 Radcliffe's Fay House at 10 Garden Street also figured prominently as a location for the Transcendentalists. It was the home of Thomas Wentworth Higginson's

Sculptor of the Transcendentalist

Perhaps the most telling episode of Daniel Chester French's childhood was when he received tutoring and supplies from a local Concord resident. May Alcott, along with her sister Louisa, did much to support and encourage French to develop his artistic skills while he was growing up in Concord and Cambridge. It was fitting, then, that the young sculptor, reared among the Transcendentalist sages of Concord, should receive his first major commission in Concord.

That first job was the minute man statue that today stands on the eastern shore of the Concord River, looking back across the North Bridge. It was given to the town to commemorate the bridge's role in the American Revolution. The first stanza of Ralph Waldo Emerson's "Concord Hymn" is inscribed on the base.

After completing this statue, French went on to win a series of prestigious commissions that established him as the nation's foremost sculptor of memorials. He created the Lincoln Memorial in Washington, D.C., the statue of John Harvard in 8 Harvard Yard, and the George Robert White Memorial in Boston's Public Garden. When he created a bust of Emerson in 1879, Emerson is reputed to have exclaimed, "That's the face I shave!"

French's bust of Emerson.

Margaret Fuller's family erected this cenotaph in Mount Auburn. She died in a shipwreck off of Fire Island; her remains were never found.

Mount Auburn Cemetery continues to attract visitors and tourists who come to pay their respects to both the famous and the not so famous who are buried here.

aunt, Mary Channing, as well as the place where George and Sophia Ripley were married in 1827 by the father of Oliver Wendell Holmes.

Another site of note, on the border of Cambridge and Watertown, is ⑨ Mount Auburn Cemetery, 580 Mount Auburn Street, which contains a cenotaph for Margaret Fuller. Mount Auburn is important not only as a pilgrimage site but also because it served as a model for Concord's Sleepy Hollow Cemetery, the final resting place of Emerson, Thoreau, and many other Transcendentalists. Founded in 1831 in a pleasant grove that was a favored walking destination of Harvard student Ralph Waldo Emerson, Mount Auburn's well-planned walks, ornamental gardens, and fountains continue to provide a pleasant place for Cantabrigians to stroll.

From Cambridge Out

While some of the Transcendentalists who had studied at Harvard found themselves at odds philosophically with their alma mater, almost all seem to have valued the sense of a scholarly community that Harvard afforded them. Once they had left Cambridge, many of them sought out a similar fellowship—and they found it in communities such as the American Unitarian Association, the Tran-scendental Club, and the collection of philosophers and writers that was beginning to form around Emerson in Concord.

Chapter 4

Concord
Heart and Soul

The Old Manse was home to the Alcott Family as well as Nathaniel Hawthorne and is now a museum.

If Transcendentalism exploded on the scene in Boston and Cambridge, its trajectory clearly pointed to Concord, nineteen miles west. The bustling New England market town was home to Ralph Waldo Emerson. Such writers and thinkers as Bronson Alcott, Nathaniel Hawthorne, Ellery Channing, and the Transcendental educator and Concord schoolmaster Franklin Sanborn were drawn there in some measure because of him. Even Thoreau, who had the best claim of any Transcendentalist to being Concord's native son, seemed to orbit the Emersonian sun.

With its roots in agriculture and market commerce, Concord was the natural home for this galaxy of writers. Some might even argue that Transcendentalism didn't come to Concord; it was already in the soil, waiting to be drawn out. In any case, Concord, with its meandering rivers and fertile ground, has served as an inspirational place for people throughout the ages, and the Transcendentalists were no exception.

Along the Grassy Banks of the Musketaquid

Much of the topography that makes Concord so suited for its role as muse was a gift of the ice age. As the mile-deep sheets of ice retreated north, they left chunks stuck in the ground to become ponds such as Walden, White, and Bateman's ponds. The freshly scrubbed earth became home to early forests of white pines, then oaks, pitch pines, and hemlocks; and two rivers, the Assabet and the Sudbury, which merge at a place called Egg Rock to form a third river, the Concord. This river flows north out of town, joining eventually with the Merrimack River on its way to the ocean just above Newburyport, Massachusetts, near Cape Ann.

Surrounding the ponds and rivers of Concord are the rolling ridges and hills that give the town many of its more appealing hikes. Thoreau favored the trip out to the Fair Haven Cliff, which gave him a view to the west of Concord. On clear days, he could see as far as Mount Monadnock. Emerson enjoyed the path above Walden now called Emerson Cliffs. Appropriately enough, Hawthorne favored the quiet seclusion of the steep hill behind the Wayside, the home he bought from the Alcotts, for his climbing.

Concord's History

The Transcendentalists who followed Emerson to Concord were not the first to sense the town's advantages. The first known humans to wander through

Take Me to the River

Many of the Transcendentalists wrote about the rivers of Concord and freely employed water imagery in their works. Journalist George Curtis claimed that the river made Concord a "dreaming, pastoral poet of a village." Ellery Channing noted the inspiration found in the river: "There is an inward voice, that in the stream / Sends forth its spirit to the listening ear." Thoreau's first published book was an account of his trip along the Concord and Merrimack rivers. Emerson likens his mind to a river in journal entries; in "Musketaquid," his poem in honor of the Concord River, he claims that his love of the river and its area has "through my rock-like, solitary wont / Shot million rays of thought and tenderness."

Hawthorne also focuses his reader's attention on the Concord River in his introduction to *Mosses from the Old Manse:*

> *We stand now on the river's brink. It may well be called the Concord—the river of peace and quietness—for it is certainly the most unexcitable and sluggish stream that ever loitered, imperceptibly, towards its eternity, the sea. . . . It slumbers between broad prairies, kissing the long meadow-grass, and bathes the overhanging boughs of elder-bushes and willows, or the roots of elms and ash-trees and clumps of maples. Flags and rushes grow along its plashy shore; the yellow water-lily spreads its broad flat leaves on the margin; and the fragrant yellow pond-lily abounds, generally selecting a position just so far from the river's brink, that it cannot be grasped, save at the hazard of plunging in.*

The Concord River, formed by the Assabet and Sudbury Rivers, drifts northward behind the Old Manse.

Although they were neither the first nor the last artists to find inspiration in moving water, the Transcendentalists' philosophy made the depth and variety of their communion with the rivers particularly notable. While Thoreau studied the movement of their currents, Emerson marveled at their sheer beauty and peaceful splendor.

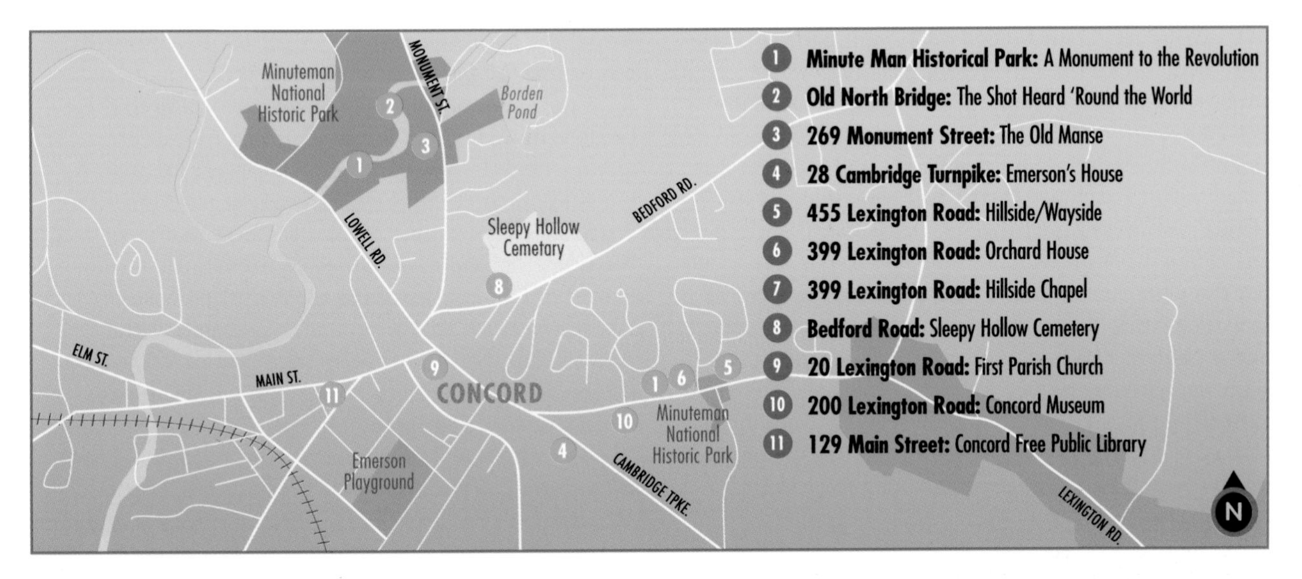

(about twelve to eighteen millennia ago) probably shared the forests with mastodons and large herds of caribou. Sometime between one and eight millennia ago, tribes started using the area as a summer camp and began planting small crop plots, including corn, beans, and melons. The flat lands near the rivers served as perfect seasonal camps. Artifacts such as stone pendants, clay pots, spears, and arrows have been found underneath what is now the Emerson Hospital parking lot.

When the British arrived in 1635, they found the friendly and open Musketaquid people living on Nashawtuc Hill, beside the slow-running river with its good, clear water. They also found a system of trails leading through the forests. Nine-tenths of the land was forested with conifers, oaks, chestnuts, and pitch pines. There were fields with grass for winter grazing and good level ground. It appeared to be the perfect place for a new town, and although the British settlers ostensibly regarded the land as already belonging to the crown, Simon Willard, Peter Bulkeley, and other early settlers opted for prudence and paid the Musketaquids for a six-mile square of land beside the river. There, they began to build the first inland Puritan settlement.

Once the settlers had established their claim to the land, they used the sacred sites of the native people for grazing their cattle and set about converting the natives

Concord's town square in the mid-nineteenth century.

to Christianity. Their houses were small, mostly single-story structures with a steep roof, massive timbers, small windows, and a big chimney. The Thomas Dane house at 47 Lexington Road, the Edward Bulkeley House at 92 Sudbury Road, and the Parkman Tavern at 20 Powder Mill Road may be the best remaining examples of this type of architecture.

For the next century and a half, the villagers were hard at work cutting their existence out of the forests. Much of the land was cleared to create firewood and open space for the roughly two hundred Concord farms that existed by the mid-eighteenth century. By the time the War of Independence came to town in 1775, Concord was an established market town with good roads to Boston as well as points west.

A Heritage of Rebellion: The First Revolution

It was in good part due to these well-maintained roads that the leaders of the revolution chose Concord to be their armory and headquarters. During the years leading up to the war, forces stockpiled weapons in the town. Then, on the night of April 18, 1775, British forces left the garrisons of Boston for Concord to seize those weapons. Paul Revere, according to the predetermined plan, rode to Concord to raise the alarms. He was captured by a patrol near Lexington, but his comrade, Dr. Prescott, made it to Concord to warn the citizens. One of Dr. Prescott's first stops was the home of Samuel Whitney. Whitney, the muster master of Concord's militia, lived in the house on Lexington Road that would later be home to the Alcotts and then the Hawthornes. When Whitney received the alarm from Prescott, his job was to rouse Concord's "minute men," the local farmers and laborers who could take up arms and become soldiers "in a minute." They gathered on the town green, accompanied by Concord's Unitarian minister, the Reverend William Emerson.

The Old North Bridge, as depicted in this painting by Alozo Chappel.

After gathering on the green, the minute men moved up to positions on the west side of the river on John Buttrick's farm. The actual battle took place on the Old North Bridge within sight of the Old Manse, the parsonage of the Reverend William Emerson. A portion of the British troops had amassed on the opposite side of the bridge from the rebels. Other redcoats, in an effort to find the reported arms caches in town, burned the Liberty Pole in the town square. Farmer Joseph Hosmer, wrongly thinking that the British had set fire to the entire town, cried out, "Will you let them burn the town down!" As the minute men advanced on the British regulars amassed on the town side of the bridge, one soldier, no one is quite sure who, fired what Emerson later dubbed "the shot heard round the world." Buttrick then gave the order to fire, and for the next two minutes the air was filled with the smoke of exploding gunpowder. As the smoke drifted down to the Manse, the death toll from this opening salvo was recorded: two British redcoats and two minute men.

The ensuing battle lasted all day and occupied most of the twenty-two miles back to Boston, costing the British nearly a third of their troops. They awoke the next day to find soldiers arriving from all corners of New England to challenge them. The Battle of Bunker Hill, one of the first major fights of the revolution, would take place a mere two months later.

Minute Man National Historical Park

❶ Minute Man National Historical Park, a national historic site comprising nearly a thousand acres, stretches across the towns of Lexington, Lincoln, and Concord. It features a five-mile Battle Road Trail that charts the route the British regulars followed after the skirmish at ❷ **the Old North Bridge.**

The original bridge no longer stands. By 1793, road rerouting and flooding had caused it to be torn down. The river remained without a bridge until 1875, when a fancier bridge was constructed and the minute man statue by Daniel Chester French was erected on the west bank of the river. That bridge lasted only thirteen years until it washed downstream in a flood. An oak bridge survived from 1889 through 1908, when flooding took its toll again. The town then tried concrete, which fared better but could not outlast Hurricane Diane in 1955. It was replaced in 1956 by the next bridge, which survived for nearly fifty years until time and constant use took their toll. In 2005, the bridge was rebuilt and now welcomes busloads of interested history buffs as well as families enjoying a sunny weekend day with a costumed park ranger and a variety of informational displays.

This bronze statue commemorating the farmers who took up arms against the British was one of the first done by Daniel Chester French. French's later projects included the Lincoln Memorial.

The park also includes Nathaniel Hawthorne's house, The Wayside, and Major John Buttrick's mansion on the bluff overlooking the river where the North Bridge was located. Buttrick's house now serves as an information booth and gift shop for the park.

This is at least the seventh bridge at the spot of the original North Bridge.

The Concord Crimson

For the 1775–76 academic year, Harvard College took an extended field trip west to the town of Concord. When the growing Continental Army needed additional barracks, headquarters, and hospitals, it occupied Harvard's dormitories and classrooms. Legend has it that it was the Reverend William Emerson who offered the town of Concord as a suitable temporary location for the college, and Harvard agreed. The "Concord Year" began on October 4 with nearly 150 students and faculty housed in private homes, taverns, and unused buildings throughout Concord.

Aside from some windows broken during snowball fights and a few romances between the young Harvard boys and the local girls, it appears that the year went well. Harvard was able to return to Cambridge to graduate its seniors in June 1776. One of the boys who studied in Concord during the year and then graduated in 1778 was Ezra Ripley, who returned to Concord after his graduation to become the minister of the First Parish Church, marry William Emerson's widow, and become owner of the Old Manse.

The Concord Hymn

By the rude bridge that arched the flood,
Their flag to April's breeze unfurled,
Here once the embattled farmers stood,
And fired the shot heard round the world.

The foe long since in silence slept;
Alike the conqueror silent sleeps;
And Time the ruined bridge has swept
Down the dark stream which seaward creeps.

On this green bank, by this soft stream,
We see to-day a votive stone;
That memory may their deed redeem,
When, like our sires, our sons are gone.

Spirit, that made these heroes dare
To die, or leave their children free,
Bid Time and Nature gently spare
The shaft we raise to them and thee.

—Ralph Waldo Emerson

Although it would be another fourteen months before the Declaration of Independence was signed, the April 19 battle was the real start of the Revolutionary War. It is now commemorated every year, on the third Monday in April, with a battle re-creation on Lexington Green. The day, a state holiday called Patriot's Day, is also known for the running of the Boston Marathon.

One of the earliest town commemorations of the April 19 skirmish was held on July 4, 1837, to dedicate a memorial at the site of the Old North Bridge. Concord usually celebrated the Fourth of July on the commons, but in the late 1830s, the town was at its political and economic pinnacle and looking to solidify its place in American history. As a suburb of Boston and the county seat of Middlesex, Concord was making a bid to be one of the major commercial centers west of Boston. Highlighting the town's role in the revolution was seen as an important part of that campaign, and so, after much political wrangling, the town finally erected an obelisk commemorating the sacrifices of the men who had fallen in battle.

Dr. Ezra Ripley donated the land behind the Old Manse for the monument at the site of the original battlefield, and the town chose a young writer and former Unitarian minister to write a dedicatory song. This man, whose roots in the town went back to the town's first minister, had only recently returned to Concord. Although born and raised in Boston, he had

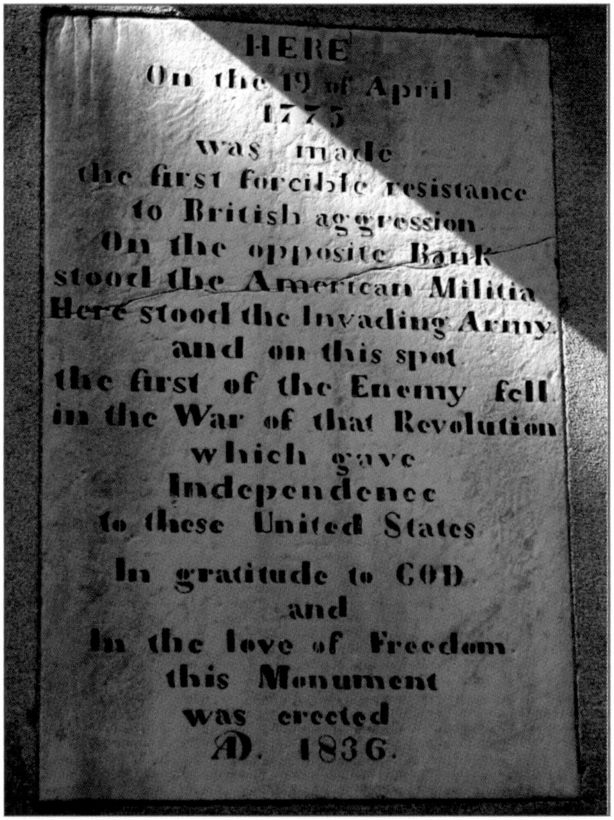

Although built in 1836, this memorial was dedicated by the town on July 4, 1837.

ties to the Old Manse as well, for it was his grandfather, the Reverend William Emerson, who had witnessed the April 19 battle from its grounds. For the occasion, the young man wrote "The Concord Hymn," to be sung by the assembled crowd.

Emerson's Concord: The Second Revolution

It was appropriate that this writer, who had also delivered a speech at the town's bicentennial celebration, should craft one of his most famous poems for the commemoration of the 1776 clash, for he would later be at the center of what Concord likes to call its "second revolution." One of the earliest events in that revolution was a speech that writer Oliver Wendell Holmes called America's "intellectual Declaration of Independence." That lecture was "The American Scholar," and the man was Ralph Waldo Emerson.

When Emerson had returned to Concord in 1834, he was in some senses adrift. His first wife, Ellen Tucker, had recently died of tuberculosis after only two years of marriage. He had resigned his post as the minister of the Second Church of Boston because he could not reconcile his changing views of religion with the orthodoxy of the Unitarian Church. It was still a full year before the start of the Transcendental Club, which would give him a sense of community, of belonging to a group of what he termed "like-minded seekers." Emerson had returned to the town where he would eventually serve as the foremost public figure, but at the time he was an out-of-work former minister moving into his grandparents' house with his mother.

The Sage of Concord

Emerson's place at the center of the Transcendentalist galaxy is due to more than talent or ambition; it can be traced to his earliest ancestors in America. His family tree was liberally sprinkled with religious men and women willing to face challenges in their daily and spiritual lives. An Emerson ancestor, Peter Bulkeley, was the first minister of Concord and author of *The Gospel Covenant*, one of the first important religious books published in the wilds of the New World. His grandfather was present and active as the revolutionary war broke out in Concord. His father, a Unitarian minister at Boston's prestigious First Parish Church, was also part of an almost unbroken line of Emersonian clergy. And young Emerson was conscious of continuing that line when he entered Harvard Divinity School in 1826.

Emerson used images such as these as advertisements for his lectures. He kept one hand balled in a fist during his speeches.

But Emerson soon discovered his own strain of rebellion, and left the church in 1832. By 1835 he had purchased his own home in the town of his ancestors; had married his second wife; and had begun a career as a writer, lecturer, mentor, and public figure. By the time of his death in 1882, Emerson had become one of the most well-known and respected men of letters in the nineteenth century.

Perhaps Emerson's most impressive accomplishment is the nearly fifteen hundred lectures he wrote and gave in almost every state in the Union and across Europe. Most were later published as essays. In addition, he wrote poetry and reviews, kept a journal, and was a diligent correspondent. Some of his most enduring works are the ones that laid the foundations for the Transcendentalist movement: his long essay, *Nature;* his address to the Phi Beta Kappa Society, "The American Scholar"; and his "Divinity School Address." These three pieces provided the framework for the movement, a framework that others would flesh out with their own contributions.

The Concord of the Transcendentalists

The town that Emerson made his home in the 1830s was a bustling center of commerce and society. The forests, which had covered almost all of the land when the first settlers arrived, occupied less than three-quarters by the start of the eighteenth century, and just one-quarter by the start of the nineteenth century. (They would cover no more than one-tenth by 1850.) Most of the landscape around the town consisted of open fields.

Manufacturing had come to Concord, and the towns-people were busy making everything from carriages and chaises to boots, bricks, guns, and pencils. The courts of Middlesex County were housed in Concord as well. The town had done away with obligatory church attendance in 1834, but social clubs and lyceums abounded, as did groups concerned about social issues such as abolition, the rights of Native Americans, and the role of women in society.

This progress came at a price, however. By the time the railroad arrived in 1844, the rivers were being polluted with industrial waste and sewage. Between 60 and 70 percent of the town's taxpayers did not own any land. Nearly a third of the population were recent Irish immigrants brought in to work in the mills and factories. Damon Mill, which employed nearly two hundred people at its peak, dominated the town, which grew from 2,200 people in 1850 to 5,700 people during the second half of the century. The mill was one of the major textile manufacturers in the area. By the close of the nineteenth century, Concord had effectively transformed itself from an agricultural market town into a Boston suburb.

Shortly after returning to the Old Manse, Emerson bought a home known as Coolidge Castle. Rather than a parsonage like the Old Manse, this was a summer house, built by Charles Coolidge in 1829. Its location at the intersection of Lexington Road and the bustling Concord Turnpike proved advantageous, for this house was to become the very center of the Transcendentalist movement. Emerson was so generous with his time and resources, so admired in his thinking and writing, and so active in a variety of causes and careers that a nearly constant stream of visitors and guests passed through the house.

Foremost among them was Henry David Thoreau, a native of Concord, who spent the vast majority of his life in the town, surveying and mastering the land, helping his father's pencil-making business, and living as close to his philosophic ideals as he could. Thoreau, a graduate of Harvard and a brilliant thinker in his own right, produced what has become the best-known work of the Transcendentalists, *Walden, or Life in the Woods*, after spending two years on Emerson's land at nearby Walden Pond in Concord (see chapter 5). Although the book made him little money while he was alive, it has become a staple of college and high school courses in literature, social sciences, philosophy, and environmental studies.

Nathaniel Hawthorne also repeatedly made his home in Concord, first renting the Old Manse, and later purchasing a house on Lexington Road that he called the Wayside. Margaret Fuller made Concord a frequent home away from home. Bronson Alcott lived with his family in a number of different Concord houses. Ellery Channing lived and wrote his poems here; Walt Whitman visited. Franklin Sanborn opened a college preparatory school here and taught the Emerson, Alcott, and Hawthorne children. Mary Peabody Mann, the widow of educational reformer Horace Mann, opened a school in Concord with her sister Elizabeth Palmer Peabody. Emerson, Thoreau, Hawthorne, Bronson and Louisa May Alcott, and many others are buried in the town cemetery. The composer Charles Ives would later complete his Concord Sonata—comprising four movements, "Emerson," "Thoreau," "Alcott," and "Hawthorne"—after visiting the town.

Given its storied past, it is not surprising that Concord has worked hard to retain its status as a major literary and historic landmark. The current town is well laid out, with a charming main street boasting the necessary bookstores and cafés for proper Transcendentalist musings. At the eastern edge of town are the major sites: the Concord Museum, Ralph Waldo Emerson's home, Bronson Alcott's Orchard House, Nathaniel Hawthorne's Wayside, the Old Manse and North

Concord prides itself as a major literary landmark.

Bridge, and Sleepy Hollow Cemetery. Many of the sixteen thousand current residents live in well-maintained, carefully preserved houses clustered around the main village.

The Old Manse: Birthplace of Emerson's *Nature*

Just north of town, set back from the road near where the Concord River bends in from the west and flows under the North Bridge, sits one of the most storied houses in all of Concord: ❸ the Old Manse at 269 Monument Street. A three-story, gambrel-roofed home, it was built in 1770 by the Reverend William Emerson, the Unitarian minister in Concord. The house was set on eleven acres of good farmland along the river and was built with low ceilings and little-box rooms to please the reverend's new bride, Phebe Bliss of Concord.

A controversy exists regarding just where the reverend stood when he observed the historic 1775 battle. In the introduction to *Mosses from the Old Manse*, Hawthorne imagines him watching from the window of the second-floor study: "It was at this window that the clergyman who then dwelt in the Manse stood watching the outbreak of a long and deadly struggle between two nations." Evidence suggests, however, that he stood on the bank of the river, just down from the British troops. The reverend's journal for the day reads as if he were in the ranks of the minute men, but that could be more of a symbolic camaraderie. We do know that when the first alarms were sounded, he appeared on the town common in his black minister's garb, rifle in his hand. A year later he departed for Fort Ticonderoga to serve as an army chaplain. Unfortunately, he died of camp fever while there and never returned to the Manse or to his wife, Phebe.

Bronson and Abigail's daughter May used the Old Manse as a subject for practicing her developing skills as an artist.

After the reverend died, his widow began taking in boarders to help with the upkeep of the house. Among these was the young preacher who had come from Harvard to fill Emerson's place in the weekly pulpit, Dr. Ezra Ripley. It was perhaps natural that Dr. Ripley would step into other of Emerson's roles as well; he and Phebe Emerson were married in 1780.

Ripley quickly became a pillar of Concord, ascending the steps of his pulpit in the First Parish Church for

Ezra Ripley replaced William Emerson in the Concord Unitarian pulpit, rented a room at the Old Manse, and eventually married Emerson's widow and became owner of the Manse.

sixty-three years and penning more than three thousand sermons while living in the Old Manse. Hawthorne liked to imagine Ripley still with him in the Manse:

> *Our ghost used to heave deep sighs in a particular corner of the parlor, and sometimes rustled paper, as if he were turning over a sermon in the long upper entry—where nevertheless he was invisible, in spite of the bright moonshine that fell through the eastern window. Not improbably he wished me to edit and publish a selection from a chest full of manuscript discourses that stood in the garret.*

When young Ralph Waldo Emerson returned to Concord in 1834 he moved into this house with his mother and took the second-floor room at the back of the house as his study. It was here, with his chair facing out the windows toward the river, that Emerson wrote his landmark book, *Nature*. It is easy to see, given the Manse's proximity to the slow-moving Concord River and the site of the 1775 rebellion, where Emerson gathered inspiration for his bold and provocative ideas. *Nature* begins with a remarkable challenge: "The foregoing generations beheld God and nature face to face; we, through their eyes. Why should not we also enjoy an original relation to the universe? Why should not we have a poetry and philosophy of insight and not of tradition, and a religion by revelation to us, and not the history of theirs?"

Then follows an Emersonian, and therefore Transcendentalist, solution: go spend time in nature, and see what new ideas this brings. "Embosomed for a season in nature, whose floods of life stream around and through us, and invite us, by the powers they supply, to action proportioned to nature, why should we grope among the dry bones of the past?" It seems particularly telling that Emerson wrote these words, with their central metaphor of the "flood of life," looking out at the river from the window of his study. As he states, however, "to go out into solitude [to achieve our 'original relation'], a man needs to retire as much from his chamber as from society." Emerson made good on this premise by going out daily to walk the hills, forests, and meadows of his chosen town. He let neither the elements nor the demands of society keep him from his walks.

Emerson is also clear about the benefits of the move into nature:

> *In the woods, we return to reason and faith. There I feel that nothing can befall me in life, — no disgrace, no calamity, (leaving me my eyes,) which nature cannot repair. Standing on the bare ground, — my head bathed by the blithe air, and uplifted into infinite space, — all mean egotism vanishes. I become a transparent eye-ball; I am nothing; I see all; the currents of the Universal Being circulate through me; I am part or particle of God.*

It is no wonder that Emerson had to leave his chamber metaphorically and physically to truly connect with nature. Remember that his chamber was, in reality, a second-floor study in a parsonage, built by his clergy grandfather, then owned by another clergyman, and decorated throughout with what Nathaniel Hawthorne called "grim prints of Puritan ministers" who "looked strangely like bad angels, or at least like men who had wrestled so continually and sternly with the devil that somewhat of his sooty fierceness had been imparted to their own visages."

When he lived at the Old Manse, Hawthorne promptly put these portraits in the attic, where he didn't have to look at them. Even so, he made the same move as Emerson, from the study to the grounds, in the beginning of *Mosses from the Old Manse*. It would seem that the study at the Old Manse, while a necessary indoor shelter for writing, particularly in bad weather, inspired a desire to head outdoors.

By the summer of 1835, Emerson was launched in a different way. Having finished *Nature*, he was engaged to be married again—to Lidian Jackson of Plymouth, Massachusetts—and he needed a more permanent living situation. He looked around town for a house that could fit his new family, his mother, and his brother and sister-in-law. He finally settled on a home called Coolidge Castle, on the other side of town, and moved out of the Manse in September 1835.

Hawthorne's Old Manse: Home of *Mosses*

After Dr. Ezra Ripley's death in 1841, the Manse lay vacant until 1842, when the young, newly married writer Nathaniel Hawthorne decided to rent it. Ownership of the house had gone to the Reverend Samuel Ripley—a relative of George Ripley, the founder of Brook Farm, where Hawthorne had been living before his marriage. Hawthorne's bride, Sophia Peabody of Salem, had good reason to push for a move from dreary Salem to Concord. Like her sister Elizabeth, Sophia was interested in the intellectual force of the man who had once lived in the Manse. The gravitational pull of Emerson's genius succeeded in drawing the Hawthornes to Concord for what they would later claim to be the happiest three years of their lives.

It is not surprising that the Hawthornes looked back favorably on their time in Concord. The Old Manse provided the famously shy Nathaniel with the privacy and seclusion he craved, as well as the natural beauty that proved as inspirational to him as it had been to Emerson years before. In his introduction to *Mosses*, Hawthorne is an almost giddy tour guide as he introduces the reader to the Manse, or what he called "Fairyland." He gives special attention to the grounds surrounding the house, particularly the garden that Elizabeth Hoar and Cynthia Thoreau, Henry's mother, had arranged as a wedding gift.

Although Hawthorne greatly enjoyed the physical and scenic comforts of the Manse, he was never one to let the natural splendor of a place blind him to its history. He keenly felt the legacy of the house and his place in it. As he notes in *Mosses*, "Nor, in truth, had the Old Manse ever been profaned by a lay occupant, until that memorable summer-afternoon when I entered it as my home. A priest had built it; a priest had succeeded to it; other priestly men, from time to time, had dwelt in it; and children, born in its chambers, had grown up to assume the priestly character." It is perhaps fitting that Hawthorne ends his introductory essay with a request that the reader sit in his study and travel back in time with him, back to the past that provided him with so much material for his stories.

Although Hawthorne seems quite joyful and content in the introduction to *Mosses*, he was reclusive and shy; the old parsonage was ideal for him. Even to his neighbors, Hawthorne was as much a dark mystery as his novels would be. Stories of a figure in dark clothes standing in the garden or walking about the orchards circulated in town and fueled speculation about the sanity of the man from Salem. Yet he did entertain guests, and both Emerson and Thoreau often stopped by. Late one December, for instance, after the river

The Transcendentalist Garden

Given the Transcendentalists' love of nature, as well as the average salary of a philosopher, it is not surprising that many kept gardens. Thoreau had his famous bean field, the Alcotts had a family garden in which each daughter was allowed to plant according to her interests and tastes, and Emily Dickinson was better known during her life as a gardener than as a poet.

Although many New England families kept gardens, most did not swoon over them as Hawthorne did his garden at the Old Manse, most of which was designed and planted by the king of the Transcendentalist philosopher-gardeners, Henry David Thoreau. "I used to visit and revisit it a dozen times a day," Hawthorne wrote, "and stand in deep contemplation over my vegetable progeny with a love that nobody could share or conceive of who had never taken part in the process of creation."

Hawthorne not only admired his garden but also worked in it regularly. Indeed, he devoted page after page of his journals to descriptions of his work in the garden each day. He felt that working in the garden helped restore "the original relation between man and nature," and he delighted in seeing the literal fruits of his labors come up from the ground.

A typical garden of the day included asparagus, beans, squash, peas, corn, and cabbage. The group Gaining Ground, a nonprofit organization feeding the hungry of Boston, has planted an authentic nineteenth-century garden at the Manse. The garden is based on Hawthorne's journals; the journal of George Bradford, a Boston friend of Emerson's; and research done at the library at Old Sturbridge Village, an educational center and re-creation of an 1830s New England town. The one anachronism is that in the nineteenth century, vegetable gardens often included fruit trees planted among the rows, while this garden does not.

Although Gaining Ground's primary mission is to provide healthy, organic food for those in need, the community building involved in creating and running this historically accurate garden is a central part of the experience.

When the Hawthornes moved into the Old Manse, they found a garden planted by Thoreau as a wedding gift.

behind the house had frozen, Emerson and Thoreau came over, and three of America's foremost authors skated until dusk, doing pirouettes and jumps on the ice.

Unfortunately, the Hawthornes' time in the Manse was limited. In October 1845, Samuel Ripley began to plan for a return to the Manse. He sent an army of carpenters, masons, and painters to begin renovations prior to his return. Hawthorne wryly compared the efforts to "rouging the venerable cheeks of one's grandmother." And so the Hawthornes moved out of the Old Manse and went back to Salem, where Nathaniel began working as the Custom House officer, an experience he would describe in the introduction to *The Scarlet Letter.*

After Samuel Ripley's death, the house remained in the Emerson and Ripley families until 1939, when it was given to the Trustees of Reservations, a nonprofit organization dedicated to preserving land and educating people. This group has operated the house as a museum for more than sixty-five years. In addition to offering tours from April through October, the Manse also hosts special events such as re-creations of mid-nineteenth-century Christmas celebrations. The Old Manse is the best symbol of Concord's dual claim to fame: as the site of the battle that started the War of Independence and as the home of two of America's greatest Transcendentalist writers.

The Hawthornes as Vandals

Although the Hawthornes were as quiet and calm a set of tenants as any landlord could want, they did leave their mark on the Old Manse. Standing at the upstairs window looking out on the orchards, Sophia inscribed on the glass with her diamond ring: "Man's accidents are God's purposes. Sophia A. Hawthorne, 1843." Hawthorne added, "Nath. Hawthorne. This is his study, 1843." Sophia then wrote, "The smallest twig leans clear against the sky," to which Hawthorne appended, "Composed by my wife and written with her diamond." Sophia finished with "Inscribed by my husband, at sunset. April 3rd, 1843. In the gold light. S.A.H." These inscriptions are still clearly visible in the glass of the north window.

Emerson's House: The Center of the Movement

In 1835, Emerson was faced with a challenge: to find a house that would be suitable for his new bride, his mother, and his role as an intellectual leader. He settled on a white two-story house at ❹ 28 Cambridge Turnpike, near the intersection with Lexington Road. It proved an excellent choice, and Emerson remained there until his death in 1882.

One of the most notable things about the house is the amount of traffic passing in front of it—which would have been the case in the nineteenth century as well. Especially before the rail line opened in 1844, the Concord Turnpike was a never-ending stream of people traveling by horseback, by stagecoach, and on foot.

The stream of people entering the front gates as guests of the Emersons' was astounding as well. Many of the major writers and thinkers of the era made it a point to visit Concord and Emerson: Margaret Fuller, Henry David Thoreau, Nathaniel Hawthorne, Ellery Channing, Elizabeth Palmer Peabody, Bronson Alcott, Franklin Sanborn, Theodore Parker, Frederic Hedge, Jones Very—and those were just the Transcendentalists. Other celebrated visitors included Walt Whitman, George Curtis, Louis Agassiz, Louisa May Alcott, Daniel Chester French, John Brown, Edwin Morton, Sarah Bradford Ripley, George Bradford, James Fields, the Hoars, and more.

Emerson bought what was called "Coolidge Castle" in 1835 and lived there until his death in 1882. The list of visitors is a veritable "who's who" of American letters: Alcott, Thoreau, Hawthorne, and Whitman are just a handful of the many guests who sat in Emerson's study (the two windows on the lower right).

The constant flow of visitors thrilled Emerson, who had long dreamed of a community of thinkers nearby. His journal entry for May 6, 1842, reads:

> *Here is a proposition for the formation of a good neighborhood. Hedge shall live at Concord, & Mr. Hawthorn: George Bradford shall come then; & Mrs. Ripley afterward. Who knows but Margaret Fuller & Charles Newcomb would presently be added? These if added to our present kings & queens, would make a rare, an unrivalled company. If these all had their hearth & home here, we might have a solid social satisfaction. . . . We might find that each of us was more completely isolated & sacred than before.*

Emerson did most of his entertaining in the study at the front of the house. Today, the Concord Museum across the street has re-created his study, complete with the original furniture. Standing in the room, it is easy to imagine the tall, intense minister embarking on one of the most prolific literary and philosophic careers of his time. In the center of the room stands his writing table, an ingenious invention: a spinning circular table with drawers fitted into the sides. Emerson stored his papers for various projects in the drawers and, as he switched from one project to the next, would spin his table like a lazy Susan to reach the appropriate drawer.

Massive bookshelves line one side of the wall from floor to ceiling. Close inspection of the shelves reveals just how important their contents were; the shelves are partitioned into blocks with handles along the side so they can be easily removed in case of fire. Bookshelves are on the other walls as well, framing a couch where many of his guests sat while they talked. Over the mantelpiece hangs a copy of Michelangelo's painting of the Fates.

Emerson wrote at the table in the center of the image, putting his papers in the drawers; he rotated the table to get papers from different drawers.

Perhaps as important as the study was the hallway, not for discussions but for the walking sticks and hat placed there at the ready for Emerson's afternoon walks. The sticks are appropriately well-polished, sturdy gems that Emerson would offer to his guests if they wished to accompany him . . . and they usually did. His favored walking companions included Thoreau, Alcott, Channing, and, when they grew old enough to keep up with his long strides, his children.

When Emerson left the house he had a variety of options, but the path he most often followed led around the back of the red barn and toward Walden Pond, a mere two miles from his backyard. His lot sloped ever so slightly down toward Mill Brook in the back, and had been planted with hundreds of apple and pear trees by Emerson himself. This location gave him plenty of directions in which to head; his other favorite walks included Sleepy Hollow and Fair Haven Cliff.

It is a testament to both Emerson and the town of Concord that when Emerson's home caught fire early on the morning of July 24, 1872, the writer had merely to run outside and shout for the town to rush to his aid. There are accounts of heroic men climbing up on the roof and spraying the house with one hand while hanging on to the peak of the roof with the other, and equally heroic stories of the Alcott daughters saving as many of Emerson's manuscripts and writings as they could.

The Emersons' furniture was taken from the house and stored in various homes, barns, and cellars to keep it safe while the house was being repaired. Townspeople and friends collected over $18,000 to rebuild the house—far more than what was needed, so Emerson and his daughter Ellen went on a tour of Europe and Egypt. On Emerson's return in the fall of 1872, the town welcomed its most famous citizen back with great fanfare and celebration. A band played while rented carriages brought the Emersons home under a special arch built for the occasion, and the town's children sang "Home Sweet Home." Emerson and his home had become symbols not just of a set of philosophic and literary tenets, but of an idealism and optimism that deeply affected those around him.

Alcott's Hillside

As soon as Bronson Alcott was able to bring his family to live in Emerson's Concord, he did so. After staying for a brief time in a rented farmhouse, he bought, with Emerson's help, what was known as the old Cogswell place at ❺ 455 Lexington Road. Alcott immediately set about renovating the colonial saltbox just down

Both Bronson Alcott and Nathaniel Hawthorne lived at 455 Lexington Road, originally built in the late seventeenth century.

Lexington Road from Emerson's house, creating terraces, arbors, and pavilions along the rear of the house by the hill, as well as a study for himself and private bedrooms for his two oldest daughters. He also took a shed on the property, cut it in two, and attached each piece to either side of the main house. Drawing his inspiration from the slope rising steeply behind the house, Alcott renamed the place Hillside.

While only a temporary stop for the Alcotts (they lived here for seven years), Hillside provided the family with a safe, comfortable place for the girls to grow up. Indeed, many of the adventures recounted by Louisa May Alcott in *Little Women* were experienced at Hillside. Plays like the ones presented by the March family were created at Hillside and staged in the barn. Louisa May pursued other literary efforts while here, too, such as putting together her first published book, *Flower Fables*.

Hawthorne's Wayside

The next owner of the house was another author who had begun to see a bit of success. By the time Nathaniel

Alcott worked hard at transforming an old colonial saltbox into a more ornate home for his family. He did this sketch of his home in 1845.

Hawthorne bought Hillside in 1852, he had already published *Twice-Told Tales*, *Mosses from the Old Manse*, *The Scarlet Letter*, and *The House of the Seven Gables*. He and his wife, Sophia, were returning to Concord after a seven-year hiatus, during which they had lived in three separate houses in Salem, one in West Newton, and one in Lenox, Massachusetts.

The Hawthornes bought the house from the Alcotts for $1,500 and immediately renamed it The Wayside. Hawthorne explained the name in a letter to Evert Augustus Duyckinck: "Alcott called it 'Hillside' as it stands close at the base of a steep ascent; but as it is also in proximity (too nigh, indeed) to the road leading into the village, I have re-baptized it 'The Wayside,'— Which seems to me to possess a moral as well as descriptive propriety."

During his first year in the house, Hawthorne completed one of his most influential pieces. His biography of Franklin Pierce, a college friend from his Bowdoin days, was important not for its contribution to the literary world but for its role in helping to elect Pierce as the fourteenth president of the United States. Hawthorne was then rewarded with a consulship in Liverpool, England. The Hawthornes spent the next seven years living in Europe.

After they returned to Concord in 1860, they completed a number of additions to the house. Perhaps the most striking was the three-story tower in the center of the building, which houses the study that Hawthorne called his "sky parlor." Hawthorne had the study built at the top of the stairs, quiet and removed from the bustle of the house. He imagined himself writing while standing with his back to the window at a specially made desk built into the outside of the stairwell. Unfortunately, the room, with its tin roof, proved unbearably hot, and in the winter dreadfully cold. So Hawthorne used it only in the early spring and autumn months, and worked out of the front parlor for the rest of the year.

Hawthorne would live for only four more years in this house; he died in 1864 of what may have been pneumonia while traveling in Plymouth, Massachusetts. His family kept the house until 1870. In 1883 Harriett Lothrop, the creator under the pen name of Margaret Sidney of the immensely popular children's book series,

Hawthorne's sky parlor writing desk.

Louisa May Alcott, 1832–88

The four daughters of Bronson and Abba Alcott (Anna, Louisa, Beth, and May) were born into an unusual and unusually talented family. Their father, a philosopher and educational reformer, and mother, an abolitionist and feminist, encouraged and fostered their daughters' creativity and intellectual pursuits. The girls also had numerous opportunities to talk with their father's friends, including Ralph Waldo Emerson, Henry David Thoreau, Ellery Channing, and Nathaniel Hawthorne, who helped foster their talents.

Given this support, it is not surprising that Louisa May decided on writing and publishing as a way to make money. Most of her early works were fables and fantastic children's stories aimed at earning enough to help support her family, but it was with the serial publication of *Little Women* in 1868 that she enjoyed her first major success. In total, she wrote more than thirty books. While she claimed she understood little of her father's philosophical musings, many Transcendentalist values are portrayed in her stories, especially in the educational models shown in *Little Women* and *Little Men*. These models continue to influence teachers and students today.

Louisa May Alcott in her study at Orchard House. She earned more from her writing than her father and nearly all of his Transcendentalist friends.

The Five Little Peppers, bought the house and did much to preserve it. The home remained in her family until 1965, when it became the first literary landmark purchased by the National Park Service. The house is now part of Minute Man National Historical Park and serves as a museum celebrating the lives and works of the Alcotts, Nathaniel Hawthorne, and Margaret Sidney. (Conducted tours take place from May to October and special literary exhibits are presented in the barn.)

Orchard House

Next door to Hawthorne's Wayside, with only a steep and forested hill separating the two, is ❻ **Orchard House at 399 Lexington Road.** This was the home of the Alcott family from 1857 to 1877, their longest residence anywhere.

When the Alcotts bought the house in 1857, it was little more than a decrepit shack surrounded by apple

The Alcott home for twenty years, the Orchard House at 399 Lexington Road now hosts thousands of *Little Women* fans who want to see the house in which Louisa May Alcott wrote the novel.

orchards, with another farming shanty farther back on the property. Besides renaming the property Orchard House in honor of its twelve acres of apple orchards, Alcott worked hard to create a livable family homestead. He literally rolled the farmer's shanty down the hill and attached it to the back of the existing house. He changed many of the thresholds from squares to arches, and put in arched recesses on either side of the fireplace.

Perhaps most important, he built a small desk right into the window-jamb for his daughter, Louisa May. It was from this room that she wrote her most famous works, including *Little Women* (although many of the events described in the book took place in the family's earlier home, Hillside).

Concord School of Philosophy

The Concord School of Philosophy, long a dream of Bronson Alcott and many of the other Transcendentalists, opened during the summer of 1879. The first summer's program was held in the study of Orchard House, after the Alcotts had moved into town. The following summer, the school was able to move into what was called ❼ **the Hillside Chapel,** next to the Orchard House at 399 Lexington Road, where it stayed for the next eight years.

Hillside Chapel.

Based on Plato's Academy, the school brought in a wide variety of lecturers to discuss a broad range of subjects, from Thomas Wentworth Higginson on American literature to Emerson on memory and Franklin Sanborn on philanthropy. Sessions lasted six weeks, with lectures and discussion sections held each day. Although the school was a success in fulfilling the goals of its founders, it was nonetheless a source of mirth among the

A lifelong dream of Bronson Alcott, the Concord School of Philosophy was a unique opportunity for adults to engage in educational and philosophical pursuits outside the confines of colleges and seminaries.

townspeople. Even Louisa May Alcott wrote wryly of the "budding philosophers" who roosted on their steps "like hens, waiting for corn."

Elizabeth Palmer Peabody and William Torey Harris outside the Concord School of Philosophy.

Orchard House was closed in 1877, after the Alcotts bought Thoreau's house in town. Bronson Alcott spent the remainder of his years running the Concord School of Philosophy, until he had a paralyzing stroke in 1882. Bronson and Louisa May died in Boston within days of each other, in March 1888.

The house is now an integral part of any literary tour of Concord, with tours offered on most days. The house offers special events and outreach programs almost year-round, including reenactments by costumed actors and "period celebrations" as well as writing workshops.

Sleepy Hollow Cemetery

In the early years of the Transcendentalist movement in Concord, a favored walk of many was ❽ Sleepy Hollow, on Bedford Road. Its quiet, shaded dells and rolling hills just one block east of Monument Square in the town center provided a refuge for shy, reclusive figures such as Hawthorne as well as inspiration for the more animated, such as Margaret Fuller and Ralph Waldo Emerson. In fact, it was here that Hawthorne and Fuller were engaged in conversation one Sunday when Emerson stumbled upon them and joined their conversation. Hawthorne noted that Emerson, despite "his clerical consecration, had found no better way of spending the Sabbath than to ramble among the woods." True enough, for Emerson had found "Muses in the woods" and "whispers . . . in the breezes." According to the tenets he set out in *Nature*, there was much to be studied and learned in the dells of Sleepy Hollow.

So it was not surprising that when the town decided in the mid-1850s to create a new cemetery, they chose Sleepy Hollow. Nor was it surprising that when the cemetery was formally consecrated in 1855, Emerson gave the address.

Along a shaded rise in the center of the cemetery, known as Author's Ridge, now reside the graves of the Hawthornes, the Alcotts, the Emersons, the Thoreaus, Ellery Channing, Elizabeth Peabody, Daniel Chester French, and others. Sleepy Hollow is a wonderful place for the citizens of Concord to spend the everlasting, as an aging Hawthorne noted to the young visiting author Rebecca Harding Davis one day when they dawdled there: "We New Englanders begin to enjoy ourselves—when we are dead."

Beyond the front gates of the cemetery is a clearly marked footpath to Author's Ridge. The first graves are those of the Thoreau family. Henry David Thoreau's grave lies just to the left of the central family marker. His simple gravestone is often decorated with natural adornments left behind by pilgrims: flowers, leaves, pinecones, and even stones.

The Alcott gravestones are clustered around a central marker, with Bronson Alcott to the left and Louisa May just in back of him. Judging from the number of decorations and gifts left behind, her fame seems to have far surpassed that of her father.

As befits his shyness in life, Hawthorne is set back from the trail. He and his wife lie near each other, one of Transcendentalism's more romantic couples. It is most likely imagination, but the Hawthorne gravesite appears darker, more shaded, and more removed than the others. One almost fears to tread there, not wanting to disturb the peace of that reclusive and occasionally tormented writer. It seems better to pass quickly by to the site that dominates the ridge, that of the Emerson family.

When approaching the Emersons' grave markers from the footpath, it is difficult to ascertain which is that of Ralph Waldo Emerson until one circles around to the front, where the ridge slopes down to the valley. Then it is clear that the enormous chunk of pink granite is Emerson's grave. Its bronze plaque reads: "The passive master lent his hand / to the vast soul that o'er him

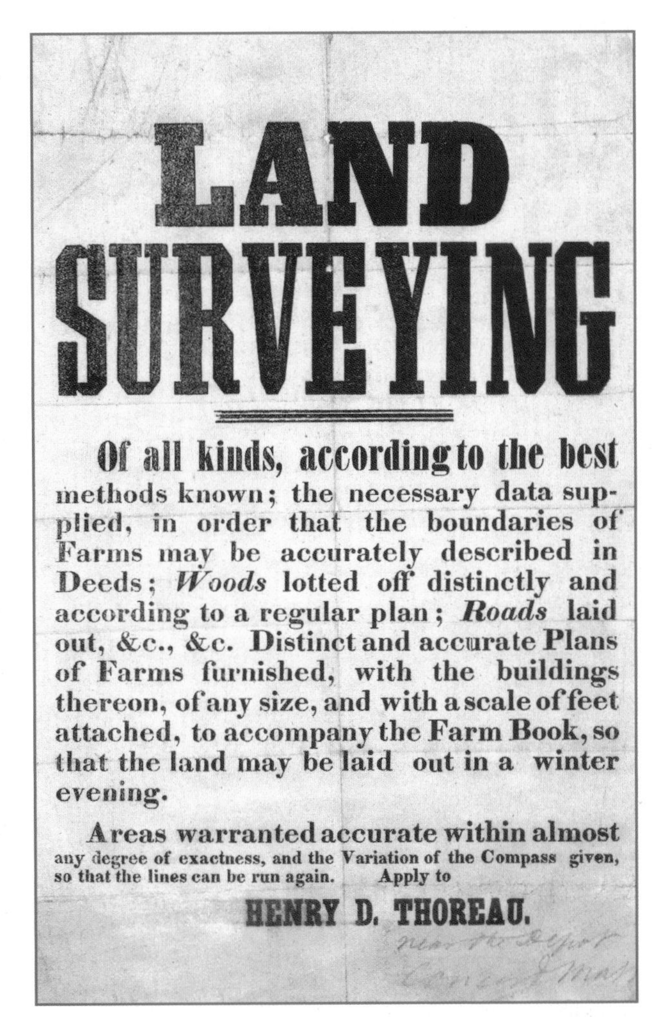

LAND
SURVEYING

Of all kinds, according to the best methods known; the necessary data supplied, in order that the boundaries of Farms may be accurately described in Deeds; *Woods* lotted off distinctly and according to a regular plan; ***Roads*** laid out, &c., &c. Distinct and accurate Plans of Farms furnished, with the buildings thereon, of any size, and with a scale of feet attached, to accompany the Farm Book, so that the land may be laid out in a winter evening.

Areas warranted accurate within almost any degree of exactness, and the Variation of the Compass given, so that the lines can be run again. Apply to

HENRY D. THOREAU.

Among his many trades, Thoreau was a skilled and busy surveyor. His assignments included surveying the area for the gates to Sleepy Hollow Cemeterey.

Numbered with the Numerous Dead

Fellow Transcendentalist and Salem resident Jones Very visited the graves of Hawthorne and Thoreau while in Concord and wrote "On Visiting the Graves of Hawthorne and Thoreau" sometime after 1864.

Beneath these shades, beside yon winding stream,
Lies Hawthorne's manly form, the mortal part!
The soul, that loved to meditate and dream,
Might linger here unwilling to depart,
But that a higher life has called away
To fairer scenes, to nobler work and thought.
Why should the spirit then on earth delay,
That has a glimpse of such bright regions caught!
And near another, Nature's child, doth rest, —
Thoreau, who loved each woodland path to tread;
So gently sleeping on his mother's breast!
Living, though numbered with the numerous dead.
We mourn! But hope will whisper in the heart,
We meet again and meet no more to part.

Thoreau's headstone is often surrounded with gifts from literary pilgrims, mostly in the form of natural decorations such as pinecones, flowers, and leaves.

Author's Ridge, where Concord's most famous writers are buried, is a short walk from the entrance gates at Sleepy Hollow.

This massive chunk of granite serves as the only marker of Emerson's grave.

planned." Sitting atop the nose of the ridge, the gravesite presides over Sleepy Hollow much as its inhabitant did over Concord during his lifetime.

Concord Today

As befits a town with so much history, Concord makes no apologies for keeping its heritage front and center. It is difficult to turn around here without running into the name of a famous author or his or her works. Concord has done an especially good job of preserving its architectural integrity. From the beautiful ❾ **First Parish Church** at **20 Lexington Road** to the rebuilt Old North Bridge, Concord takes great pride in what it was and what it has become.

Perhaps the easiest place to get a sense of this heritage is at ❿ **the Concord Museum** at **200 Lexington Road,** across the street from Emerson's home on the Concord Turnpike. The museum uses Thoreau's collection, as well as that of early Concord

Concord today.

Emerson's grandfather, William Emerson, was the minister at the First Church at 20 Lexington Road. He was succeeded by Ezra Ripley, who held the post for sixty-three years. It remains a Unitarian church.

memorabilia collector Cummings Davis, to introduce the visitor to the Concord of yesterday. The emphasis is on Emerson and Thoreau, but the collection also provides glimpses of Concord before the British settlers arrived in 1635, as well as the Concord of Damon Mill and the Concord that became the twentieth-century suburb of Boston.

From the museum, it's an easy walk to the former homes of Emerson, Alcott, and Hawthorne, as well as into

Concord Free Public Library.

of Concord and beyond, the collection is one of the top resources for those interested in the Transcendentalists.

Concord is also home to the Concord Academy, a modern-day college preparatory school near the location of Franklin Sanborn's academy, as well as the Fenn School and a number of public schools. Many of the town's residents commute to Boston on the railroad, just as the townspeople did in the mid-nineteenth century, although the train depot is now a store and the walls of the station are painted with murals of Walden Pond.

town, where one can buy a good cup of coffee, a used book, or any of the goods one might find in any New England small town.

At the far end of Main Street, in the center of the fork of Main Street and Sudbury Road, is another of Concord's treasures. ⓫ The Concord Free Public Library is enjoying its newly remodeled home at 129 Main Street, which boasts an array of wonderful features. The Special Collections department is particularly impressive, with great primary and secondary resources pertaining to Concord and its people. From the correspondence of Emerson, Alcott, and Thoreau to Herbert Wendell Gleason's nineteenth-century photos

All in all, Concord is that rarity: a livable tourist destination. It has perhaps lost a bit of the radicalism and intellectual drive that its most famous citizens brought here, but it continues to attract new residents and visitors thanks to its convenience to Boston, its great sense of history, and the striking beauty of its rivers, meadows, and hills.

Chapter 5

Walden

Secular and Sacred

The still waters of Walden invite reflection.

Walden

It is not far beyond the Village church,
After we pass the wood that skirts the road,
A Lake,—the blue-eyed Walden, that doth smile
Most tenderly upon its neighbor Pines,
And they, as if to recompense this love,
In double beauty spread their branches forth.
This Lake has tranquil loveliness and breadth,
And of late years has added to its charms,
For one attracted to its pleasant edge,
Has built himself a little Hermitage,
where with much piety he passes life.
Thrice happy art thou, Walden! in thyself,
Such purity is in thy limpid springs;
In those green shores which do reflect in thee,
And in this man who dwells upon thy edge,
A holy man within a Hermitage.

—Ellery Channing

A mere two miles from the center of Concord is a small lake surrounded by low hills and dense forests. Framed on two sides by the busy Routes 2 and 126, Walden Pond is a lovely swimming hole and fishing pond. The trails around the lake are wonderful for hiking and jogging. This area is enjoyed by hundreds of thousands of visitors each year, many of whom give little or no thought to Transcendentalism.

For Thoreauvians, though, Walden Pond is unique among cultural landmarks for its role as the inspiration for, birthplace of, and monument to a single masterwork. While it may be true that more people have heard of Walden Pond, or even *Walden*, than of the Transcen-dentalist who made them famous, Henry David

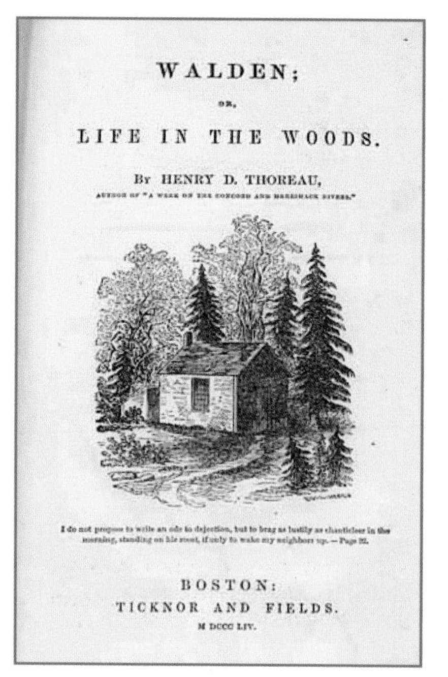
WALDEN;

OR,

LIFE IN THE WOODS.

By HENRY D. THOREAU,

I do not propose to write an ode to dejection, but to brag as lustily as chanticleer in the morning, standing on his roost, if only to wake my neighbors up. — Page 92.

BOSTON:
TICKNOR AND FIELDS.
M DCCC LIV.

The title page of Thoreau's *Walden; or, Life in the Woods* featured a line drawing based on one done by Sophia Thoreau, Henry's younger sister. Toward the end of his life, Thoreau asked that the subtitle be dropped.

Thoreau's two-year stint at the pond has inspired countless people from all walks of life, from political leaders and environmental activists to philosophers, literary devotees, rock stars, and Transcendentalist seekers. To those who have been touched by *Walden's* message, Walden Pond looms large in the imagination. It is both an ideal and a location. It is a system of thought, an American gem, a cause worth fighting for, and a quiet place just outside the center of Concord.

Even though Thoreau was not the first to consider moving to Walden (Ellery Channing had contemplated the idea a few years earlier) or even the first to accomplish it, he succeeded in ways others had not. Not only did he carefully live the Transcendentalist ideals espoused in his own poetry, Thoreau also created one of the most influential works in American literature out of his experiment in living "deliberately."

Walden; or, Life in the Woods is, on its most basic level, an account of Thoreau's time at Walden Pond. But even in its structure (Thoreau collapsed two years into one, and the book moves from summer to spring), *Walden* is not a straightforward narrative of day-to-day existence. As many have pointed out, it is a journey taken by staying still and paying attention. It is about Thoreau's quest to seek his own original relationship to the universe by seeing the universe in everything around him.

Transcendentalism's Native Son

Thoreau himself was not immune to the scrutiny and criticism of those who were mystified by the choices he was making. Many of his neighbors did not understand the Concord-born philosopher; they wondered why a Harvard-educated man seemed to do little with his college degree. Even in the arena of progressive education, he did not quite fit in. Although he landed an excellent teaching job at the Center School in Concord, he quit after only two weeks because he could not accept the school's policy of flogging its students. After some self-examination and an essentially fruitless job search, he reached the conclusion that he wanted to be a writer.

But if one can judge by the way he describes the requirements for the act of reading in *Walden*, Thoreau was not necessarily interested in writing for a popular audience. What he envisioned was a more careful and deliberate endeavor:

> *To read well, that is, to read true books in a true spirit, is a noble exercise, and one that will task the reader more than any exercise which the customs of the day esteem. It requires a training such as the athletes underwent, the steady intention almost of the whole life to this object. Books must be read as deliberately and reservedly as they were written.*

Thoreau's Face

Thoreau's face hinted at his cantankerous and intense personality—what Hawthorne politely called his "wild original nature." Hawthorne less politely summed up his contemporary's looks: "He is as ugly as sin, long-nosed, queer-mouthed, and with uncouth and somewhat rustic, although courteous manners, corresponding very well with such an exterior."

Hawthorne liked Thoreau, however, and softened his description thus: "His ugliness is of an honest and agreeable fashion, and becomes him much better than beauty." Perhaps Thoreau's visage is better immortalized in bronze, forever scanning the woods near Walden.

Of the three known portraits of Thoreau, this daguerreotype is perhaps the most familiar.

This bronze version of Thoreau's face is kinder and warmer than the famous daguerreotype.

By the time Thoreau retired to the woods, many in the town assumed that he was merely a cranky hermit going off to the woods to avoid people. And it's easy to see how they might have gotten this impression. After all, here was a man who declared in *Walden*: "the mass of men lead lives of quiet desperation. What is called resignation is confirmed desperation." And who wrote, "I do not wish to flatter my townsmen, nor to be flattered by them, for that will not advance either of us. We need to be provoked, — goaded like oxen, as we are, into a trot." Or who proclaimed, even more pointedly, "Society is always diseased, and the best is most so." And who wrote, "Men tire me."

However, to view Thoreau only as a misanthrope would be to miss the point, for *Walden* is full of hope and humor as well as soaring, ecstatic descriptions of natural splendor that both clearly describe the objects in front of him and serve as symbols of a system of thought that is perhaps Thoreau's most enduring legacy. In *Walden*, Thoreau teaches his readers to view the pond and its environs as a microcosm of the greater world. He sees the clash of nations in a war between the ants, citizens of town in the fish, a life in the earth or in the river, a year in a day, and a day in the pond. Not just evidence of divinity but Divinity itself is everywhere; it just needs to be studied closely.

Part of the reason Thoreau is often misinterpreted may be a lack of understanding about what he actually did and why. As he described in his journal in the spring of 1845, Thoreau was looking for a place to work on his writing and gain some distance from his obligations in town. By the time he wrote about this in *Walden*, he

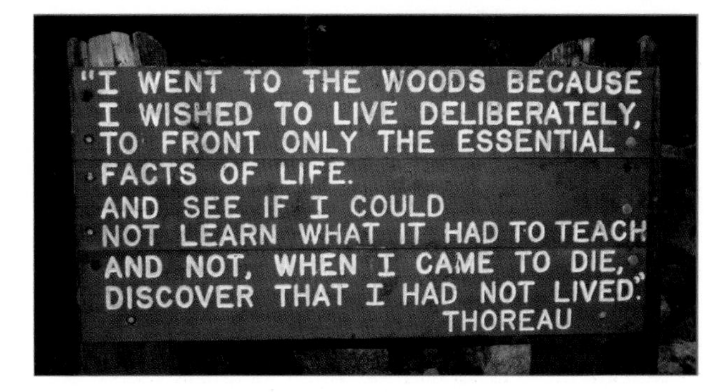

Perhaps one of Thoreau's most famous passages, these words adorn the sign marking the site of his house.

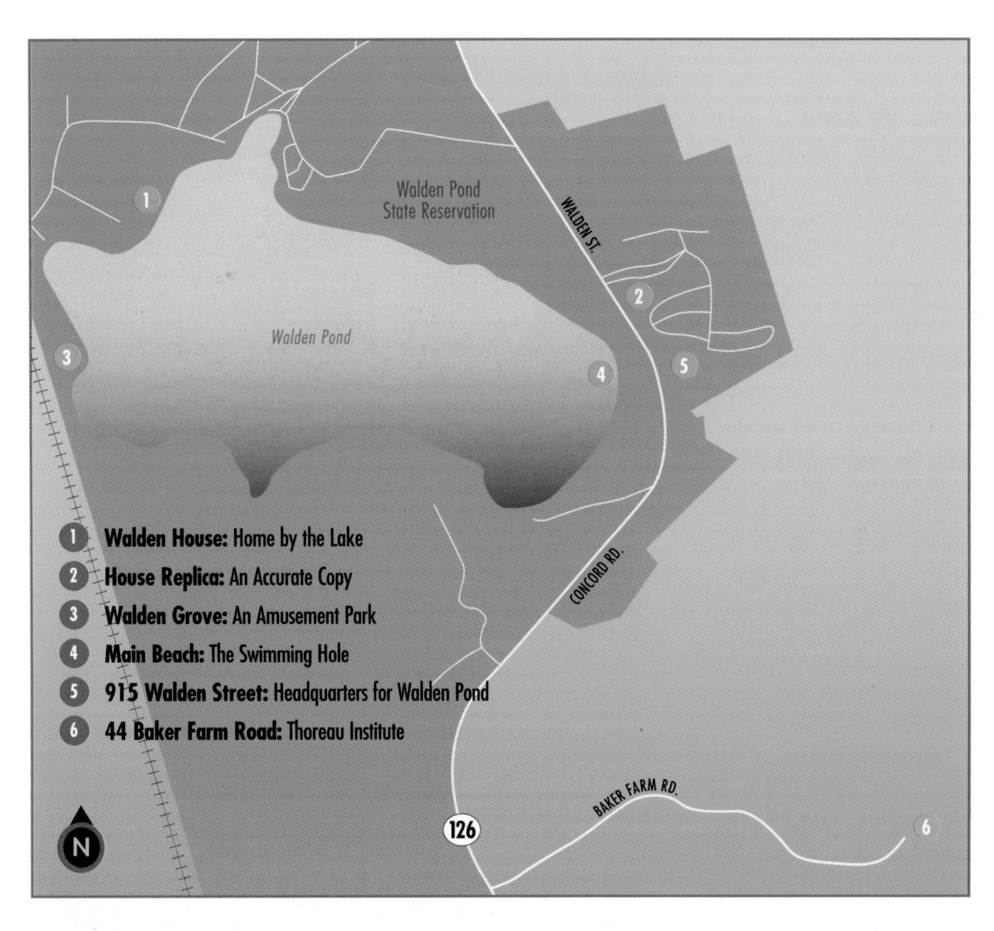

Thoreau investigated and considered a number of different locations before settling on Walden. According to Ellery Channing, Thoreau considered sites along the Sudbury River, on Fair Haven Hill, on Cliff Hill, and at Baker Farm. He may have also considered Flint's Pond, but ultimately settled on the pond that was the favorite walking destination of his Concord friends.

In some ways, it was also a homecoming; he had visited the pond as a child and remembered that visit as a wonderful experience. But the deciding factor may have been the fact that Emerson had recently purchased eleven acres of land bordering the lake and was willing to let his young protégé use it rent free. Thoreau chose a site along the longest inlet (what is now called "Thoreau's Cove") and built ❶ Walden House just back from the water.

claimed, "My purpose in going to Walden Pond was not to live cheaply nor to live dearly there, but to transact some private business with the fewest obstacles." Later, he clarified this "private business" in one of the best-known passages from *Walden* (it is even on the sign that stands today at the site of his cabin): "I went to the woods because I wished to live deliberately, to front only the essential facts of life, and see if I could not learn what it had to teach, and not, when I came to die, discover that I had not lived." This was not an idle sojourn but an active quest.

A Pond of His Own

Excursions to Walden Pond, literary or otherwise, certainly did not begin (or end) with Thoreau's experiment. Emerson often journeyed to Walden Woods

The House

Thoreau's ten-by-fifteen-foot house was a model of engineering and craftsmanship. Made completely from pine, most of it felled and hewn by Thoreau himself, the house kept him warm and dry for the two years of his experiment. When Thoreau left Walden, Emerson took possession of the cabin and then sold it to his gardener, Hugh Whelan. Whelan then tried to move the house to the site of Thoreau's bean field near Walden Pond. In 1849, James and Daniel Clark brought it to the far side of Concord, where it was used, among other things, to store grain. From there, its fate is uncertain, but at some point it was dismantled and its timber used to repair barns and other farm buildings.

History is never lost in Concord, however; the area now boasts a number of versions. One ❷ **house replica** is in the parking lot of Walden Pond State Reservation; another stands just outside the Concord Museum. The most historically accurate one is being constructed at the Thoreau Institute, a research and conservation facility near the site of Thoreau's cabin. The framing and siding were conducted according to information from *Walden*, Thoreau's journal, and other primary sources.

This re-creation of Thoreau's house is one of three in the Concord area. It sits in the Walden Pond parking area.

A view through the window of the version of Thoreau's house that stands in the Walden Pond parking lot.

for inspiration and rejuvenation. As he describes in his journal and as the accounts of his children confirm, Walden was Emerson's most favored and frequent destination. And although Hawthorne had spent only a few years in Concord by the time Thoreau went to Walden, he, too, was a fan of the pond:

> *Walden Pond was clear and beautiful as usual. It tempted me to bathe; and, though the water was thrillingly cold, it was like the thrill of a happy death. Never was there such transparent water as this. I threw sticks into it, and saw them float suspended on an almost invisible medium. It seemed as if the pure air were beneath them, as well as above. It is fit for baptisms; but one would not wish it to be polluted by having sins washed into it. None but angels should bathe in it; but blessed babies might be dipped into its bosom.*

Once Thoreau decided to build himself a house by the pond, he did not idle. He planned his experiment through the late winter and early spring, dug the foundation for his house in March, framed it in April, raised the walls and roof in May with the help of friends, and covered the ten-by-fifteen-foot structure with recycled shingles bought from an Irish immigrant who had been working to build the Boston-Fitchburg rail line. In early summer he planted beans and a vegetable garden, and moved in officially on July 4, 1845. He added a chimney in November and plastered the house at the end of that month.

The house he settled into was a wood-frame cabin based on the cottage-style architecture imported from England. About the size of a garden shed, it was a far cry from the grand houses along Main Street in Concord. His friend Ellery Channing called it "a wooden inkstand." Thoreau embraced the size, however: "My dwelling was small, and I could hardly entertain an echo in it; but it seemed larger for being a single apartment and remote from neighbors. All of the attractions of a house were concentrated in one room; it was kitchen, chamber, parlor, and keeping-room." Thoreau's only complaint about the size was that it sometimes got too crowded, not with people but with thoughts: "One inconvenience I sometimes experienced in so small a house, the difficulty of getting to a sufficient distance from my guest when we began to utter the big thoughts in big words." Philosophy, for Thoreau, was an epic battle, better suited to the outdoors:

> *You want room for your thoughts to get into sailing trim and run a course or two before they make their port. The bullet of your thought must have overcome its lateral and ricochet motion and fallen into its last and steady course before it reaches the ear of the hearer, else it may plough out again through the side of his head.*

This is not philosophy for the timid.

For the next two years, Thoreau made his primary home by the lake. His front porch was about a hundred paces from the water, and while it may be difficult to imagine now, since the trees have closed in significantly since his time, Thoreau was able to watch the sun rise over the water and observe the lake at any time of the day from his doorstep.

The Pond

Although Walden Pond is not geologically much different from the lakes and ponds surrounding it (it is a so-called kettle lake, left behind by receding glaciers), it does hold one mystery that stumped even the astute naturalist Thoreau. Walden's water does not fluctuate with droughts or intense rain. Thoreau noted that there are no visible inlets or outlets to Walden, and pondered the scenarios. His theory was that the pond was fed by a spring seeping in from deep underground.

The view from the actual house site down to Walden Pond.

Over the years, many others have proposed theories as well, such as the pond's being fed by an underground stream making its way from the White Mountains of New Hampshire to the Long Island Sound. Another more far-fetched theory was that Walden really had no bottom and was therefore unaffected by surface changes. In fact, Walden is fed by seepage from the surrounding hills through the sandy soil on top of the solid hardpan just underneath the topsoil.

Thoreau was able to disprove the bottomless theory by carefully mapping the depths of Walden just before the ice broke up in the spring. Although he proved that the pond has a bottom, he was perhaps even more satisfied with the metaphor he found by plumbing the lake:

> *This is a remarkable depth for so small an area; yet not an inch of it can be spared by the imagination. What if all ponds were shallow? Would it not react on the minds of men? I am thankful that this pond was made deep and pure for a symbol. While men believe in the infinite some ponds will be thought to be bottomless.*

Although unable to solve the mystery of Walden's water source, Thoreau did not lack the ability to describe that water in soaring poetical terms:

> *Walden is blue at one time and green at another, even from the same point of view. Lying between the earth and the heavens, it partakes of the color of both. Viewed from a hill-top it reflects the color of the sky; but near at hand it is of a yellowish tint next the shore where you can see the sand, then a light green, which gradually deepens to a uniform dark green in the body of the pond. In some lights, viewed even from a hill-top, it is of a vivid green next the shore. Some have referred this to the reflection of the verdure; but it is equally green there against the railroad sandbank, and in the spring, before the leaves are expanded, and it may be simply the result of the prevailing blue mixed with the yellow of the sand. Such is the color of its iris.*

In Thoreau's view, Walden (and nearby lakes) became the very window into the soul of the earth and the mirror of oneself: "A lake is the landscape's most beautiful and expressive feature. It is earth's eye; looking into which the beholder measures the depth of his own nature." It was in these "great crystals on the surface of the earth, Lakes of Light," that the Transcendentalists could see the spiritual forces at work in the natural world and define their relationship to the universe.

Nor did Thoreau limit his interaction with the water to the shore. Aboard his boat, he plumbed the depths of the lake, observed fish, and chased loons. He also spent nights trolling for pickerel by moonlight, or drifting through the dark fishing for metaphors: "It was very queer, especially in dark nights, when your thoughts had wandered to vast and cosmogonal themes in other spheres, to feel this faint jerk, which came to interrupt your dreams and link you to Nature again. . . . Thus I caught two fishes as it were with one hook."

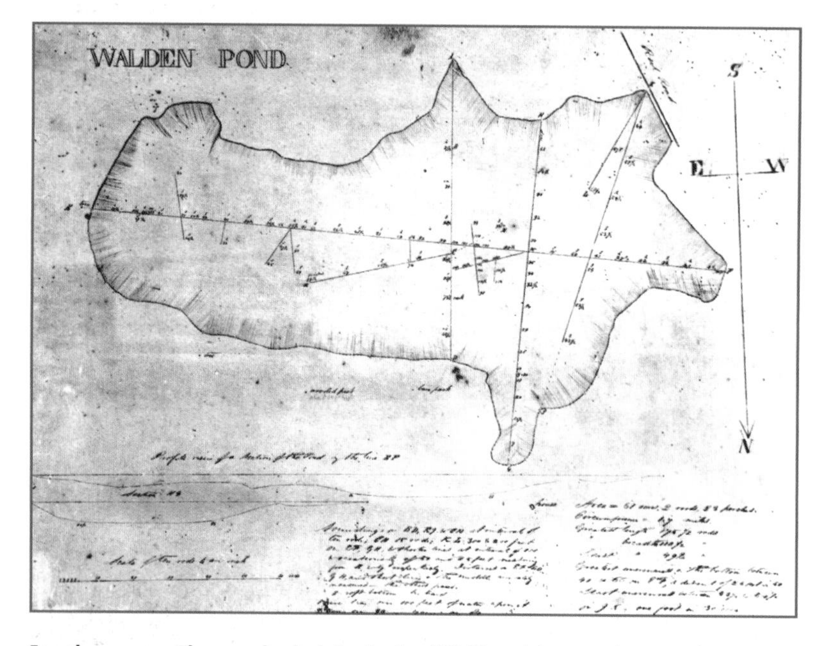

Ever the surveyor, Thoreau plumbed the depths of Walden while it was frozen and created this surprisingly accurate map of the pond.

The Woods

Another subject of Thoreau's close scrutiny was the forest surrounding the pond. Already well versed in the woods before he came to the pond to live, he found in Walden a forum to describe those trees left standing in an already well-logged area:

Sometimes I rambled to pine groves, standing like temples, or like fleets at sea, full-rigged, with wavy boughs, and rippling with light, so soft and green and shady that the Druids would have forsaken their oaks to worship in them; or to the cedar woods beyond Flint's Pond, where the trees, covered with hoary blue berries, spiring higher and higher, are fit to stand before Valhalla, and the creeping juniper covers the ground with wreaths full of fruit; or to swamps where the usnea lichen hangs in festoons from the black-spruce trees, and toadstools, round tables of the swamp gods, cover the ground, and more beautiful fungi adorn the stumps, like butterflies or shells, vegetable winkles; where the swamp-pink and dogwood grow, the red alderberry glows like eyes of imps, the waxwork grooves and crushes the hardest woods in its folds, and the wild holly berries make the beholder forget his home with their beauty, and he is dazzled and tempted by nameless other wild forbidden fruits, too fair for mortal taste.

In addition, his time among these trees gave Thoreau the opportunity to observe how trees disperse their seeds and succeed each other. These studies led to his more scientific later works such as the essays "The Succession of Forest Trees" and "The Dispersion of Seeds." Both were given, either in part or whole, as lectures in front of farmers and merchants.

It is the loss of these trees that Thoreau later mourns. When he first came to Walden at the age of four, the land was completely forested, but as the nineteenth century advanced, the forests were decimated and the future turned grim for both the natural area and the mythic source of his imagination: "Since I left those shores the woodchoppers have still further laid them waste, and now for many a year there will be no more rambling through the aisles of the wood. . . . My Muse may be excused if she is silent henceforth. How can you expect the birds to sing when their groves are cut down?"

Never one to miss the forest for the trees, Thoreau gave his readers a thorough examination of the ecosystem surrounding the pond, including the plants and animals that also made Walden Woods their home. Some, such as the mice who listened to his flute, even took up residence in his home. In *Walden*, Thoreau mentions the names of nearly a hundred different species of plants and animals that he observed while at the pond. This extraordinary catalog is part of the legacy that Thoreau left us: being witness to the beauty and variety in nature is often an important first step to preserving it. For Thoreau, as for many

In Thoreau's time, the woods often rang with the sounds of axes and saws.

of the Transcendentalists, the outer landscape corresponded to an inner state.

These forests were wild places, not just literally but metaphorically. The wilderness may have offered the peace and serenity found in communion with nature, but Thoreau was attracted to its darker, more predatory side as well: "I caught a glimpse of a woodchuck stealing across my path, and felt a strange thrill of savage delight, and was strongly tempted to seize and devour him raw; not that I was hungry then, except for that wildness which he represented." According to Thoreau, this sense of the natural and animal plays an integral role in understanding human nature. The balance between the animal side and "higher nature" must be examined, however, for its lessons on how to live a more healthy existence. "We are conscious of an animal in us, which awakens in proportion as our higher nature slumbers. It is reptile and sensual, and perhaps cannot be wholly expelled; like the worms which, even in life and health, occupy our bodies."

Neighbors

Besides the woodchucks crossing his path, Thoreau also shared the woods with a few human neighbors. Although he devotes a chapter to "Brute Neighbors" and another to "Former Inhabitants and Winter Visitors," many people still think that Thoreau was the only one who ever came to Walden. Not true, as Thoreau himself, as well as Concord's town records and Hawthorne's notebooks, bear witness. For those who wished to avoid close monitoring by the town's busybodies, Walden Woods afforded a measure of freedom and independence—a place where blacks such as Zilpha White and Brister Freeman could live on their own terms and drunks could drink in peace. An earlier settlement of freed and escaped blacks had also since vanished, and Thoreau wonders about it. He also mentions Hugh Quoil, an Irishman who had been a soldier at Waterloo and a ditch digger, and who lived half a mile away. Quoil died just a few months after Thoreau moved to Walden.

Also interesting were the people who came to visit him. According to Mary Hosmer Brown, Thoreau would signify his willingness to have guests by placing one of his chairs outside. Then Channing or Alcott, or sometimes Emerson, would show up for a talk or, more often, a walk. Occasionally the neighbor farmer, Joe Hosmer, would come.

The most frequent visitor appears to have been Channing. Thoreau believed nothing could deter Channing from coming to Walden for a chat, not even the "deepest snows and most dismal tempest" that would stop "a farmer, a hunter, a soldier, a reporter, even a philosopher." Thoreau gives an account of Channing's visits at the start of the "Brute Neighbors" chapter of Walden: "Sometimes I had a companion in my fishing, who came through the village to my house from the other side of the town, and the catching of the dinner was as much a social exercise as the eating of it." Thoreau then presented a constructed dialogue in which "The Hermit" (Thoreau) consents to go fishing with "The Poet" (Channing) once his meditation is finished. This passage is just one example of the type of social interaction Thoreau enjoyed.

Another group of people came, not for the philosophy or exercise, but for safety and comfort. Escaped slaves on their way to Canada passed by Thoreau's cabin or were brought there. Because the cabin offered less protection than houses in town, it was not an ideal location, but Thoreau helped the slaves in any way he could, often accompanying them on the trains north to Canada. He also hosted the Antislavery Women of Concord's annual meeting on

The Ice King

Thoreau shared the forest, in a sense, with the most unlikely of bedfellows, a businessman. While Thoreau was at Walden, Frederic Tudor (otherwise known as the Ice King) was a visitor, not for the conversation but for the ice. He had begun in 1805 with the idea that he could harvest the Massachusetts ice and ship it to warmer climates. By the mid-1820s, he was shipping nearly two thousand tons of ice a year—two-thirds of the total shipping from Boston. His longtime partner, Nathaniel Wyeth, had developed an efficient way of cutting and harvesting ice, and the two of them shipped it to more than fifty different places around the globe, including India and China. By the winter of 1846, the two were shipping sixty-five thousand tons of ice a year.

In the age before refrigeration, the business of cutting frozen pond water into chunks to preserve through summer made fortunes for the few who were willing to risk the dangers.

By the winter of 1847, however, the two had broken off their partnership and were involved in a trade war that left almost no body of freshwater in Massachusetts unravaged. Tudor came to Walden Pond with his crew of workers and cut out nearly one thousand tons of ice a day for shipment to Martinique. Thoreau described the process as an invasion: "In the winter of '46–7 there came a hundred men of Hyperborean extraction swoop down on to our pond one morning, with many car-loads of ungainly-looking farming tools,—sleds, ploughs, drill-barrows, turf-knives, spades, saws, rakes, and each man was armed with a double-pointed pike-staff, such as is not described in the New-England Farmer or the Cultivator." Fortunately, Tudor's and Wyeth's dispute ended that winter, and the ice trade war fell off. As Thoreau notes in *Walden*, an enormous pile of ice was abandoned to melt its way back into Walden Pond rather than be shipped to Martinique.

Frederic Tudor, a.k.a. the Ice King.

August 1, 1846. Thoreau engaged in antislavery actions throughout his life and was an ardent supporter of the radical abolitionist John Brown, whom Thoreau called a "true Transcendentalist." His lectures "Slavery in Massachusetts" and "A Plea for Captain John Brown" were among the most political writings of his career.

The Town

Thoreau had an ambivalent relationship with the nearby town of Concord. On one hand, it represented food, comfort, and friendship. But it also represented criticism, gossip, and a government connected to the distant Mexican-American War. So although Thoreau walked into town most days or at least every other day, he also found that "to be in company, even with the best, is soon wearisome and dissipating. . . . We are for the most part more lonely when we go abroad among men than when we stay in our chambers."

Thoreau's journals show that the most common sites in town that he visited were his parents' home, Emerson's home, Channing's home, the post office, and Hillside, where Bronson Alcott was living at the time. It was not unusual for him to drop in on his friends, unexpected and unannounced, to learn the news and gossip of the day, and then sneak out the back door to his "snug harbor" at the pond. He describes this habit as being entertained well, but his friends did not always see it that way. In Emerson's words, "Thoreau goes to a house to say with little preface what he has just read or observed, delivers it in a lump, is quite inattentive to any comment or thought which any of the company offer on the matter, nay, is merely interrupted by it &, when he has finished his report, departs with precipitation."

It wasn't just his friends whom Thoreau provoked into squabbles. Some readers of *Walden* have protested his seeming inconsistency about how he survived in the woods. He claimed that his food cost him only twenty-seven cents a week, for instance. The truth was that he often received food from his mother or ate with friends in town. Clearly, the reality does not match what he wrote. As Edward Emerson notes, however, that does not detract from the truth of what Thoreau described. His experiences at Walden gave him the material for the book, but *Walden* is, as he reminds us throughout, a deliberately

Anti-Slavery Fair.

This Fair will commence on Wednesday August 3rd at Shepherd's Hall. Among the articles which will make it worthy of attention, will be a great variety of clothing for children, Frocks, Caps, Aprons, Shoes &c, also a large collection of very beautiful bags from Cork, & worsted work of all descriptions. Brooches from Rome, Books, Engravings, Card cases, & medals.

The Liberty Bell, an annual, containing articles in prose & verse contributed by John Q. Adams, Harriet Martineau, Dr. Bowring & other eminent writers in England & America will be for sale.

A. Tewksbury, M. M. Brooks,
A. Tolman, E. Bellows,
M. J. Stacy, S. E. Thoreau.

An announcement for an abolition meeting similar to the one Thoreau hosted at Walden Pond.

constructed narrative compressed into one year, not an exact account of his two-year, two-month, and two-day experiment.

One episode in which the discrepancy between fact and fiction is particularly apparent is the night he spent in jail. Here is how he describes it in *Walden*:

The Fire of April 30, 1844

Thoreau may have disparaged the town's criticisms of him, but some of that censure was warranted. One event that lowered the town's estimation of Thoreau was his burning of nearly three hundred acres of woods at Fair Haven Bay a little over a year before moving to Walden. Thoreau and his friend Edward Hoar had lit a fire in a tree stump to cook a fish chowder made from the fish they had caught that day. Unfortunately, a spark lit the dry grass near the stump, and the fire quickly spread out of control. By the time it was put out some hours later, it had caused more than $2,000 damage. The May 3 article in the *Concord Freeman* did little to help Thoreau's reputation:

> *The fire, we understand, was communicated to the woods through the thoughtlessness of two of our citizens who kindled it in a pine stump, near the Pond, for the purpose of making a chowder. As every thing around them was as combustible almost as a fire-ship, the flames spread with rapidity and hours elapsed before it could be subdued. It is to be hoped that this unfortunate result of sheer carelessness, will be borne in mind by those who may visit the woods in future for recreation.*

For years, Thoreau had to deal with people calling him "woods burner"—a harsh moniker for a budding naturalist.

At first he made little comment, nor did he offer to pay the farmer for the woods destroyed. By 1850, however, Thoreau had gained enough distance to offer his perspective on the event—if only to his journal:

> *I once set fire to the woods. Having set out, one April day, to go to the sources of Concord River in a boat with a single companion, meaning to camp on the bank at night or seek a lodging in some neighboring country inn or farmhouse, we took fishing tackle with us that we might fitly procure our food from the stream, Indian-like. At the shoemaker's near the river, we obtained a match, which we had forgotten. Though it was thus early in the spring, the river was low, for there had not been much rain, and we succeeded in catching a mess of fish sufficient for our dinner before we had left the town, and by the shores of Fair Haven Pond we proceeded to cook them. The earth was uncommonly dry, and our fire, kindled far from the woods in a sunny recess in the hillside on the east of the pond, suddenly caught the dry grass of the previous year which grew about the stump on which it was kindled. We sprang to extinguish it at first with our hands and feet, and then we fought it with a board obtained from the boat, but in a few minutes it was beyond our reach; being on the side of a hill, it spread rapidly upward, through the long, dry, wiry grass interspersed with bushes. . . . I walked slowly through the wood to Fair Haven Cliff, climbed to the highest rock, and sat down upon it to observe the progress of the flames, which were rapidly approaching me, now about a mile distant from the spot where the fire was kindled. Presently I heard the sound of the distant bell giving the alarm, and I knew that the town was on its way to the scene. Hitherto I had felt like a guilty person,—nothing but shame and regret. But now I settled the matter with myself shortly. I said to myself: "Who are these men who are said to be the owners of these woods, and how am I related to them? I have set fire to the forest, but I have done no wrong therein, and now it is as if the lightning had done it. These flames are but consuming their natural food." (It has never troubled me from that day to this more than if the lightning had done it. The trivial fishing was all that disturbed me and disturbs me still.)*

One afternoon, near the end of the first summer, when I went to the village to get a shoe from the cobbler's, I was seized and put into jail, because, as I have elsewhere related, I did not pay a tax to, or recognize the authority of, the State which buys and sells men, women, and children, like cattle, at the door of its senate-house.

What is clear is that Thoreau had come into town to do some errands and get a shoe fixed when he ran into Sam Staples, the town tax collector and jailer. Staples confronted Thoreau about the missing tax payments, and Thoreau still declined to pay. According to legend, Staples pleaded with him, even offering to pay the tax for him or at least lend him the money; still Thoreau declined, so Staples had no choice but to put him in jail. Although Thoreau's fine was paid anonymously that evening, Staples had already taken his boots off by the fire and had no inclination to get up to let him out. And so Thoreau spent the night in jail, and the experience became the foundation of a lecture he gave entitled "Resistance to Civil Government." This, in turn, became the landmark essay "Civil Disobedience."

In his typical style, Thoreau took an experience that was not completely uncommon (Bronson Alcott had been jailed for the same reason two and a half years before), and created an epic event in which the small details are loaded with heroic and symbolic weight:

I could not help being struck with the foolishness of that institution which treated me as if I were mere flesh and blood and bones, to be locked up. I wondered that it should have concluded at length that this was the best use it could put me to, and had never thought to avail itself of my services in some way. I saw that, if there was a wall of stone between me and my townsmen, there was a still more difficult one to climb or break through, before they could get to be as free as I was. I did not for a moment feel confined, and the walls seemed a great waste of stone and mortar.

The Legacy

More than any other Transcendentalist, Thoreau has been acknowledged as a major influence on many of the most progressive thinkers and leaders in a variety of fields. His antiwar and antislavery stances have been cited as influences by such leaders as Gandhi, the Jewish theologian Martin Buber, back-to-the-land advocates Helen and Scott Nearing, and Martin Luther King Jr. Authors as diverse as Leo Tolstoy and William Butler Yeats have acknowledged a literary debt to Thoreau. Environmental leaders such as John Muir and Rachel Carson credit his close examinations of nature with inspiring the conservation and environmental movements in the United States. Even Native American studies can, in some measure, trace its beginnings to the interests of this intrepid scholar. And websites on everything from Unitarianism to yoga to the simplicity movement appropriate his name and words for their purposes. In progressive ideology and practice, Thoreau is ubiquitous.

This stamp was issued by the U.S. Postal Service in 1967 to commemorate the 150th anniversary of Thoreau's birth.

Thoreau and Native Americans

Although Thoreau did not join any of the philanthropic movements dedicated to addressing the injustices suffered by Native Americans at the hands of white settlers, he strived for a deeper and more complex understanding of the area's original inhabitants. Appreciative of their relationship with and knowledge of the natural world, Thoreau struggled against his impulse to idealize the "noble savage" by undertaking a systematic study of Native Americans, reading a wide variety of sources and compiling pages and pages of excerpts in what are now called the "Indian notebooks."

These scholarly efforts were augmented by an uncanny knack for finding artifacts. One evening after he had returned to Concord from Harvard, for example, he was talking with his brother, waxing nostalgic about the previous inhabitants of the area. He pointed to a spot where the former Chief Tahatawan had supposedly stood and said, "And here is his [Tahatawan's] arrowhead." He then reached down and picked up a stone at random to display as an example of what could have been the chief's arrowhead. To his great surprise, it was an arrowhead.

His propensity for finding artifacts amazed his friends, particularly Channing and Hawthorne, who remarked that Thoreau "seldom walks over a ploughed field without picking up an arrow-point, spear-head, or other relic of the red men—as if their spirits willed him to be the inheritor of their simple wealth." He accumulated nearly nine hundred Native American artifacts before his death, most of which are now at Harvard University.

Thoreau's Flute

Perhaps the most touching tribute to Thoreau came from pen of Louisa May Alcott. The Alcott girls spent much time with Thoreau, learning from him the wonders of nature. After his death, Louisa wrote "Thoreau's Flute," which was originally published in the *Atlantic Monthly* in 1863:

We sighing said, "Our Pan is dead;
His pipe hangs mute beside the river;
Around it wistful sunbeams quiver,
But Music's airy voice is fled.
Spring came to us in guise forlorn;
The bluebird chants a requiem;
The willow-blossom waits for him; —
The Genius of the wood is gone."

Then from the flute, untouched by hands,
There came a low, harmonious breath:
"For such as he there is no death; —
His life the eternal life commands;
Above man's aims his nature rose.
The wisdom of a just content
Made one small spot a continent,
And turned to poetry life's prose.

"Haunting the hills, the stream, the wild,
Swallow and aster, lake and pine,
To him grew human or divine, —
Fit mates for this large-hearted child.
Such homage Nature ne'er forgets,
And yearly on the coverlid
'Neath which her darling lieth hid
Will write his name in violets.

"To him no vain regrets belong
Whose soul, that finer instrument,
Gave to the world no poor lament,
But wood-notes ever sweet and strong.
O lonely friend! he still will be
A potent presence, though unseen, —
Steadfast, sagacious, and serene;
Seek not for him—he is with thee."

–Louisa May Alcott

A Good Deal of Travel

Thoreau's night in jail was not his only notable absence from Walden during the *Walden* years. Although he did not describe the experience in the book, he left his cabin to go to Maine in August and September 1846. This trip, taken with a cousin, lasted roughly two weeks and served as the basis for the first chapter of *The Maine Woods* and as inspiration for his later voyages to Maine.

Thoreau journeyed to Maine to experience firsthand the Native Americans he had read so much about, as well as to climb to the top of Mount Katahdin. Although the Penobscot Indian guides he and his cousin hired never showed up, Thoreau managed to reach what he thought was the summit of Katahdin by himself (historians have since figured out that he stopped just short of the true summit). He was struck by the power of the landscape as he returned to camp: "Nature was here something savage and awful, though beautiful. I looked with awe at the ground I trod on, to see what the Powers had made there. . . . This was the Earth of which we have heard, made out of Chaos and Old Night. Here was no man's garden, but the unhandselled globe."

Thoreau left Walden to attempt to summit Mount Katahdin in Maine. Although he was sure he reached the summit, later researchers ascertained that he didn't get quite as far as he thought he did.

Walden after *Walden*

Thoreau left Walden after his second year at the pond. In *Walden*, he gives only this reason: "I left the woods for as good a reason as I went there. Perhaps it seemed to me that I had several more lives to live, and could not spare any more time for that one." The reality was that he moved into Emerson's home to help out Emerson's wife, Lidian, while Emerson traveled in Europe. And although he had moved away, the pond continued to draw him back: "I had not lived there a week before my feet wore a path from my door to the pond-side." He also notes that others were using the same path, and their traffic helped keep the trail to the pond open.

Traffic to the pond ebbed and flowed throughout the nineteenth century. Men such as Emerson, Alcott, and Channing continued to visit, even after, and perhaps especially after, Thoreau's death in 1862. Those who wanted to commune with Thoreau's spirit, however, have had to compete with others who simply want to enjoy the pond.

The widely varying motivations of the visitors to Walden Pond have led to some uneasiness over the years. Recreational users have clashed with literary fans over what constitutes wise use of the land. One of the most notable recreational innovations was the Lake Walden Amusement Park, better known as ❸ Walden Grove, which existed from 1866 to 1902. Built by the Boston-Fitchburg rail line, which owned a chunk of land from the tracks on the north shore of Walden down to the water, this "park" included concessions, fairgrounds, pavilions, picnic areas, dancing platforms, merry-go-rounds, sports fields, a beach constructed with soft sand brought in by freight trains, and a train stop right by the pond. The lake itself was host to gala boats with ribbons and streamers as well as hordes of swimmers and bathers. Groups from the greater Boston area rented the area for outings, retreats, and recreation.

The Cape

Maine was not the only place that had the power to draw Thoreau from Concord. He made a number of trips outside Middlesex County—not as many as Emerson made, but certainly more than taken by the average citizen of mid-nineteenth-century New England. He spent time in New Hampshire, in Canada, in New York, and on Cape Cod.

Thoreau's *Cape Cod* was never published as such during his lifetime. He wrote the manuscript originally as a series of articles for *Putnam's Monthly*, but only three of the original five pieces were published. After Thoreau's death, his sister Sophia and Ellery Channing helped edit his remaining work, and *Cape Cod* was first published in 1865.

Using the same format as *Walden*, Thoreau collapses three trips into one and works his way geographically out the arm of the Cape. He starts in Eastham and walks with an unnamed companion (Ellery Channing) up to Provincetown, where the two board a ferry back to Boston. Thoreau's observations range from a darkly morbid account of a shipwreck complete with floating and bloated corpses to a thrilling description of fishermen in pursuit of mackerel.

Published in 1865, this volume is still one of the best walking guides to Cape Cod.

Walden Grove was a popular destination for Bostonians who ventured out of the city to swim, go for boat rides, and picnic.

The amusement park burned down in 1902 and was left in ashes. The next development was the construction of bathhouses at the west end of the pond in 1917, after the town of Concord began offering swimming lessons there. By the 1930s, although *Walden* had drifted into obscurity, the popularity of Walden Pond had grown tremendously, and the pond sometimes hosted nearly 30,000 people a day. A concrete jetty was added in the 1950s to help facilitate swim lessons at ❹ the Main Beach. Fortunately, the Department of Conservation and Recreation, which took over management of the pond in 1975, realized that this crush of people would eventually destroy the treasure. The department instituted limits on the number of visitors at one time and on pond access and use. It also took down the concrete jetty and restored the beach to its more natural state.

This photo shows the docks coming out from the beach where the Red Cross offered swim lessons in the mid-twentieth century.

Walden Today

Walden Pond has now become ❺ Walden Pond State Reservation, managed by the Massachusetts Department of Conservation and Recreation at 915 Walden Street. It has also been designated a National Historic Landmark. In 1922 the Emerson, Forbes, and Haywood families gifted the land to the state to preserve it as a park, along the model of what Thoreau had called for in his journal just before his death: "All Walden Woods might have been preserved for our park forever with Walden in its midst." Unfortunately, by the time the land was granted to the state, most of the Walden Woods had been cut down, much as Thoreau had foreseen. It is only because of careful planning and close attention that the forests have grown back to nearly what they were when Thoreau was at the pond.

The headquarters at Walden Pond.

As the only public swimming hole in the area, Walden Pond can see upward of five thousand swimmers, boaters, and sunbathers a day during the hot summer months. The four-hundred-acre reservation receives nearly 800,000 visitors a year. Of those, a small percentage come purely to pay homage to Thoreau. These admirers and philosophers ramble the woods, stand inside the re-creation of his house, and generally seek to connect with the place on a transcendent level. Some meditate, others write, and many add a stone to the cairn that stands as a monument to Thoreau.

Another place of interest to literary pilgrims is ❻ the Thoreau Institute at Walden Woods, a research and education facility located at 44 Baker Farm Road, in Lincoln, just a mile from the site of Thoreau's cabin. It also houses the Walden Woods Project. Continuing the efforts of such local heroes as Tom Blanding and Mary Sherwood, the Walden Woods Project has raised more than $23 million for its conservation initiatives.

The gem of the institute is the Henley Library, named for musician Don Henley, who heeded the call and founded the Walden Woods Project. The library is a gorgeous wood-paneled room with views of the woods. Its collection includes nearly every published work on Walden or Thoreau: some eight thousand books and fifty thousand documents. It also boasts a wonderful array of primary sources and artifacts, including manuscripts, maps, and photographs of the pond and nearby Concord, as well as collections on Emerson, Helen and Scott Nearing, and Paul Brooks. The collection's curator, Jeffrey Cramer, edited the definitive annotated *Walden*.

Part of the Thoreau Institute, the Henley Library is, so far, the best embodiment of Thoreau's vision of a library "in the depths of the primitive forest."

These efforts have done much to ensure the preservation of Walden Pond and about 70 percent of the surrounding 2,680 acres of land known as Walden Woods. The remaining 30 percent of the woods face a more uncertain future, however. The biggest issue is what to do with the site of a thirty-five-acre landfill, which was built in the late 1950s and closed in 1994. Proposals have included a number of public works projects as well as cell phone towers. Condominiums were

The Rock Cairn

In 1872, Bronson Alcott and Ralph Waldo Emerson began to construct a rock cairn as a memorial to Thoreau and his time at Walden Pond. It grew modestly at first, but Alcott had high hopes: "The pyramid is insignificant as of yet; but could Thoreau's readers add theirs the pile would rise above the treetops to mark the site of his hermitage." Over the years, Thoreau's readers have added theirs to the pile, and while not yet above the treetops, it is a fitting memorial. Some visitors simply deposit stones, while others decorate and sign them. Walt Whitman added his in 1881, and John Muir made his contribution in 1883.

In 1975, park rangers moved the stone cairn because the park commissioner felt the stones were "unsightly." The resulting outcry from Thoreauvians prompted the park to replace the cairn in 1978.

Alcott and a friend started this cairn as a monument to Thoreau in 1872; it has grown stone by stone throughout the years.

Though the efforts of the Walden Woods Project, much of the woods surrounding the pond have been preserved for recreational uses.

proposed for one site, which has since been protected from development, but as yet there is no guarantee for the rest of the woods.

There are other, more positive projects in the works as well. The Walden Woods Project has undertaken a feasibility study for a wildlife overpass that would allow animals to cross Route 2 in safety. And visitors can walk Thoreau's Path on Brister's Hill, a one-mile path in Concord adjacent to the town forest introducing Thoreau's life, writings, and legacy through his own words and through quotations from those who influenced him.

Despite the passing of the years, Thoreau would still recognize the pond that has become synonymous with his name. As he reminds readers in *Walden*, the pond retains no visible record of the changes around it. The water still changes from blue to green to gray, and the area is still enjoyed by a mix of fishermen and philosophers. The pond has stayed, and will ideally always remain, a mixture of the secular and the sacred.

Chapter 6

Salem

Sins of the Past

Salem's natural beauty and protected harbor attracted many early settlers; the town was an important shipping port in the early 1800s.

In many ways, Salem had the potential to be just as much a center of Transcendentalism as Boston or Concord. Only some fourteen miles north of Cambridge and Boston, this busy seaside port of the early nineteenth century was home to such Transcendentalist stars as Nathaniel Hawthorne, Elizabeth Palmer Peabody, and the poet Jones Very. It boasted a strong Unitarian church, a well-endowed Athenaeum, and one of the first lyceum programs in the Northeast. The city was also blessed with the natural splendor of the sea and forests. Its history and sense of Puritan destiny, however, may have kept it from reaching its potential as a major cultural center of nineteenth-century New England.

That history began in 1624, when British settlers from nearby Cape Ann, led by Roger Conant, moved farther inland in search of more temperate weather and safer ports. They settled at the mouth of the river the Native Americans called the Naum-Keag and, in 1629, named the town after the Hebrew word for peace, shalom. In the following years, the settlement did enjoy peace and prosperity, deriving its living from fishing and trade. This prosperity did not ensure safe times forever, though; the citizens eventually struggled through the stresses of smallpox epidemics, warring tribes, the dangers of a seagoing life, and a Puritanical worldview. The fears connected with Puritan teachings contributed to the hysteria and resulting tragedy that gripped the town in 1692.

The Witch Trials

When a pair of Salem girls fell sick in January 1692 and did not improve, the village doctor, William Griggs, diagnosed them as "bewitched." Suddenly, the whole town was whipped into a frenzy of accusation and terror. Inculcated with fears of the devil and sin, residents quickly turned on each other. By June, a hundred and fifty people had been imprisoned for witchcraft. A special court was convened and, based on "spectral evidence" (the testimony of those who had been "bewitched"), fourteen women and five men were sent to the gallows. A sixth man was crushed to death as punishment for the sin of witchcraft. Finally, in October, Massachusetts governor William Phipps closed down the court and replaced it with the Superior Court of Judicature, which did not allow the use of spectral evidence and acquitted the rest of the accused. The Salem witch trials were over.

The reverberations of the trials, however, have cast a strong spell over Salem. A sense of guilt and Puritanical excess have long affected the town's concept of itself, even though it became a prosperous port, rivaling its neighbor to the south for most of the eighteenth century. The trials have maintained a firm grip on the cultural imagination of America as well. From Nathaniel Hawthorne's *The Scarlet Letter* to Arthur Miller's *The Crucible* (remade as a movie as recently as 1996), the Salem witch trials continued to intrigue and appall.

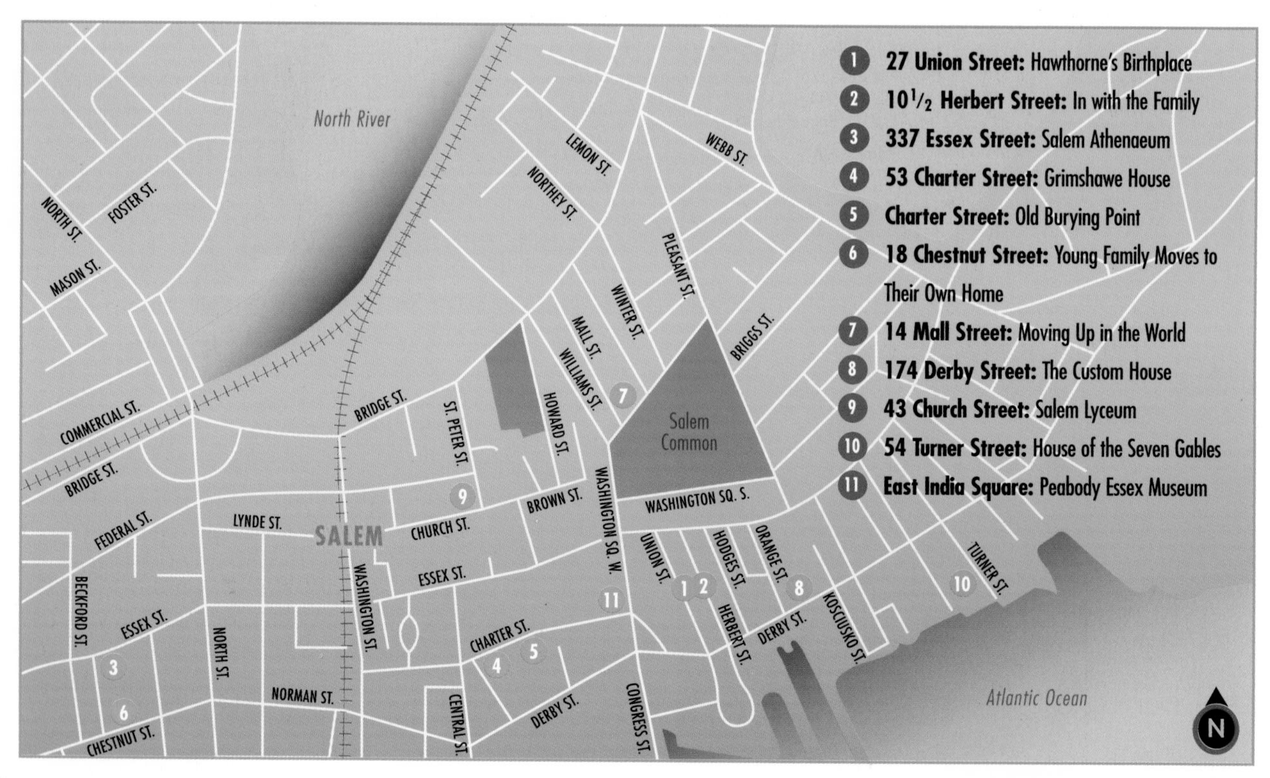

Salem's Decline

Salem's prosperity as a port did not last. In 1807, American authorities placed an embargo on shipping to Britain and France in retaliation for those countries' attacks on American ships. When the War of 1812 followed, Salem's maritime grandeur was lost to Boston and New York.

It wasn't until the industrial revolution of the mid-nineteenth century that the cotton mills and leather tanneries drew in hordes of Irish and French Canadian immigrants to revitalize the town.

Hawthorne's Neighborhood

It was against this backdrop of the ebb and flow of commerce that Nathaniel Hawthorne came of age both as a man and a writer. Born in Salem on July 4, 1804, he was to spend much of the next forty-five years there, and by the time he left for good he had written *Twice-Told Tales* and *The Scarlet Letter*, and was beginning to earn a reputation as one of America's most intriguing writers.

His father was a ship's captain who wrote poetry in the margins of the ship's log while at sea. His mother, by all accounts, was loving and beautiful. He had two sisters. When he was born, his family was living at ❶ 27 Union Street, a gambrel-roofed two-story house that was only a few feet away from the street but was a pleasant place for the Hathornes (as it was spelled by the American branch of the family until Hawthorne added the "w" sometime after college).

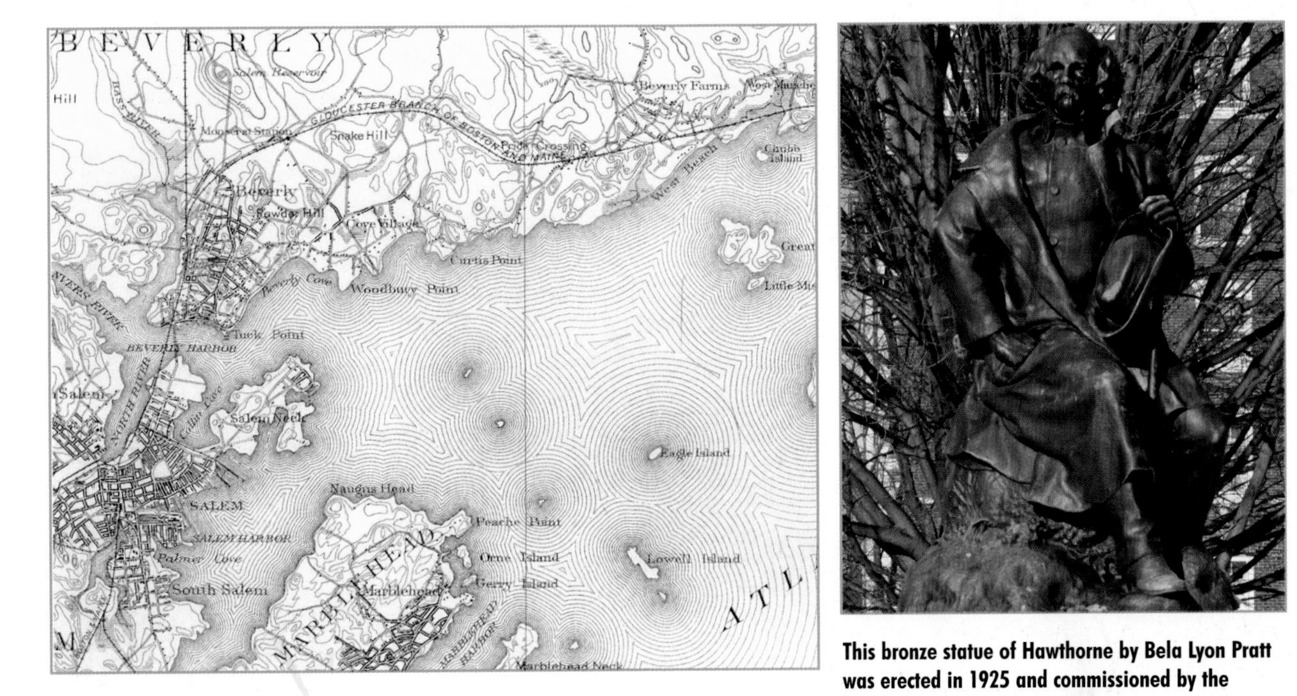

A map of Salem in the late nineteenth century.

This bronze statue of Hawthorne by Bela Lyon Pratt was erected in 1925 and commissioned by the Hawthorne Memorial Association.

This domestic idyll was shattered, however, in 1808, when Hawthorne's father died in Suriname, leaving his mother nearly destitute. Pressed by lack of money, the mother sold the house on Union Street and moved less than a block away to her family's house at ❷ **10½ Herbert Street.** In this crowded two-story house, Hawthorne shared a room and even a bed with his uncles. Although some critics like to raise their eyebrows at this, it was a normal enough situation for a struggling nineteenth-century family.

Sometime around his ninth birthday, Hawthorne injured his foot playing ball. When all the doctors in Salem couldn't cure him, he accompanied his mother north to her brother's house in Maine, where it was hoped the change would help him heal. This did the trick, and Hawthorne looked back at his time in Maine as a wonderful experience:

> *Here I ran quite wild, and would, I doubt not, have willingly run wild till this time, fishing all day long, or shooting with an old fowling-piece; but reading a good deal, too, on the rainy days, especially in Shakespeare and "The Pilgrim's Progress," and any poetry or light books within my reach. Those were delightful days; for that part of the country was wild then, with only scattered clearings, and nine tenths of it primeval woods.*

Although his mother eventually sent him back to Salem to resume his education and prepare for college, this experience in the north country clearly

This house, built in 1750, was where Hawthorne was born. His family lived there until his father died when Nathaniel was five.

In 1958, to preserve the house, workers loaded it onto a truck and drove it through town to the House of the Seven Gables, where it was added to the museum.

had a lasting effect on Hawthorne. He never lost his love of rambling through nature, nor his appreciation of what it could signify. When Hester Prynne is banished from town in *The Scarlet Letter*, she does not flee to another settlement but heads to the natural world, halfway between ocean and forest.

Upon returning to Salem, Hawthorne again took up residence in the house on Herbert Street and attended school nearby. In the months leading up to his matriculation at Bowdoin College, he began to exercise his talents as a writer and develop his skills as a businessman. For nearly two months, from the end of August to October 1820, Hawthorne put out seven issues of a weekly newspaper, based on the *Salem Gazette*, titled the *Spectator*. For this publication, Hawthorne published the poetry of his sister as well as his own; news stories about reported sea serpents and school examinations; and advertisements for paper, subscribers, contributors, and even a husband for his aunt, Mary Manning. As editor, Hawthorne wrote virtually all of the content (his sisters helped some), and the newspaper showcased his growing wit and style before he truly considered being a writer. For example, his tongue-in-cheek essay "On Industry" pokes fun at the perceptions of his own laziness:

> *It has been somewhere remarked, that an Author does not write the worse for knowing little or nothing of his Subject. We hope the truth of this saying will be made manifest in the present article. With the benefits of Industry, we are not personally acquainted, (it not being one of the attributes of literary men) . . . but we have often seen them conspicuously displayed in others. By the aid of industry almost every undertaking is ultimately successful, and without it even the easiest enterprises generally fail.*

From 1820 to 1824, Hawthorne was a student at Bowdoin College in Brunswick, Maine. Attracted by its lower tuition and more orthodox Christian views as compared to Harvard, Hawthorne's mother sent him to Bowdoin, with his uncle paying the bills. Although he didn't have much extra money, Hawthorne managed to enjoy himself (he was fined fifty cents for playing cards), learn enough to get by (he described himself as an "idle student"), and develop a few lasting friendships that would serve him well for the rest of his life. Fellow students Franklin Pierce, Henry Wadsworth Longfellow, and Horatio Bridge became lifelong friends, and the politician, the poet, and the naval officer helped Hawthorne throughout his career. He remained as dedicated to them as they were to him.

It was from the bosom of this freedom and friendship that Hawthorne began to consider, on paper, his

Hawthorne hand-produced seven issues of this newspaper covering the events and issues of his family and his life.

Salem Athenaeum

Like the other Transcendentalists, Hawthorne was an avid and wide-ranging reader. He enjoyed John Bunyan, William Shakespeare, John Milton, and Alexander Pope. When in Salem, he borrowed many of his books from the Athenaeum.

Although this is not the same building Hawthorne visited, the Salem Athenaeum is still a private library open to visitors. The room to the right of the front entrance is the "Hawthorne Room."

The Salem Athenaeum started as the Social Library in 1760; it became known as the Athenaeum when it merged with the Philosophical Library in 1810. The Athenaeum operated much like its brethren in Boston and Cambridge, offering shares to be purchased in return for borrowing privileges. The 100 shares in the Salem Athenaeum were sold for $100 apiece. Hawthorne's uncle, William Manning, had a share that he gave to his sister Mary, who in turn let Hawthorne use her borrowing card until she finally just gave him the share in 1828.

By 1837, two years before Hawthorne left Salem, the library had eight thousand volumes and, according to a compilation of his borrowing record by Marion Kesselring, Hawthorne read widely in the collection. Although his tastes seemed to return most often to histories and books of travel, he also checked out the fictional and poetic works of Montague, Dryden, Swift, Coleridge, and Scott. The library moved often while Hawthorne was in Salem, but in 1858 the bequest of Caroline Plummer made it possible to build and occupy Plummer Hall at 132 Essex Street, which now houses the Phillips Library of the Peabody Essex Museum. ❸ **The Salem Athenaeum** moved to **337 Essex Street** in 1906 and remains a private library open to visitors.

No. ....

Name, ...

Address, ...

Salem • Public • Library,

SALEM, MASS.

This card must always be presented on returning a book; also, WITH A SLIP, when asking for, or renewing a book.

☞ The proper holder is in all cases responsible for books drawn on this card and IF LOST it will not be replaced until 7 days after notice is given.

Immediate notice of a *change of residence* must be given and this card must be surrendered on ceasing to be a resident.

One volume allowed each day.

Books labelled "Seven Days' Book" must not be retained more than one week, and cannot be renewed.

Other books may be retained two weeks and may be renewed.

A fine of two cents a day, including Sundays and holidays, must be paid on each volume kept over time.

No book will be delivered to the party incurring fine till all indebtedness is paid.

Borrowers finding any book mutilated or unwarrantably defaced are expected to report it.

The intentional injury of books or other property of a Public Library incurs, by statute, a liability of a fine of $50, or imprisonment for six months.

The borrowing card in use during Hawthorne's time. He used his mother's card to borrow books from the Athenaeum.

options for the future. In an 1821 letter to his mother from college, he floated the idea of becoming a writer:

> *I have not yet concluded what profession I shall have. The being a minister is of course out of the question. I should not think that even you could desire me to choose so dull a life. Oh, no, mother, I was not born to vegetate forever in one place, and to live and die as calm and tranquil as—a puddle of water. As to lawyers, there are so many of them already that one half of them (upon a moderate calculation) are in a state of actual starvation. A physician, then, seems to be "Hobson's choice;" but yet I should not like to live by the diseases and infirmities of my fellow-creatures. And it would weigh very heavily on my conscience, in the course of my practice, if I should chance to send any unlucky patient "ad inferum," which being interpreted is, "to the realms below." Oh that I was rich enough to live without a profession! What do you think of my becoming an author, and relying for support upon my pen?*

There is no evidence of his mother's reaction or of Hawthorne's taking any definitive steps toward being an author at this point, but he was beginning to think of life beyond the fun of college.

His time at Bowdoin was not all joyful, however. He was given to occasional lapses of judgment (he was eventually nearly suspended for gambling) and fits of homesickness. Imploring his sister Louisa for help in getting home early, Hawthorne wrote, "It is so long since I saw the land of my birth that I am almost dead of homesickness, and am apprehensive of serious injury to my health if I am not soon removed from this place." Whether it was a desire to return to Salem or merely restlessness picked up from his father, Hawthorne was rarely happy in one place for long. He moved often, never staying longer than five years in any single place after leaving Salem in 1840. His son, Julian, describes this restlessness in his biography of his father:

> *In fact, after freeing himself from Salem, Hawthorne never found any permanent rest anywhere. He soon wearied of any particular locality. A novelist would say that he inherited the roving disposition of his seafaring ancestors. Partly necessity or convenience, but partly, also, his own will, drove him from place to place; always wishing to settle down finally, but never lighting upon the fitting spot.*

Hawthorne did return to Salem in 1825, however, to move in with his sisters and mother in the house on Herbert Street that he liked to call Castle Dismal. In no hurry, Hawthorne pondered his future and gradually withdrew from the world:

> *And year after year I kept on considering what I was fit for, and time and my destiny decided that I was to be the writer that I am. I had always a natural tendency (it appears to have been on the paternal side) toward seclusion; and this I now indulged to the utmost, so, that, for months together, I scarcely held human intercourse outside of my own family; seldom going out except at twilight, or only to take the nearest way to the most convenient solitude, which was oftenest the seashore, the rocks and beaches in that vicinity being as fine as any in New England.*

While much has been made critically of this seclusion, Hawthorne gave his own interpretation: "My long seclusion had not made me melancholy or misanthropic, nor wholly unfitted me for the bustle of life; and perhaps it was the kind of discipline which my idiosyncrasy demanded, and chance and my own instincts, operating together, had caused me to do what was fittest." In any case, it was a time of incubation during which Hawthorne freed himself from society to embark on his career as a writer. Unfortunately, most of the stories he wrote during that time he burned.

Hawthorne, like many of the Transcendentalists, did not think of himself as one of Emerson's protégés (he even mocks Emerson's followers as "a variety of queer, strangely-dressed, oddly behaved mortals, most of whom took upon themselves to be important agents of the world's destiny, yet were simply bores of a very intense water"). However, many of the central tenets of Transcendentalism (awareness of the creative and imaginative power of nature, the breaking away from form and tradition, and the emphasis on the individual experience) can be seen in stories like "Young Goodman Brown" and novels such as *The Scarlet Letter*.

Dueling Stories

Apparently Hawthorne was not always in deep seclusion, for he found the time to get embroiled in a juicy bit of social drama. During Hawthorne's time in Salem, he met a beautiful woman of society, Mary Sillsbee, who, after befriending Hawthorne, reading her poetry to him, and sharing with him intimate details, expected to receive the same details of Hawthorne's soul. When she did not, she used a different stratagem: she made up a story about one of Hawthorne's friends, John O'Sullivan, whom she claimed had impugned her dignity as a woman.

When Hawthorne rashly challenged O'Sullivan to a duel, he refused and explained the matter to Hawthorne. The duel was dropped. Unfortunately, the original story continued to make the rounds, and a friend of Hawthorne's, Jonathan Cilley, was challenged by a man named William Graves to fill Hawthorne's place, as Graves would fill O'Sullivan's place. The two men met, and Cilley was killed. Hawthorne's guilt over this was tremendous.

Or at least that is the story told by Hawthorne's son, Julian, in his biography of his father. Although a wonderfully dramatic tale, it may in fact be completely false. In the more credible version put forth in Brenda Wineapple's biography of Hawthorne, Cilley and Graves dueled in the nation's capital over a completely unrelated political issue.

This oil painting, done in 1840 by Charles Osgood, is the best-known image of Hawthorne, who has been described as "smolderingly handsome."

The lasting product of these years was Hawthorne's anonymously published volume of short stories, *Twice-Told Tales*, in which he began to explore the Puritan past that had so haunted his hometown and nearby Boston. This collection comprises thirty-five stories in two volumes. Most of the tales are set in a colonial New England fraught with the dangers of a society turned too far inward. Although the book did not sell well, it did provide Hawthorne with an introduction into literary circles. The stories present the quintessential themes that Hawthorne turned to again and again: long-held dark secrets ("Roger Malvin's Burial"), historical events ("The Gray Champion"), and inner torment ("The Minister's Black Veil").

The Peabody Connection

Although they failed to find a large audience within Salem and New England, these stories did attract the attention of at least one other intellectual resident of Salem. Just a few blocks over on Charter Street lived the Peabody family. Their house at ④ 53 Charter Street, now known as the Grimshawe House, was home to the three Peabody girls and their parents from 1835 to 1840. In 1837, after reading *Twice-Told Tales*, Elizabeth Palmer Peabody did some investigative work to ascertain the author's identity, and then invited the young writer and his two sisters over. The usually reticent Hawthorne accepted the invitation, and the three Hawthornes arrived on November 12, 1837, for a visit.

It was on a second visit that Hawthorne was transfixed by the beauty of the youngest Peabody sister, Sophia, and asked her to accompany him to a play. She declined because she never went out at night; he rarely went out in the day. In the end they compromised on a late afternoon stroll, and within two years they were engaged. The couple kept the engagement a secret,

Hawthorne met Sophia Peabody at this house in 1837 and quickly fell in love with her. The house was to serve as the setting for Hawthorne's posthumously published novel, *Dr. Grimshawe's Secret.*

One of the oldest burial grounds in all of New England, the Burying Point provided Hawthorne with a secluded and peaceful place to walk.

however, because they believed that neither of their families would be happy with the match. Not until a few weeks before the wedding, in 1842, did the families find out.

The house where Hawthorne met his future bride is directly adjacent to the oldest cemetery in Salem, ❺ the Old Burying Point. The cemetery, established in 1637, was a favorite ramble of Hawthorne, who liked to walk its paths and read the stones. Of particular interest to him was the grave of John Hathorne, his great-great-grandfather.

The Hathornes had come to Salem a generation before, when John's father, William Hathorne, arrived in Salem "with his Bible, and his sword, and trode the unworn street with such a stately port" and made a name for himself as "a soldier, legislator, judge; he was a ruler in the Church. . . . He was likewise a bitter persecutor" of the Quakers, whom he had whipped for trespassing on Puritan soil. William Hathorne's son John was one of the justices of the Salem witch trials, a legacy Hawthorne struggled with, as he describes in "The Custom House," the introduction to *The Scarlet Letter*:

> *His son, too, inherited the persecuting spirit, and made himself so conspicuous in the martyrdom of the witches, that their blood may fairly be said to have left a stain upon him. So deep a stain, indeed, that his old dry bones, in the Charter Street burial ground, must still retain it, if they have not crumbled utterly to dust! I know not whether these ancestors of mine bethought themselves to repent, and ask pardon of heaven for their cruelties; or whether they are now groaning under the heavy consequences of them, in another state of being. At all events, I, the present writer, as their representative, hereby take their shame upon myself for their sakes, and pray that any curse incurred by them—as I have heard, and as the dreary and unprosperous condition of the race, for many a long year back, would argue to exist—may be now and henceforth removed.*

The cemetery at the Old Burying Point furnished Hawthorne with more than heavy guilt and a historical perspective; many of the characters that populate the dark pasts of Hawthorne's fiction received their names from stones at this cemetery.

Jones Very: Salem's Mystic Poet-Seeker

It was during the late 1830s that Hawthorne met another Transcendentalist who happened to be a "project" of Elizabeth Peabody: Jones Very. He, like Hawthorne, was born in Salem to a ship's captain; however, Very's parents never married. He also lost his father and had to live within limited means. Hawthorne went to Bowdoin College; Very went to Harvard, entering as a sophomore in 1833.

Here, though, the similarities end. Whereas Hawthorne was, at best, an uninspired student, Very was an extraordinary scholar, winning the prestigious Bowdoin Prize at Harvard two years in a row for his essays. His prize-winning essay on epic poetry, given as a lecture to the Salem Lyceum in December 1837, attracted the admiration of Peabody, who brought it to the attention of Emerson. Emerson, in turn, invited him to repeat the lecture in Concord in April 1838. A month later, Very attended his first meeting of the Transcendental Club; the night's topic was, appropriately enough, mysticism. Very would become the ultimate Transcendentalist mystic poet.

By this time, Very had graduated from Harvard but stayed on as a Greek tutor and divinity student. During the summer of 1838, he began an essay on Shakespeare. At the same time, he was attempting to completely erase his identity in order to be an empty vessel for God's light. These two projects proved too much for him: the twenty-five-year-old poet and scholar began to develop a reputation among the young undergraduates of Harvard for a madness that culminated in telling his students to "flee to the mountains, for the end of all things is at hand" and storming Professor Henry Ware Jr.'s rooms, asserting that he was the second coming of Christ. When Ware questioned him, Very responded, "I had thought you did the will of the Father, and that I should receive some sympathy from you—But I now find that you are doing your own will, and not the will of your father." Not surprisingly, Harvard quickly let him go, and Very returned to Salem under the care of his younger brother, then a freshman at Harvard.

Pale and drawn Jones Very lost his teaching position at Harvard College when he became convinced he was the second coming of Christ and told his students to "flee to the mountains, for the end of all things is at hand!"

The change of scenery did little to change his perspective. By the following Sunday morning, Very had decided to spread the news of his transformation through his Federal Street neighborhood and beyond. Around ten in the morning, he visited Elizabeth

McLean Hospital, founded in 1811, was originally known as "asylum for the insane" and has a long-standing reputation for treating patients with mental illnesses. Jones Very and Emerson's younger brother Bulkeley Emerson were occasional residents at McLean.

Peabody on Charter Street, who let him say his piece, baptize and pray over her, and then precipitously depart. Unfortunately, one of his later visits was to the Reverend Charles Wentworth Upham, a Harvard Divinity School classmate of Emerson's and a vigorous opponent of Transcendentalism (he later worked hard to get Hawthorne dismissed from the Salem Custom House). On the night of September 16, Upham had Very taken from his home in Federal Street and sent to McLean Asylum in Charlestown.

Very spent thirty-one days at McLean before returning to his home in Salem to write poetry and further channel the divine grace that would fill him for the next year. He did not return to Upham's home but did visit Emerson in Concord for a six-day stay in October 1838. A year later, by September 1839, the divine spirit had left him and he was once again the quiet scholar he had been before. In 1843, he was sanctioned to preach in Salem and served as a supply (or substitute) preacher from time to time, but he never received a congregation of his own. Although he continued to write poetry, many critics feel that the poetry of his early years was never matched in vision, fervor, and sensibility.

A Return to Salem

Following their marriage, the Hawthornes rented Emerson's Old Manse in Concord. When their time there came to an end in October 1845, they returned to the Herbert Street house and moved in with Hawthorne's mother and two sisters. Although Hawthorne continued to think of it as Castle Dismal, the return was less painful than the young couple had imagined. As Nathaniel told Horatio Bridge, he was even able to write in the house: "Here I am, again established in the old chambers where I wasted so many years of my life. I find it rather favorable to my literary duties, for I have already begun to sketch out the story for Wiley & Putnam."

Several other events helped make Salem palatable again. The first was the announcement of Sophia's second pregnancy. The Hawthornes' oldest daughter, Una, had been born at the Manse and was now charming Hawthorne's sisters and mother. The second piece of good news was that after much political wrangling, Hawthorne had secured a position as the surveyor of revenue for the Salem Custom House. This, in turn, allowed the Hawthornes to move out of Castle Dismal in the fall of 1846 to a house at ❻ 18 Chestnut Street, and then, a year later, to ❼ 14 Mall Street. It was in this house that Hawthorne wrote *The Scarlet Letter*.

The Custom House

Hawthorne chose to open *The Scarlet Letter* with the same type of autobiographical sketch that prefaces *Mosses from the Old Manse*. Although the ostensible purpose of the sketch was to inform his readers how he came across the scarlet letter and the details of the story, it also introduces the reader to Salem, ❽ the Custom House at 174 Derby Street and his colleagues there, and his ancestors before divulging the "origins" of the novel.

Although the Salem that Hawthorne describes in 1846 is "now burdened with decayed wooden warehouses, and exhibits few or no symptoms of commercial life," he claims mild contentment at having returned to the town of his birth:

> *This old town of Salem—my native place, though I have dwelt much away from it, both in boyhood and maturer years—possesses, or did possess, a hold on my affections, the force of which I have never realized, during my seasons of actual*

The Son

Father! I wait thy word—the sun doth stand,
Beneath the mingling line of night and day,
A listening servant waiting thy command
To roll rejoycing on its silent way;
The tongue of time abides the appointed hour,
Till on our ear its solemn warnings fall;
The heavy cloud withholds the pelting shower,
Then every drop speeds onward at thy call;
The bird reposes on the yielding bough
With breast unswollen by the tide of song;
So does my spirit wait thy presence now
To pour thy praise in quickening life along
Chiding with voice divine man's lengthened sleep,
While round the Unuttered Word and Love their vigils keep.

—Jones Very

Hawthorne worked at the Salem Custom House from 1846 to 1849. The preface to *The Scarlet Letter* details his experiences as the customs official for Salem.

> *residence here. Indeed, so far as its physical aspect is concerned, with its flat, unvaried surface, covered chiefly with wooden houses, few or none of which pretend to architectural beauty, — its irregularity, which is neither picturesque nor quaint, but only tame, — its long and lazy street, lounging wearisomely through the whole extent of the peninsula, with Gallows Hill and New Guinea at one end, and a view of the alms-house at the other, — such being the features of my native town, it would be quite as reasonable to form a sentimental attachment to a disarranged checker-board. And yet, though invariably happiest elsewhere, there is within me a feeling for old Salem, which, in lack of a better phrase, I must be content to call affection.*

His "affection" for the town, he supposes, rests on his unique Salem heritage. While his progenitors may have committed grave sins in the name of justice, Hawthorne imagines his role as a "writer of story-books" is enough "retribution" for their sins.

Turning from his own ancestry to the Custom House itself, Hawthorne brings his readers face to face with the "veterans" who formed his staff: "Thus, on taking charge of my department, I found few but aged men. They were ancient sea captains, for the most part, who, after being tossed on every sea, and standing up sturdily against life's tempestuous blast, had finally drifted into this quiet nook." Hawthorne even embraced the change of pace and scenery with a type of contented resignation:

> *After my fellowship of toil and impracticable schemes with the dreamy brethren of Brook Farm; after living for three years within the subtile influence of an intellect like Emerson's; after those wild, free days on the Assabeth, indulging fantastic speculations, beside our fire of fallen boughs, with Ellery Channing; after talking with Thoreau about pine-trees and Indian relics, in his hermitage at Walden; after growing fastidious by sympathy with the classic refinement of Hillard's culture; after becoming imbued with poetic sentiment at Longfellow's hearth-stone, — it was time, at length, that I should exercise other*

faculties of my nature, and nourish myself with food for which I had hitherto had little appetite.

This peace, however, was not to last. Merely three years after assuming his office, Hawthorne was removed when Zachary Taylor replaced James Polk as the twelfth U.S. president in 1849. In a letter to Longfellow, Hawthorne described his politically motivated termination as like having his head chopped off.

But while it was a blow to Hawthorne's income and ego, the forced removal was a blessing for American literature, for Hawthorne had begun to suffer from a writer's block that could not be overcome, even by the usual Transcendentalist remedy of communing with Nature:

> *It was not merely during the three hours and a half which Uncle Sam claimed as his share of my daily life, that this wretched numbness held possession of me. It went with me on my sea-shore walks, and rambles into the country, whenever—which was seldom and reluctantly—I bestirred myself to seek that invigorating charm of Nature.*

Whether his state was caused by bureaucratic ennui or the stifling atmosphere of Salem, steeped in the past and suffering in the present, Hawthorne had been stuck. It wasn't until he came home in the middle of the day in September 1849 and told his wife that his tenure at the Custom House was over that he felt he could move on and finish *The Scarlet Letter.*

Once he got going, though, Hawthorne worked quickly and intensely, finishing the novel literally as James Fields was preparing to begin printing it. As he described it in a letter: " I finished my book only yesterday, one end being in press in Boston, while the other was in my head here in Salem; so that, as you see, the story is at least fourteen miles long." Later, in that same letter, Hawthorne

The Secret Manuscript

In publisher James Fields's 1871 memoir, *Yesterdays with Authors*, the proprietor of the Old Corner Bookstore crafts a wonderful story about how the manuscript of *The Scarlet Letter* came into his possession.

THE

SCARLET LETTER,

A ROMANCE.

BY

NATHANIEL HAWTHORNE.

BOSTON:

TICKNOR, REED, AND FIELDS.

M DCCC L.

When *The Scarlet Letter* arrived on the scene in 1850, it attracted immediate attention: the title page was printed with bright red ink.

When Fields went to visit the Hawthornes in 1849, Nathaniel was quite depressed and despaired of writing anything good again. Fields pressed Hawthorne to show him what he had been working on, telling him that he would publish whatever he had written. Hawthorne declined, claiming that he had no new work and that he was the least popular writer in American literature. Fields, sensing that Hawthorne had been working on something, pushed harder. Hawthorne again told him no.

As he gathered his things to leave, Fields noticed a dresser against the wall and, acting on a wild speculation, told Hawthorne he knew there was a manuscript in it. Hawthorne denied it but, after Fields left, caught up to him and handed him a sheaf of papers he had been hiding in a drawer. Fields read the germ of *The Scarlet Letter* on the train back to Boston and immediately offered to publish the novel.

The Salem Lyceum

Coincidentally, the only club Hawthorne was ever part of was a branch of the only club that Thoreau ever joined, the lyceum. ❾ **The Salem Lyceum, 43 Church Street,** was founded in 1830 to provide "mutual education and rational entertainment" for the citizens of Salem. In its sixty-year career, more than one thousand lectures were offered there, although none by Hawthorne.

Hawthorne was elected corresponding secretary for the 1848–49 season—much to his surprise, because apparently he hadn't campaigned or even proposed himself as a candidate. As secretary he did very little: he didn't introduce the speakers and often didn't even go to the lectures. He did, however, book many of his Transcendentalist friends to speak. Emerson, Thoreau, and Fields were all invited by Hawthorne, as was Daniel Webster.

Emerson was the most frequent guest, giving thirty lectures to the Salem Lyceum over his career. Thoreau read parts of *Walden*, and Fields spoke on American literature. Other notable speakers included Frederick Douglass, Horace Mann, Oliver Wendell Holmes, and Jones Very, whose lyceum lecture on epic poetry served as his calling card into Transcendentalist circles. Bronson Alcott also used the Salem Lyceum to host his "conversations."

The early lectures were given in either the Methodist church on Sewall Street or the Universalist church on Rust Street. The society was quickly able to raise $4,000 for a new building. The original structure could hold seven hundred guests. Men were charged a dollar, and women, who had to be invited by a male, paid seventy-five cents. The building now houses the Lyceum Bar & Grill, but while the plaque outside takes note of Alexander Graham Bell's first demonstration phone call from that location, it offers no recognition of the building's role as a lyceum.

describes reading the final chapter to Sophia before sending it off to Fields in Boston: "It broke her heart and sent her to bed with a grievous headache, which I look upon as a triumphant success."

Once finished with *The Scarlet Letter*, Hawthorne moved his family again, this time to the opposite end of the state, to Lenox, a small village nestled in the Berkshires. The Hawthornes lived there for nearly two years before returning to Concord. Nathaniel's time in the Berkshires was surprisingly busy for such a serene and secluded location. While there, he developed a friendship with Herman Melville and wrote *The House of the Seven Gables*, set in Salem, as well as *The Blithedale Romance*, a fictional account of his time at Brook Farm. As he joked in a letter to Bridge, his wife was hard at work as well: "Mrs. Hawthorne published a little work two months ago, which still lies in sheets, but I assure you it makes some noise in the world, both by day and night. In plain English, we have another little daughter."

Although Hawthorne had left Salem, it was still in his consciousness. His next novel after *The Scarlet Letter* also took its cue from a historic past and a crime left unpunished. In this work, Hawthorne took the Salem home of his cousin, Susannah Ingersoll, and made it famous. Hawthorne was well acquainted with the house, having played cards there often, and easily transformed its many chambers into the home of a long-lived curse.

❿ **The House of the Seven Gables, 54 Turner Street,** today is a testament to Hawthorne and his legacy. It was purchased in 1908 by Caroline Emerton and opened as a museum in 1910 with the mission of "educating people of all ages, preserving its historic buildings and collections for future generations, and providing community services for families and children." It hosts 150,000 visitors a year, who come to see one of the oldest surviving mansions in New England.

Another of Salem's highlights is ⓫ the Peabody Essex Museum, in East India Square on New Liberty Street. The museum is one of the largest on the East Coast, comprising a main campus running nearly three blocks as well as a number of historic houses nearby. The main museum's atrium, a soaring glass and brick space designed by architect Moshe Safdie, is worth visiting just for itself.

The House of the Seven Gables museum covers more than three hundred years of Salem history with two thousand artifacts, a staff of costumed guides, and numerous art pieces and photographs.

These two museums are an integral part of a citywide drive to promote Salem's historic heritage. With one of the highest museum-per-square-mile densities in the Northeast, the town is actively pursuing tourism as a major industry. For those fascinated by the witch trials, of course, Salem offers a plethora of attractions: the Salem Witch Museum, Salem Witch Village, Salem Wax Museum of Witches and Seafarers, the Witch Dungeon Museum, the Witch History Museum, and the Witch House.

But Salem isn't just about witches. Anchored by the Peabody Essex Museum and supported by the USS *Friendship* (a reconstruction of a three-masted nineteenth-century sailing vessel) and the House of the Seven Gables historic site, Salem has plenty of history to share with visitors.

The architecturally striking Peabody Essex Museum is the center of Salem's downtown.

Chapter 7

Utopian Societies

Transcendent Communities

This house was home to the Fruitlands community and was under the direction of Abigail Alcott, who did her best to keep the entire community fed, clothed, and warm.

Transcendentalism was, from its earliest beginnings in Unitarianism, a breaking away from the past toward a new way of thinking and living. Emerson opened his landmark work *Nature* with the declaration that "there are new lands, new men, new thoughts. Let us demand our own works and laws and worship." The new "American scholar" he described to the graduating seniors of the Phi Beta Kappa Society would break away from the cultural ties that bound America to Europe. And much as his "Divinity School Address" tried to persuade young soon-to-be preachers to move past "corpse-cold Unitarianism" to a more intuitive and vital relation with God, the Transcendental Club encouraged young men and women to break free from the philosophic and theological traditions of the past to create new ideas. The America of the nineteenth century, the Transcendentalists felt, demanded new actions for a new society.

While some of the Transcendentalists strived for the type of "self-reliance" Emerson spoke of and Thoreau lived, many also sought the dynamic interchange that comes from groups of people. This dynamic mixed well with the Transcendentalists' natural inclination toward social reform and produced discussion clubs, societies for social activism, and experiments in communal living, including Brook Farm and Fruitlands.

Brook Farm in West Roxbury was the most famous and longest lasting of the Transcendentalist utopian communities. Founded in 1841 by George and Sophia Ripley, it disbanded in 1847 after a series of mishaps and missteps. While it existed, it was viewed by many in Transcendentalist circles, especially in its early years, as a venture born of pure motives and forward thinking.

Fruitlands was less successful. Bronson Alcott and Englishman Charles Lane moved to a farm they called Fruitlands, near Harvard, Massachusetts, in 1843 with a circle of thirteen people: the Alcotts with their four girls, Charles Lane and his young son, and five other adults. This community managed to survive only seven months before disbanding in January 1844.

Although these were the only two Transcendentalist communities that formally separated themselves from the outside world, other individuals and small groups attempted to live the ideals of the Transcendentalist movement through utopias. In this sense, utopias are communities that formally set themselves apart from mainstream society so members can live according to their beliefs while creating new societal structures that are more equitable and productive. Thus, Thoreau, who was trying to live as close to the earth as he could, and Dickinson, living in a world limited to her household because it helped her write the poetry she needed to, were also utopian.

Emerson had his progressive social ideas as well. He was a notoriously bad gardener and found that great physical labor made him too tired and distracted for intellectual labor, so he opted not to join Brook Farm or Fruitlands. Instead, he tried to address the issue of class within his own house and requested that his cook and servant girl sit down to dinner with his family. The cook, however, was too shy and would not budge from the kitchen, and the servant girl did not want to leave the cook by herself. So ended Emerson's experiment in domestic social equality.

The Transcendentalists' desire to create a perfect society was a product not only of their own philosophy but also of their place and time. From John Winthrop's "City on a Hill" (the belief that the Puritan pioneers were the chosen few) to the Manifest Destiny doctrine (which claimed it was the United States' destiny to expand westward), Americans have long felt it was their duty to create the ideal society. In the first seventy-five years of the country,

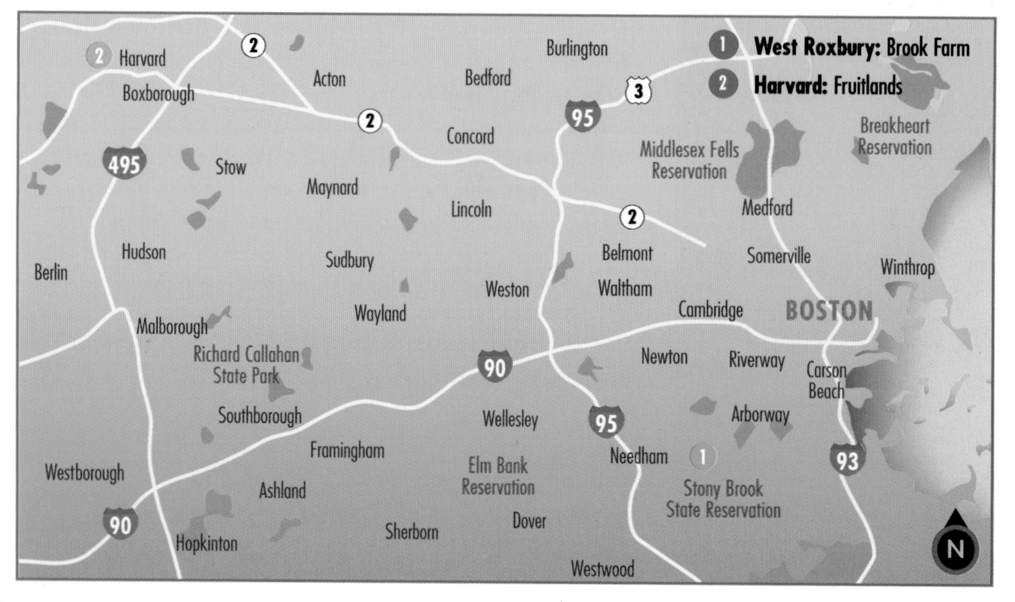

more than one hundred utopian communities were started in the United States, though most lasted only a short time. This utopian impetus grew particularly strong in the middle of the nineteenth century; more than sixty utopian societies were started in the 1840s alone, nearly a third of them based to varying degrees on the work of Charles Fourier. The largest of these Fourieristic societies, in Red Bank, New Jersey, at one point had nearly 130 members.

Brook Farm

When George Ripley graduated from Harvard Divinity School in 1826, he quickly landed a position with the Purchase Street Church in Boston, where he was the minister for fifteen years. An insightful and diligent scholar, Ripley's first ten years as a minister were relatively quiet. By the fall of 1836, however, he had grown increasingly frustrated with the current theological opinions and jumped at the chance to join Emerson and Frederic Henry Hedge in starting the Transcendental Club. He even hosted the first meeting at his house.

A year later, when Andrews Norton attacked Emerson's "Divinity School Address," it was Ripley who defended Emerson and engaged Norton in a prolonged debate. And when the Transcendental Club was ready to start its own journal, Ripley agreed to be the assistant editor, under Margaret Fuller.

At the same time, a journalist and writer by the name of Albert Brisbane was translating the works of Charles Fourier, a French utopian socialist, into English. He published many of them as *The Social Destiny of Man* in 1840. Fourier believed that the problem with society was how society was organized: how work was divided, where people lived, and how children were educated. He proposed a highly structured alternative community called a phalanx, in which men and women would do

George Ripley left his post as a Unitarian minister to found the Brook Farm Institute of Agriculture and Education on a two-hundred-acre farm in West Roxbury. It was the longest-lasting, best-known Transcendentalist utopian community.

what work naturally appealed to them and social classes would be erased.

Fourier successfully exported his ideas to America through men such as Brisbane and *New York Tribune* editor Horace Greeley. Inspired by *The Social Destiny of Man*, Ripley announced at an October 1840 meeting of the Transcendental Club that he had decided to start his own community, ideally with the help of those present. Intuitively understanding that he had not convinced Emerson at the meeting, Ripley wrote him a few days later, on November 9, to press his case:

> *Our objects, as you know, are to insure a more natural union between intellectual and manual labor than now exists; to combine the thinker and the worker, as far as possible, in the same individual; to guarantee the highest mental*

freedom, by providing all with labor, adapted to their tastes and talents, and securing to them the fruits of their industry; to do away the necessity of menial services, by opening the benefits of education and the profits of labor to all; and thus to prepare a society of liberal, intelligent, and cultivated persons, whose relations with each other would permit a more simple and wholesome life, than can be led amidst the pressure of our competitive institutions.

Charles Fourier, a French utopian socialist, had a tremendous impact on the American utopian movement of the mid-nineteenth century. He advocated highly structured communities he called phalanxes.

Ripley had high hopes for this dream and envisioned it as the dawn of a new world: "If wisely executed, it will be a light over this country and this age. If not the sunrise, it will be the morning star." Emerson remained unconvinced. Writing back a month later, he thanked Ripley for the invitation and pledged his moral support but noted that "if the community is not good for me neither am I good for it."

Undaunted, in April 1841 Ripley started ❶ the Brook Farm Institute of Agriculture and Education on a two-hundred-acre farm at 679 Baker Street in West Roxbury, some nine miles southwest of Boston. To purchase the land and the buildings, as well as to pay for supplies for the first year, Ripley created a joint stock company that sold twenty-four shares at $500 each. Among the original contributors were George Ripley and his wife, Sophia; the newspaper editor Charles Dana; George's sister Marianne; Minot and Maria Pratt; William Allen; Sarah Stearns; Charles Whitmore; and a young writer from Salem looking for a peaceful life in the country, Nathaniel Hawthorne.

Each of the shareholders was entitled to a single vote, and many also held director positions. Each would annually receive either 5 percent interest on their share or free tuition for one student. In addition, all members of the community were expected to do three hundred days of work during the course of a year in payment for room and board.

The Grounds

When the intrepid social reformers moved to the farm in April 1841, they found themselves in the middle of a rare springtime blizzard. Fortunately, a two-story farmhouse already existed on the property. They named the farmhouse the Hive because of its central role in their existence. Its dining room held fifty people, and

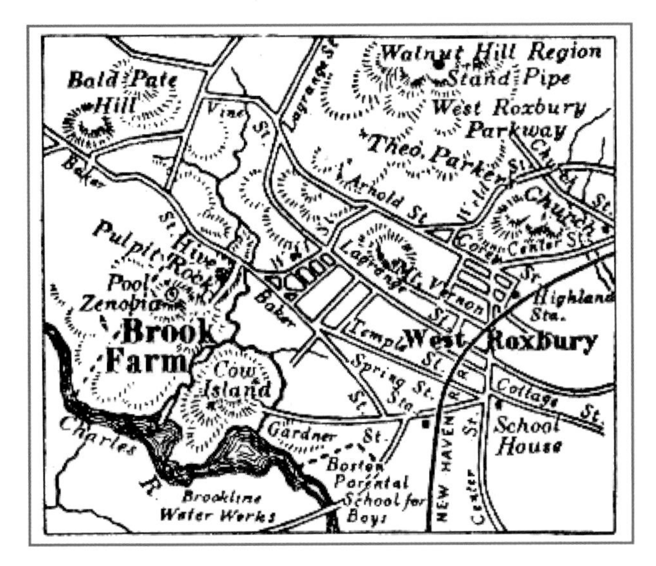

The two-hundred-acre farm in West Roxbury proved delightful and bucolic but difficult to farm.

One of the preexisting buildings on Brook Farm, this large farmhouse was named "the Hive" and served as the center of the community.

the parlor served as a gathering place for social and community events. Ripley's personal library, which was part of his contribution to the community, was laid out on open bookshelves for everyone to enjoy.

Across the street was another house, which the farmers rented and named the Nest. This home served as the school for the community as well as providing housing for some of the teachers and students. The first new building constructed was a house on the highest part of the farm, given the name the Eyrie. It provided Mr. and Mrs. Ripley with their own home as well as small rooms for students. Ripley's library followed him up the hill and was established in the Eyrie as well.

After this came the oddly named Margaret Fuller Cottage (she never spent a night there and had no intention of living there) and the Pilgrim House, built by Ichabod Morton, whose tenure in the house lasted only two weeks. Both buildings were used as lodging for Brook Farmers, and the Pilgrim House also contained the laundry facility and the offices for the *Harbinger*, a weekly journal. In 1843, members constructed a two-story workshop some three hundred yards from the Hive, which housed a mill, machinery, and, later, the printing press for the *Harbinger*.

The Arcadian Life

While Brook Farm never achieved the ambitions Ripley set out for it in his letter to Emerson, it did succeed on a number of levels. The community, which grew to nearly two hundred members at one point, consisted predominantly of young people, who brought a sense of joy and optimism to many aspects of farm life. At night, the members would dance and play music, play cards and charades, create tableaux vivants, and perform plays. Daytime recreations included picnics, sledding, skating, and swimming.

Affectionately known as Ripley's Farm among its inhabitants, the community had a reputation for a type of idyllic eccentricity best illustrated by its custom of the daily circle, the "symbol of Universal Unity." Members of the community joined hands in a circle at the end of each day and vowed "truth to the cause of God and Humanity."

Among the largest draws for young people were the highly successful schools at Brook Farm. Education at the farm included a nursery school, a primary school for children up to ten years old, and a college preparatory school. The primary school was under the direction of Sophia and Marianne Ripley and used a progressive, child-centered pedagogy that some scholars have compared with John Dewey's model of education. In any case, the students appeared to be happy, and many were successfully sent on to Harvard. The community also offered evening courses to the adults on such topics as moral philosophy, German, and modern European history.

The *Harbinger*

The *Harbinger*, a weekly journal published at Brook Farm (and later in New York), was edited by George Ripley. In the introductory notice of June 15, 1845, Ripley, never one to leave his ministerial rhetoric far behind, described the mission of the *Harbinger* with typical zeal:

> *The interests of Social Reform will be considered as paramount to all others in whatever is admitted into the pages of the* Harbinger. *We shall suffer no attachment to literature, no taste for abstract discussion, no love of purely intellectual theories, to seduce us from our devotion to the cause of the oppressed, the down trodden, the insulted and injured masses of our fellow men. Every pulsation of our being vibrates in sympathy with the wrongs of the toiling millions; and every wise effort for their speedy enfranchisement will find in us resolute and indomitable advocates.*

The weekly, which lasted for four years, featured writing by many of the brightest minds from both within the Transcendentalist movement and outside the circle. The Transcendentalist poet and critic Christopher Cranch contributed poems, while John Dwight wrote about music. Thomas Wentworth Higginson published his poetry, Charles Dana wrote poetry and book reviews, Albert Brisbane and Horace Greeley discussed social reforms, and George Ripley reported on Brook Farm.

Geo P Bradford

THE

HARBINGER,

DEVOTED TO

SOCIAL AND POLITICAL PROGRESS.

"All things, at the present day, stand provided and prepared, and await the light."

VOL. I.

PUBLISHED BY THE BROOK FARM PHALANX.

NEW-YORK:
BURGESS, STRINGER, AND COMPANY.
BOSTON:
REDDING AND COMPANY.
MDCCC XLV.

Although the *Harbinger* claimed to have "no taste for abstract discussion," essays with titles like "Hymn of Humanity" and "The Universality of Providence" regularly ran in the weekly magazine.

However, this vision of Eden glosses over the very real stresses of trying to make the community a success. The soil in West Roxbury was sandy and full of rocks. The intrepid utopians managed to farm only about twenty acres of the nearly two hundred that came with the farm, in part because only a handful of the men at Brook Farm had ever been farmers before. Five—William Allen, Francis Farley, Charles Salisbury, John Orvis, and John Brown—listed farming as their occupation on the Brook Farm roster. The other men ranged from ministers and attorneys to shoemakers, hotelkeepers, fishermen, and even an apothecary. Although Brook Farm ran a successful school and was able to sell milk, vegetables, and hay, it had to struggle continually for economic stability.

In an effort to erase social classes and increase comfort, these simple clothes were designed for Brook Farm members.

Part of the reason was the basic premise behind dividing the duties of the farm: that everyone would share in both the work and the leisure time, but each chore would be done by the person who most wanted to do it. This inevitably led to some inequities. As Emerson noted in his 1883 "Historic Notes of Life and Letters in New England," "The country members naturally were surprised to observe that one man ploughed all day and one looked out of a window all day, and perhaps drew his picture, and both received at night the same wages."

To combat the sense that some members were not doing their fair share, the community adopted the following standards when they formalized the Brook Farm Institute of Agriculture and Education: ten hours of work in the summer and eight hours in the winter would constitute a day's work. Three hundred days of work a year was required for full membership in the community. Those who did less than a full year's work would have to pay for room and board at four dollars a day.

In addition, the community decided in 1845 to become an official Fourieristic phalanx, after Albert Brisbane, Fourier's foremost American popularizer, had lived there for a time. The formal adoption of Fourierism was, in part, a strategy to generate a much-needed influx of capital. But it also brought a more structured daily routine that eclipsed some of the more carefree aspects of community life. For example, with the change to a phalanx, voting rights were distributed according to how many shares a family owned rather than by apportioning one vote to each member. This disenfranchised a number of longtime members, who then left the community.

Decline

Brook Farm began a big project in the summer of 1844, starting construction on a building to be known as the Phalanstery. This three-story building, nearly sixty

Farmer Hawthorne

In some ways, Nathaniel Hawthorne's seven-month sojourn in West Roxbury reflects the trajectory of the entire experiment: early enthusiasm, weary contentment, growing disillusionment, and a disappointing exit.

He came to the farm cheerfully hoping to establish a peaceful home and enjoy an agrarian life among equals. In his first weeks, he worked with diligence and enthusiasm; his first real success came on April 16, three days after he arrived, when he learned to milk a cow belonging to Margaret Fuller. Hawthorne had nicknamed the cow the Transcendentalist Heifer and attributed human characteristics to her: "Miss Fuller's cow hooks the other cows, and has made herself ruler of the herd, and behaves in a very tyrannical manner."

He also took on the duties of chopping hay, bringing in firewood, and pitching manure. A week later he was chopping wood, turning a grindstone, and seeing himself as quite the farmer: "It is an endless surprise to me how much work there is to be done in the world; but, thank God, I am able to do my share of it,—and my ability increases daily. What a great, broad-shouldered, elephantine personage I shall become by and by."

His growing confidence in his abilities as a manual laborer came at a cost, however. Just two weeks into his farm life, Hawthorne began to note how difficult it would be for him to carry on his career as a writer while at Brook Farm. At first the work was merely physically challenging; he complained that chopping wood disturbs "the equilibrium of the muscles and sinews," making it difficult for him to write.

The farm work soon became mentally challenging as well, however. On June 1 he wrote, "I think this present life of mine gives me an antipathy to pen and ink, even more than my [Boston] Custom-House experience did. . . . In the midst of toil, or after a hard day's work in the goldmine, my soul obstinately refuses to be poured out on paper." A month and a half later, he had had enough:

> *And, joyful thought! in a little more than a fortnight; I shall be free from my bondage,— . . . free to enjoy Nature,—free to think and feel! Even my Custom-House experience was not such a thraldom and weariness; my mind and heart were free. O, labor is the curse of the world, and nobody can meddle with it without becoming proportionably brutified! Is it a praiseworthy matter that I have spent five golden months in providing food for cows and horses? It is not so.*

After a few weeks' break in September, Hawthorne lasted until November, when he was released from his "contract." Unfortunately, he had to sue the corporation to get his initial investment back, and even then, he never saw his money.

yards long, was to be the center of the community. Located at the top of the hill, just in front of the Eyrie, the Phalanstery was to house all the public rooms. Parlors, reading rooms, reception rooms, single bedrooms, a great hall for assemblies, a full kitchen with a bakery, and a dining hall for three hundred people were all nearly completed when the entire structure burned to the ground on March 3, 1846. It was uninsured.

The probable cause of the conflagration was a spark from a defective chimney. Because of the remoteness of the farm, little could be done to save the building. John Thomas Codman, writing about the fire, described it as quite a spectacle: "Ere long the flames were chasing one another in mad riot over the structure; running across long corridors and up and down the supporting columns of wood, until the huge edifice was a mass of firework. . . . It was a grand and magnificent sight!"

The construction of the Phalanestry had been funded primarily through loans, and its destruction presented Brook Farm with a loss of $7,000. This was too much for the community to bear, and it was forced to disband the following year, in 1847. George Ripley had to sell most of his personal library to pay the debts of the association.

The farm and lands were sold to John Plummer in 1849. James Freeman Clarke, the Transcendentalist Unitarian minister, bought the property in 1855 with the intention of establishing another community there. During the Civil War, he offered it to President Lincoln for an army base, and the Second Massachusetts Regiment trained at "Camp Andrew" on the grounds.

In 1870, the farm became the Martin Luther House for orphans. It operated for nearly a hundred years, under a variety of names, until the last remaining building, the Margaret Fuller Cottage, burned down in the 1970s. Now all that is left to mark the spot is a display at the original location of the Hive and the nearly hidden remains of the cottage.

This small informational display is all that marks one of most successful utopian attempts in the nineteenth century.

Hidden in the bushes is the foundation of what was called the Margaret Fuller Cottage, although she had no intention of ever living there.

Many key figures in the venture moved on to gain success in other ways. Ripley, for example, went to work for Horace Greeley's *New York Tribune* while Hawthorne, of course, became a renowned writer—and used his Brook Farm experiences as the basis for his novel *The Blithedale Romance*.

Perhaps Brook Farm's finest epitaph was written by Emerson, a man who could never bring himself to uproot his family to West Roxbury but who recognized the nobility of the enterprise. Writing in 1883, Emerson commented:

> *It was a noble and generous movement in the projectors, to try an experiment of better living. They had the feeling that our ways of living were too conventional and expensive, not allowing each to do what he had a talent for, and not permitting men to combine cultivation of mind and heart with a reasonable amount of daily labor. At the same time, it was an attempt to lift others with themselves, and to share the advantages they should attain.*

West Roxbury Today

When the Brook Farmers arrived in West Roxbury, it was only a western hamlet of the main town of Roxbury. West Roxbury split from Roxbury in 1851. The same year rail service arrived in the town, allowing residents to commute easily to Boston. Since then, West Roxbury has grown into a Boston suburb of thirty thousand people and is now officially considered part of Boston.

Although all the buildings associated with Brook Farm are gone, the land connected with the farm is now listed as a National Historic Landscape under the jurisdiction of the Massachusetts Department of Conservation and Recreation. The farmland borders on West Roxbury's Millennium Park, a hundred-acre park on the capped Gardner Street Landfill. Hiking and mountain-biking trails lead through the property, and the Gethsemane Jewish cemetery occupies much of the high ground.

What used to be a thriving community of more than seventy people is now open grassfields hedged in by busy suburban sprawl.

Fruitlands

When Bronson Alcott returned from his intellectual tour of England in the fall of 1842, he was accompanied by Charles Lane and Lane's young son, William. The two men had been in town for only a month when they gathered a group of Brook Farmers for a meeting at Emerson's house to lay out the plans for their own communal society. While it was to model itself on Brook Farm in many ways, ❷ Fruitlands, just outside of the small village of Harvard, Massachusetts, would not be a Fourieristic phalanx. Instead, Alcott and Lane opted for a structure that they called a "consociate family," which meant to Alcott and Lane an ideal merging of familial and societal structures. What it meant to Abigail Alcott was that she had more people to take care of.

The two men suggested to Emerson that he buy them "a farm of a hundred acres in excellent condition with good buildings, a good orchard, and grounds." As he had when presented with a similar request from George Ripley, Emerson declined the invitation. Their enthusiasm undimmed, Alcott and Lane continued to scout for possible locations, and finally found a ninety-acre farm some fourteen miles northwest of Concord, near the town of Harvard. Using $1,800 of Lane's money, they bought it. Wyman Farm, as it was known, ran along the ridge of Prospect Hill, offering views of Mounts Watchusett and Monadnock in the distance. The central farmhouse and barn were about a quarter of a mile below the ridge. The property had few fruit trees, but Alcott and Lane renamed it "Fruitlands," in honor of the community's vegetarian diet. They moved in on June 1, 1843, in a driving rainstorm. (Mother Nature seems not to have smiled on Transcendentalists starting utopian communities.)

Those who joined Lane and the Alcotts in the venture were an eclectic and eccentric group. Samuel Larned, who had worked in a countinghouse before coming to Fruitlands, believed that foul language, when uttered with a pure heart, uplifted its listeners. Therefore, he

Thanks to Clara Endicott Sears, who bought the land in 1910, Fruitlands has been opened to the public as a museum for nearly one hundred years. It now includes smaller museums of Shaker life, Native American arts, and nineteenth-century paintings.

greeted most people with a "Good morning, goddamn you!" and a cheery smile. Joseph Palmer, a butcher from Harvard, grew a beard when beards were considered socially taboo (Thoreau grew one too). Abraham Wood insisted that everyone call him Wood Abraham. Samuel Bower left Fruitlands to embrace nudism. The one woman (aside from the Alcotts) at Fruitlands was supposedly exiled from the community because she ate fish at a neighbor's dinner party.

Planting Aspiring Vegetables

Although neither Alcott nor Lane was a farmer, the new community managed to plant a dozen acres by July: eight acres of grains, two of potatoes, one of vegetables, and one of melons. Their approach to farming was novel for the time, to say the least. After some early help from an ox and a cow, the men decided to work the farm without the "subjugation of animals"—their spadework, however, proved ineffective and they were forced to "enslave" some cattle to till the land. The community chose to plant only "aspiring vegetables," those that grew upward, while the baser vegetables, those that grew downward, were forbidden. The community also decided to produce only enough food to sustain themselves, because they felt that selling food might degrade the purity of their mission.

Lane and Alcott's fanaticism was not limited to farming. According to Louisa May Alcott's wry short story "Transcendental Wild Oats," which was based on her experiences at Fruitlands, the men declared that "nothing was to be admitted [to the community] which has caused wrong or death to man or beast." Prohibited items included meat, dairy products, leather, and even lamp oil. Cotton, silk, and wool were also banned, because they were products of slave labor. When not working, the small community engaged in self-improvement through daily meditation, reading, and philosophic discussion. The children were schooled in the morning, after their chores were done.

The philosophy underpinning the Fruitlands experiment held that only by reforming every individual could society as a whole be reformed. (This approach contrasted

"Transcendental Wild Oats"

Beyond the announcements in the *Dial*, there is one surviving description of the Alcotts' time at Fruitlands. In December 1873, Louisa May Alcott published her version of the experiment as a six-thousand-word story, "Transcendental Wild Oats." From the sarcasm of the opening lines ("On the first day of June, 184—, a large wagon, drawn by a small horse and containing a motley load, went lumbering over certain New England hills, with the pleasing accompaniments of wind, rain, and hail") to the tongue-in-cheek descriptions of the various members of the community, Louisa May touches on most of the important elements of the experiment. Casting Charles Lane as "Timon Lion" and her father as "Abel Lamb," Alcott is as unstinting in her criticism of Lane and Alcott's impractical idealism as she is generous in her praise for her mother (who she christens "Sister Hope").

One notable passage is her description of bringing in the hay while the men are out lecturing:

> *About the time the grain was ready to house, some call of the Oversoul wafted all the men away. An easterly storm was coming up and the yellow stacks were sure to be ruined. Then Sister Hope gathered her forces. Three little girls, one boy (Timon's son), and herself, harnessed to clothes-baskets and Russia-linen sheets, were the only teams she could command; but with these poor appliances the indomitable woman got in the grain and saved food for her young, with the instinct and energy of a mother-bird with a brood of hungry nestlings to feed.*

with that embraced at Brook Farm, which sought to restructure all of society.) Alcott and Lane declared that "each member is to perform the work for which experience, strength, and taste best fit him." In practice, this meant that the men devoted themselves to their own self-improvement, leaving Abba Alcott to do almost all the hard physical work. For example, Alcott and Lane left on a lecture tour during harvest season, leaving Abba to bring in the hay with the help of the girls and Lane's young son.

A Quick Decline

By the end of the year, Abba Alcott was fed up with the tremendous workload, strict dietary requirements, and sexual abstinence demanded by Lane. She gave her husband an ultimatum: she was going to leave the farm and take the children; he could chose to join them or he could opt to stay. Out of food and firewood, she moved the family to a nearby farmer's house, where they could rest, take stock, and support themselves by taking on work in the village of Still River. Defeated, Alcott went with his family and took to his bed in a combination of exhaustion and depression. Lane, for his part, foresaw the demise of the community and left with his son for a nearby Shaker community at the beginning of January. After less than seven months, the experiment at Fruitlands had failed miserably.

By October of the following year, the Alcotts were back in Concord. Shortly after their return, they were able to purchase, with an inheritance from Abba's father and help from Emerson, the house on the Lexington Road that they called Hillside and later sold to Nathaniel Hawthorne. Bronson Alcott moved on to other dreams, later sharing his perspective on the venture:

> *Our "Fruitlands" was an adventure undertaken in good faith for planting a Family Order here in New England, in hopes of enjoying a pastoral life with a few devoted men and women, smitten with the sentiments of the old heroism and love of holiness and humanity. But none of us were prepared to actualize practically the ideal life of which we dreamed. So we fell apart, some returning to the established ways, some soured by the trial, others postponing the fulfillment of his dream to a more propitious future.*

Alcott was never able to fulfill his dream of the ideal "consociate family," but he did accomplish another lifelong dream when, at eighty years of age, he opened the Concord School of Philosophy in 1879.

Fruitlands Today

The farm (located at 102 Prospect Hill Road) has retained both its rural flavor and its heritage as the site of a utopian experiment, thanks to the efforts of Clara Endicott Sears, who bought Fruitlands in 1910 and opened the farmhouse to the public as a museum in 1914. The Fruitlands Museum now comprises several smaller museums of Shaker life, American Indian arts and crafts, and nineteenth-century paintings, in addition to the original farmhouse with its many artifacts from the Alcott and Lane families.

It was perhaps inevitable that the Transcendentalists would envision communities of seekers who were both equal and free to express themselves as the spirit moved them, just as it was probably inevitable that those communities would fail. Philosophers do not necessarily make good farmers, and the sandy, rocky soil of New England demands the very best of farmers. These attempts at creating a more just and harmonious society exemplified some of the best tendencies of the Transcendentalists as well as some of their shortcomings. The communities highlighted their hope and faith, while illustrating the lack of practicality that too often accompanied their philosophic ideals.

Chapter 8

Amherst

"Paradise"

Emily Dickinson's house on Main Street has been carefully restored and now serves as the centerpiece of the Emily Dickinson Museum.

Poem #215

What is — "Paradise" —
Who live there —
Are they "Farmers" —
Do they "hoe" —
Do they know that this is "Amherst" —
And that I — am coming — too —

Do they wear "new shoes" — in "Eden" —
Is it always pleasant — there —
Won't they scold us — when we're homesick —
Or tell God — how cross we are —

You are sure there's such a person
As "a Father" — in the sky —
So if I get lost — there — ever
Or do what the Nurse calls "die" —
I shan't walk the "Jasper" — barefoot —
Ransomed folks — won't laugh at me —
Maybe — "Eden" a'n't so lonesome
As New England used to be!

—Emily Dickinson

Amherst's recollections of its most famous Transcendentalist seeker are tantalizing and mysterious: the reclusive poet in her white dress tending her gardens; neighbors catching no more than a glimpse of the ghostly lady among the trees; bundles of poems wrapped with twine and stuffed into drawers; children eagerly watching for the wicker basket of gingerbread to be mysteriously lowered from a second-story window; unverified stories of unrequited passion for her sister-in-law. Although this eccentric and talented poet was quiet and demure while alive, she has since become the center of attention for countless scholars and visitors.

This oil portrait, based on the one known daguerreotype of Dickinson, attempts to portray her in color and was meticulously researched by Guillermo Cuellar before he began painting.

Emily Dickinson was called the "myth of Amherst" even during her lifetime, but it is not just the stories about her that spark wonder and fascination. It is the nearly eighteen hundred poems she wrote over the course of almost forty years. Only eleven of those were published in her lifetime; it wasn't until her friend Mabel Loomis Todd (who also happened to be her brother's mistress) took on the project of editing and publishing Dickinson's work after her death that the public began to catch a fuller glimpse of the striking talent of the woman who is now known as the "belle of Amherst."

In the ensuing years, Dickinson has grown into a full-blown industry. The house that served as her home, along with her brother's house next door, is now the Emily Dickinson Museum. Mabel Loomis Todd's home has been made into a bed-and-breakfast, and the town library has a special Emily Dickinson collection with an international reputation. At least four literary journals are dedicated to examining her work, and a Google search of her name yields nearly two million hits. Her poetry is a staple of literary anthologies and appears as often in elementary schools as it does in graduate courses. Both Amherst and the literary world continue to take Emily Dickinson very seriously.

Although Dickinson never attended the meetings of the Transcendental Club or discussed utopian visions in Elizabeth Peabody's bookstore, she clearly sought to develop her own relationship with the universe. Her poetry sits within the broad confines of the philosophic ideals set out by Ralph Waldo Emerson, whose work she much admired and who came to her brother's home, the Evergreens, for a visit. In addition, Dickinson's subjects and language have much in common with those of Henry David Thoreau, whose *Walden* was published just as Dickinson was beginning to write poetry seriously. Emerson has the "transparent eye-ball" (his concept that when a person is out communing in nature, he takes everything in because he is both part of and a microcosm of what he sees—see chapter 4);

Dickinson has the soul. She also wants to clear away everything that stands between her and whatever it is that is out there:

Poem #327

So safer — guess — with just my soul
Upon the Window pane —
Where other Creatures put their eyes —
Incautious — of the Sun —

It is through this "window pane" that the reality of the outside world floods into Dickinson's consciousness and permeates her poetry. It is because she is open to the ideas and feelings that flow into her soul through the "window" that she is able to see the world with new eyes. And through this window, we can catch a glimpse of the Amherst of Emily Dickinson, her paradise that allowed her to look within for a poetry of possibility—poetry that is not limited by sensory experience but moves wherever her imagination and experience can take her.

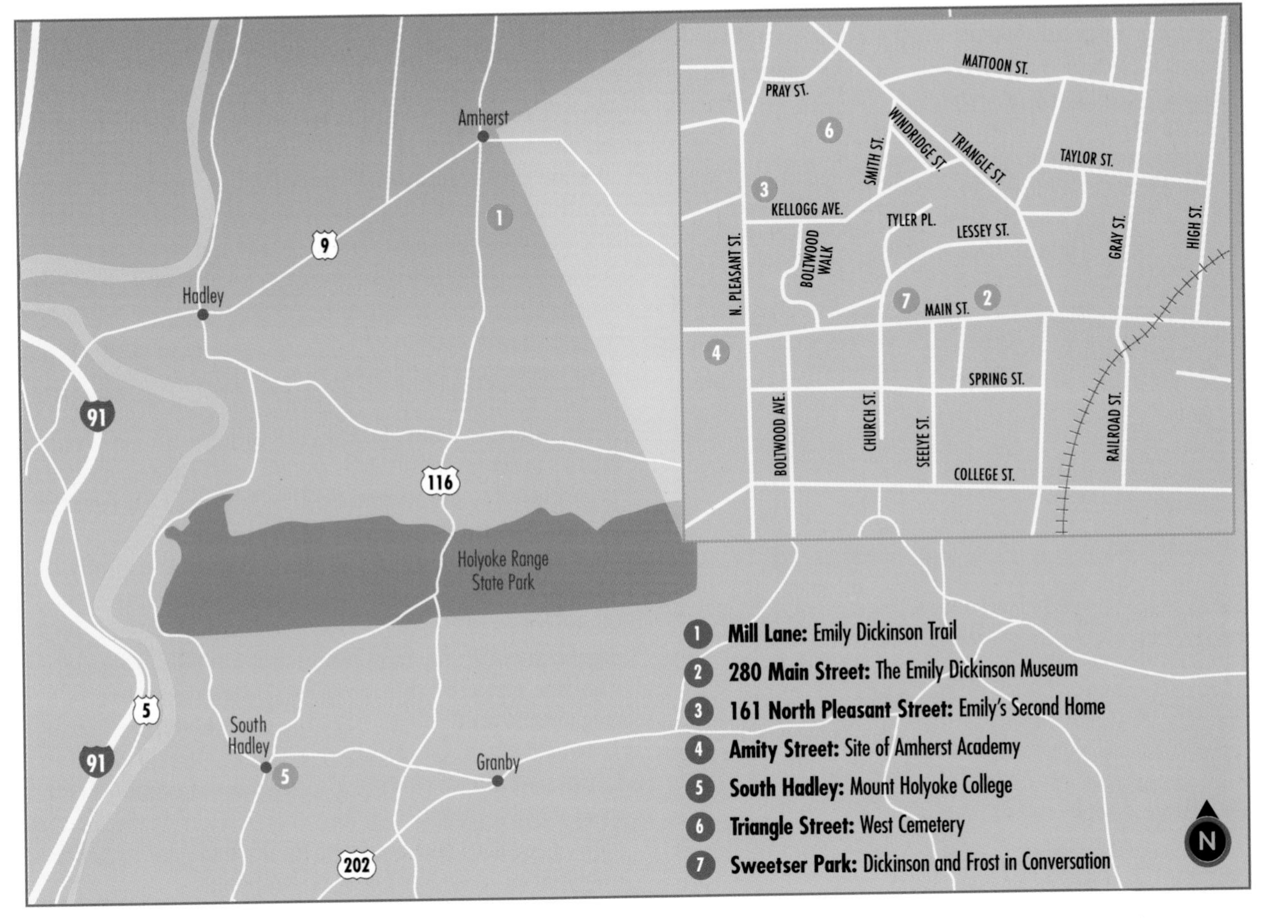

The Emily Dickinson Trail

In Hollywood, the famous get a star on a sidewalk; in the Amherst area, the famous get a trail through the woods. What began with the Robert Frost Trail, a forty-two-mile path leading from South Hadley to Wendell, has now blossomed into an entire trail system honoring local authors including Emily Dickinson, the dictionary writer Noah Webster, and the activist and novelist Helen Hunt Jackson.

❶ **The Emily Dickinson Trail** leads along the Fort River just south of town. It starts at the very popular Groff Park, just off Route 116, and meanders through woods and fields to the Mill Lane parking lot. Although it is a lovely walk, there is no evidence that Dickinson ever followed such a path.

"Home Is the Definition of God"

Poem #657

I dwell in Possibility —
A fairer House than Prose —
More numerous of Windows —
Superior — for Doors —

One way into Dickinson's world, both figuratively and literally, is through the front door. While the other writers in the Transcendentalist movement gathered, lectured, and worked in very public places, Dickinson traveled only within her imagination, and her poetry remains firmly rooted in her life at home. As she wrote to her friend Perez Cowan in 1870, "Home is the definition of God." For her, home was a miniature world—a Transcendentalist notion that allowed her to plumb her daily life for the larger meanings that Emerson and Thoreau sought in nature.

Dickinson held her connection to home and family against the backdrop of changing conceptions of what "home" meant. During the nineteenth century, houses grew increasingly intimate as shops and offices began moving out of middle-class homes. This led to a growing distinction between the public sphere of commercial life and the private sphere of the family, what one critic has called the macro and micro experiences of Dickinson's world. Social standards and advice given in magazines and architectural books of the time reflected this move by describing homes as sanctuaries and refuges from the outside world.

Dickinson did not let the confined space of a house or even a town restrict her, however. Rather, it was her base of security and comfort, from which she let her imagination take her far from Amherst:

Poem #1052

I never saw a Moor —
I never saw the Sea —
Yet know I how the Heather looks
And what a Billow be.

Indeed, her world was much larger than where she lived or what she owned:

Poem #466

'Tis little I — could care for Pearls —
Who own the ample sea —
Or Brooches — when the Emperor —
With Rubies — pelteth me —

Or Gold — who am the Prince of Mines —
Or Diamonds — when have I
A Diadem to fit a Dom —
Continual upon me —

Amherst Fixtures

Emily Dickinson was born on December 10, 1830, to Edward Dickinson and Emily Norcross Dickinson in the Homestead, now part of ❷ **the Emily Dickinson Museum, 280 Main Street,** a house that her grandfather, Samuel Fowler Dickinson, had built some seventeen years before. Although their grandfather had to sell the Homestead in 1833 to David Mack, who owned a straw hat business in town, the Dickinsons continued to live in half of the house, which they rented from the Macks until Dickinson's father bought a house at ❸ **161 North Pleasant Street** in 1840.

North Pleasant Street, where Dickinson lived for fifteen years.

During the next fifteen years, Dickinson led a fairly typical life for a daughter of a well-to-do New England family. Her father was a prominent lawyer in the village of Amherst, and she was the middle child between her older brother, Austin, and her younger sister, Lavinia. Her letters from the time speak of parties, sleigh rides, and visits from friends. In part due to her grandfather's dedication to education and his financial support of ❹ **Amherst Academy,** which he had helped found in 1814, Dickinson was allowed to study in the school on Amity Street, now a parking lot across the street from the Amherst Public Library. She followed a rigorous curriculum with an emphasis on science and logic before spending her sixteenth year studying chemistry, physiology, algebra, astronomy, and rhetoric at the nearby Mount Holyoke Female Seminary, now ❺ **Mount Holyoke College,** in **South Hadley.** Although she generally enjoyed her time at the seminary, she suffered occasionally from homesickness. As she wrote to her friend, Abiah Root, "Thoughts of

Mount Holyoke continues to be one of the finest single-sex colleges in the country.

home and friends 'come crowding thick and fast, like lightnings from the mountain cloud' and it seems very desolate."

The House on Pleasant Street

However, she was soon back home, and it was in the house at North Pleasant Street that much of the foundation for her poetry was laid. One of her most intriguing notions about homes and houses is that each possesses secret places and inner rooms. Perhaps this idea was inspired by her experiences with secret treasures hidden away from daily life. For example, when she was young and her father wanted her to read only from the Bible, her brother hid a copy of Longfellow's *Kavanagh* under the pianoforte for her to read in private. Another visitor hid a copy of Lydia Maria Child's *Letters from New York* just outside the front door. It's not surprising that Dickinson learned from an early age to look past exteriors to the treasures that might be hidden within.

Amherst Academy is long gone, but this stone tablet across the street from the library and next to the recently renovated Amherst Cinema marks the spot where Emily received an unusually demanding education for a young woman of the time.

Although the house on North Pleasant Street has now become a gas station, the abutting ❻ West Cemetery on Triangle Street has been renovated and remains an important literary pilgrimage site. Much has been made of Dickinson's proximity to the cemetery during her formative years. Funeral processions would often pass by her windows, and as she watched quietly from inside, her thoughts would also travel toward the grave. As she noted in one of her letters: "I have just seen a funeral procession go by of a negro baby, so if my ideas are rather dark you need not marvel." Graveyard imagery appears frequently in some of her most famous poetry:

Poem #216, 1861 version

Safe in their Alabaster Chambers
Untouched by Morning
And untouched by Noon —
Lie the meek members of the Resurrection —
Rafter of Satin — and Roof of Stone!

Where others might be upset or put off by thoughts of death, Dickinson embraces funereal imagery and brings it back inside her domestic world:

Poem #1743

The grave my little cottage is,
Where "Keeping house" for thee
I make my parlor orderly
And lay the marble tea.

It was a poetic inevitability that the cemetery that inspired some of Dickinson's most striking poetry would serve as her final home. When she died in 1886, her coffin was carried over the hill behind the Homestead down to the Dickinson plot behind the iron railings in the center of the West Cemetery and laid next to her father and grandfather.

In 2005, the town of Amherst renovated West Cemetery, fixing the cemetery gates, replacing the stolen iron fence around the Dickinson plot, and adding a mural along the back of a neighboring building. The mural features some fifty people from Amherst's history.

The West Graveyard Cemetery contains the gravesites of some of Amherst's most famous citizens, including Emily Dickinson.

The Homestead

This connection between the grave and the home seems to have been a comforting one for Dickinson, whose own large family home had many "chambers" in which to hide and withdraw from the near-constant stream of business visitors and social callers. Stories abound of Dickinson carrying on conversations with visitors from behind corners or closed doors or in the shadows of hallways. There are many theories about why Dickinson became so reclusive, but the truth remains as elusive as the poet.

In 1855 the Dickinson family was able to buy back the Homestead. Although it was a personal victory for her father, whose legal business was booming, the return to the Homestead was initially very difficult for Dickinson and her mother. Mrs. Dickinson suffered from ill-health and, according to Dickinson, was an "invalid" restricted

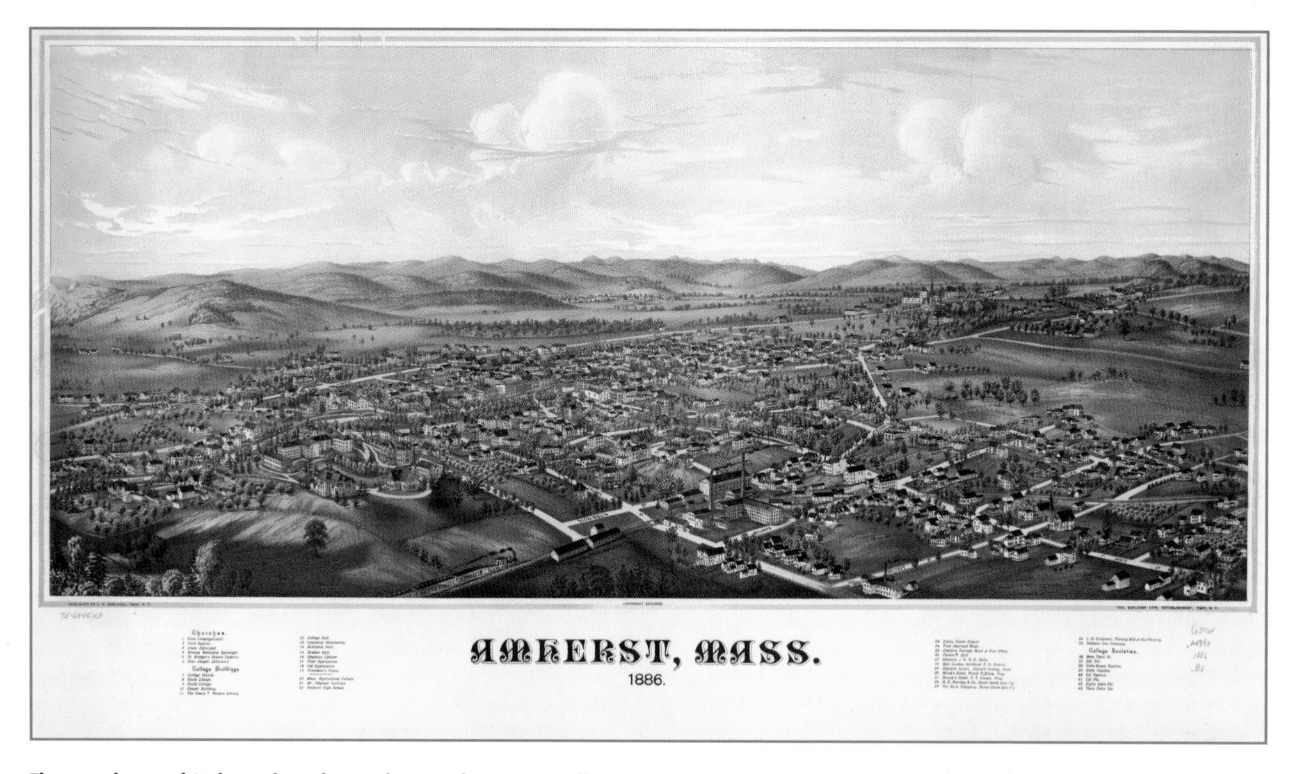

This aerial view of Amherst shows how wide open the Pioneer Valley was in the late nineteenth century. It is now much more forested.

to the lounge or easy chair. The move back into the Homestead was a physical strain on Mrs. Dickinson, and Emily's sister Lavinia was apparently put in charge of the house while Emily nursed her mother back to health.

Nevertheless, Dickinson eventually made her father's house her own and settled into a spacious, sparsely furnished corner bedroom on the second floor. The room, on the southwest corner of the building, is notable for both the sunlight and the cooling breezes it receives. From her room, Dickinson had a clear view across the hay fields her father owned, past the newly built Amherst College, all the way to the Mount Holyoke Range, rising up from the valley floor some eight miles away. Indeed, maps and pictures from the second half of the nineteenth century are particularly striking to the modern visitor because they show an almost total lack of trees in the town and the surrounding Pioneer Valley. The valley, now quite densely forested, was almost entirely cleared of standing trees during Dickinson's time, just as Concord was. Today both the Homestead and the Evergreens are quietly tucked away behind rows of hemlocks, white pines, and massive oaks. Looking out from her window now, one can see only trees, the street, and a row of houses.

To get a better sense of what the poet saw and what she did, many take a tour through the Emily Dickinson

Renovating the Homestead

The Homestead was built in 1813 as the first residential brick building in the area. It was originally a two-story house with a fanlight over the center front door, three chimneys, and a hipped roof. It is unclear whether the one-story west wing was original or added early on. David Mack added Greek Revival embellishments when he owned it from 1833 to 1855.

When the Dickinsons moved back into the house in 1855, they removed the west wing (which had grown to two stories), put in a porch on the west side, and built a two-story brick ell in the back. By then, the house had been painted an ochre color with a dark green trim. Edward Dickinson added the fashionable Italianate upgrades to signify his position as a man of wealth and style. One of the main additions was a cupola that is just slightly higher than the tower of the Evergreens, the house he built for his son, Austin.

The Parks family, who owned the house after the Dickinsons, sandblasted the brick back to its original unpainted surface and made other minor structural changes. The Emily Dickinson Museum, after much research, decided to return the Homestead to the ochre color Dickinson knew during her lifetime.

The two windows on the second floor to the left of the door lead into Emily's room.

Museum, which includes both the Homestead and the Evergreens next door—the home of Austin and Susan Dickinson, Emily's brother and sister-in-law. Highlights of the tour include discussions of nineteenth-century Amherst and readings of Dickinson's poetry.

For "Poem of the Season" (a poem picked specially to match the season), a tour group gathers in what was once Lavinia's bedroom, and a volunteer from the group reads the poem. If the volunteer presents it well, the words seem to ring differently here than anywhere else. It's an eerie feeling, as if the words are themselves ghosts returning home.

Right across the hall is Dickinson's bedroom, where she wrote much of her poetry. It is easy to imagine her sitting and meticulously crafting her poems at the table in the corner (which is, like most of the furniture in the museum, not the actual piece but a close approximation; Harvard University has most of the remaining original furniture). What is more difficult to imagine is how, especially after her mid-thirties, Dickinson almost never left the property. The town, even before the railroad arrived in 1853, had much to offer.

Although it was very much the bucolic country village of New England postcards, Amherst boasted a number

This view, similar to what Emily saw out her window, is now obscured by houses and white pines.

Dickinson wrote hundreds of poems and then neatly packed them into small bundles, called fascicles, that she hid in the drawers in her bedroom.

of attractions. Amherst College was founded (with significant help not only from Dickinson's grandfather, Samuel Fowler Dickinson, but also from Noah Webster) in 1821 as a reaction to the more liberal Unitarian influences of Harvard and Yale. The other major factor in town life was the Hills Hat Factory, which produced more than half of all the palm leaf hats in the country by 1855. The Hills factory, along with its rival, the Henry D. Fearing Hat Factory, employed nearly six hundred people.

In 1853 the railroad came to Amherst (with much help from Edward Dickinson), and the town began to change, growing rapidly. The station was quite close to the Dickinson property, so Emily could see the trains arriving and departing from her window.

Amherst's transition from country village to bustling town brought with it a wide variety of problems, from fights between rival hat-factory workers to the morphine addiction of Harriet Beecher Stowe's daughter, who lived in town. The burgeoning town also attracted visitors such as Ralph Waldo Emerson, P. T. Barnum, and naturalist John Burroughs.

Dickinson took no interest in seeing these things firsthand, however. That is not to say she did not care about the outside world; she read the *Springfield Republican* religiously and corresponded with many people. By 1865, however, she rarely left the house, even to walk the hundred yards to her brother's home. When her brother entertained her Transcendentalist idol, Ralph Waldo Emerson, Dickinson did not even come over to meet the man she so admired.

If Dickinson herself did not move about town or publish widely, the Dickinson name still had tremendous influence over the town. Emily's brother and his wife made the Evergreens into a social center by hosting important visitors and town meetings.

Although Dickinson did not take part in the varied comings and goings of either house, one location continued to draw her out: her garden. Situated at the east end of the property, the garden provided Dickinson with both an activity and the seeds for some of her most striking poetry:

Poem #32

When Roses cease to bloom, Sir,
And Violets are done —
When Bumblebees in solemn flight
Have passed beyond the Sun —
The hand that paused to gather
Upon this Summer's day
Will idle lie — in Auburn —
Then take my flowers — pray!

Two Poets

At the west end of ⑦ Sweetser Park, right next to the Evergreens on Main Street, two poets are engaged in an eternal conversation. Emily Dickinson sits with her back to the street, facing Robert Frost. At Dickinson's side is an iron book with a brief biography and this poem:

Emily Dickinson and Robert Frost are always to be found in conversation at Sweetser Park.

Poem #245

I held a Jewel in my fingers —
And went to sleep —
The day was warm, and winds were prosy —
I said "'Twill keep" —

I woke — and chid my honest fingers,
The Gem was gone —
And now, an Amethyst remembrance
Is all I own —

On the iron pages next to Frost's statue is his reply:

The Road Not Taken

Two roads diverged in a yellow wood,
And sorry I could not travel both
And be one traveler, long I stood
And looked down one as far as I could
To where it bent in the undergrowth;

Then took the other, as just as fair,
And having perhaps the better claim,
Because it was grassy and wanted wear;
Though as for that the passing there
Had worn them really about the same,

And both that morning equally lay
In leaves no step had trodden black.
Oh, I kept the first for another day!
Yet knowing how way leads on to way,
I doubted if I should ever come back.

I shall be telling this with a sigh
Somewhere ages and ages hence:
Two roads diverged in a wood, and I—
I took the one less traveled by,
And that has made all the difference.

Frost was hired by Amherst College to teach English in 1917 and, after his initial two-year stint, returned often to Amherst until his death in 1963.

The statues were commissioned in 1995 and executed by Michael J. Virzi. They are just one example of the valued place of poetry in Amherst.

Poem #106

The Daisy follows soft the Sun —
And when his golden walk is done —
Sits shyly at his feet —
He — waking — finds the flower there —
Wherefore — Marauder — art thou here?
Because, Sir, love is sweet!

We are the Flower — Thou the Sun!
Forgive us, if as days decline —
We nearer steal to Thee!
Enamored of the parting West —
The peace — the flight — the Amethyst —
Night's possibility!

In fact, Emily's family and friends thought of her more as a gardener than a poet. She planted and cared for nearly two acres of gardens, had an impressive conservatory where she cultivated hothouse flowers, and often gave dried flowers or bulbs as gifts, occasionally with a small poem tucked in.

Amherst Today: "Plain and Whole and Permanent and Warm"

In the nineteenth century, the Dickinson name was connected primarily to the social and business interests of Amherst. Today, however, the name lures writers of all types—poets and novelists, the famous and the unknown, the practiced and the practicing. (To be fair, a good chunk of the credit for attracting the literary set must also go to Amherst's other famous poet, Robert Frost.) Amherst boasts perfect spots for sipping a cappuccino and writing in a journal, and wonderful bookstores for browsing. To nourish the soul and intellect, the town provides a wide array of writing groups, lectures, performing arts, and political events. And to nourish the body, it offers a wide variety of good places—much frequented by the local student population—to eat for only a few dollars. Amherst is a wonderful town for spending a morning working hard on a novel, working hard at pretending to work hard on a novel, or working hard at nothing much at all.

This view up Main Street toward the center of town is still recognizable today.

Timeline

April 4, 1780 — William Ellery Channing is born in Newport, Rhode Island.

November 29, 1799 — Amos Bronson Alcott is born in Wolcott, Connecticut.

Amos Bronson Alcott, friend to Emerson and father of Louisa May Alcott, was occasionally brilliant and consistently eccentric.

May 25, 1803 — Ralph Waldo Emerson is born in Boston.

Emerson did much to spread the tenets of Transcendentalism through the fifteen hundred lectures he gave throughout New England and across the United States.

May 16, 1804 — Elizabeth Palmer Peabody is born in Billerca, Massachusetts.

July 4, 1804 — Nathaniel Hawthorne is born in Salem.

1805 — Henry Ware Sr.'s appointment to the Hollis Chair of Divinity at Harvard provides momentum for liberal Christianity.

May 23, 1810 — Margaret Fuller is born in Cambridgeport, Massachusetts.

August 24, 1810 — Theodore Parker is born in Lexington, Massachusetts.

July 12, 1817 — Henry David Thoreau is born in Concord.

August 21, 1820 — The first issue of Nathaniel Hawthorne's short-lived newspaper the *Spectator* is published.

February 11, 1825 — Emerson enrolls in Harvard's Divinity School.

September 28, 1828 — William Ellery Channing delivers his landmark sermon, "Likeness to God," which will provide the intellectual foundation for both Unitarianism and Transcendentalism.

March 11, 1829 — Emerson is ordained as pastor of the Second Church of Boston.

The son of a Unitarian minister, Ralph Waldo Emerson left his ministry at the Second Church of Boston when he felt he could not in good conscience administer the sacrament.

September 30, 1829 — Emerson marries Ellen Tucker.

May 23, 1830 — Bronson and Abba Alcott marry in Boston.

December 10, 1830 — Emily Dickinson is born at the Homestead in Amherst.

December 25, 1832 — Emerson sails for England.

August 1836 — Jones Very graduates from Harvard.

September 9, 1836 — Emerson's *Nature* is published.

September 19, 1836 — The first meeting of the Transcendental Club is held.

August 30, 1837 — Thoreau graduates from Harvard.

August 31, 1837 — Emerson delivers "The American Scholar" address at Harvard.

November 12, 1837 — Nathaniel Hawthorne, whose *Twice-Told Tales* is published anonymously this year, and his sisters visit Elizabeth Peabody and her sisters in Salem.

July 15, 1838 — Emerson delivers the "Divinity School Address" at Harvard.

1839 — Elizabeth Peabody opens her West Street bookstore in Boston.

1839–44 — Margaret Fuller conducts "conversations" for women at Peabody's bookstore.

August 31, 1839 — Thoreau and his brother John leave for a two-week canoe trip on the Concord and Merrimack rivers.

1840 — The Alcotts move to Concord for the first of a number of times.

1840–42 — The *Dial* magazine is published.

April 1, 1841 — George Ripley and others move to Brook Farm.

May 19, 1841 – Theodore Parker delivers his radical sermon "Discourses on the Transient and Permanent in Christianity" in Boston.

July 9, 1842 — Nathaniel Hawthorne marries Sophia Peabody in Boston, and the couple move into the Old Manse in Concord.

October 2, 1842 — William Ellery Channing dies in Vermont.

June 1, 1843 — The Alcotts move to Fruitlands to launch a utopian community.

FITCHBURG RAILROAD.

Hoosac Tunnel Route.

The Short Line between

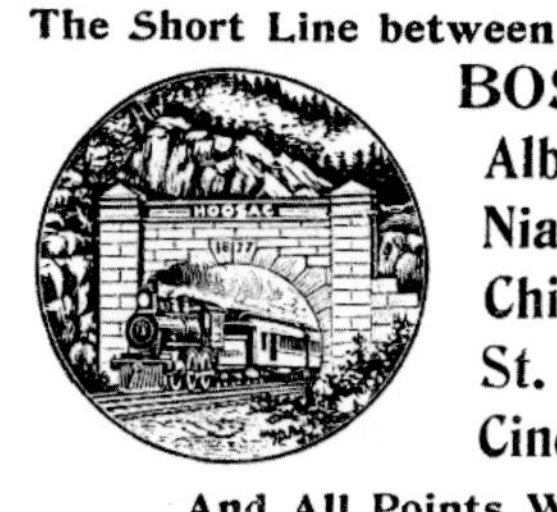

BOSTON and
Albany,
Niagara Falls,
Chicago,
St. Louis,
Cincinnati,

And All Points West.

Lake Champlain Route

Between BOSTON and
Burlington, Vt., Montreal, Ottawa
And all Canadian Points.

Palace, Sleeping, or Drawing Room Cars on all through trains.
For Time-Tables or space in Sleeping Cars call on any Ticket Agent of the Company, or address
A. S. CRANE, Gen. Traffic Mgr.
C. M. BURT, Gen. Pass. Agt., Boston, Mass.

The Boston-Fitchburg railroad reached Concord in 1844 and immediately began to change Concord from a village to a suburb.

June 17, 1844 — The Boston-Fitchburg rail line opens in Concord.

1845 — The Hawthornes return to Salem.

July 4, 1845 — Thoreau moves to Walden Pond.

March 2, 1846 — The Brook Farm Phalanstery burns to the ground.

July 1846 — Thoreau is arrested and spends the night in jail for refusing to pay the poll tax.

August 1, 1846 — The annual meeting of the Anti-Slavery Women of Concord is held at Thoreau's cabin at Walden.

August 1, 1846 — Margaret Fuller sets sail for Europe.

September 1847 — Thoreau leaves the cabin at Walden to move in with the Emersons.

July 19, 1850 — Margaret Fuller dies in a shipwreck off Fire Island with her husband and son. Her body is never recovered.

1852 — The Hawthornes buy the Hillside from the Alcotts and rename it the Wayside.

July 4, 1854 — Thoreau delivers his lecture "Slavery in Massachusetts" in Framingham, Massachusetts.

August 9, 1854 — Thoreau's *Walden* is published.

December 1860 — Emerson meets Walt Whitman.

The poet Walt Whitman greatly admired Emerson and Thoreau, coming to Concord for repeated visits, but was not himself a Transcendentalist.

1857 — The Alcotts purchase Orchard House and move there in the spring of 1858.

1859 — Bronson Alcott is appointed superintendent of the Concord schools.

May 10, 1860 — Theodore Parker dies in Florence, Italy.

June 28, 1860 — The Hawthornes return to the Wayside after seven years in Europe.

April 16, 1862 — Writer and reformer Thomas Higginson receives a letter from Emily Dickinson, a poet he's never heard of, asking whether her verse "lives or no."

May 6, 1862 — Thoreau dies in Concord.

May 19, 1864 — Nathaniel Hawthorne dies in Plymouth, New Hampshire.

1872 — Bronson Alcott and others begin building a rock cairn at the site of Thoreau's cabin at Walden Pond.

Louisa May Alcott's growing fame as a writer enabled her to buy the Thoreau house in the center of Concord for her family.

July 24, 1872 — Emerson's house is partly burned before volunteer firemen can put out the fire.

November 14, 1877 — Louisa May Alcott buys the Thoreau house in Concord, and the Alcott family moves in.

1879 — Bronson Alcott and Franklin Sanborn open the Concord School of Philosophy at Alcott's Orchard House.

April 27, 1882 — Emerson dies in Concord.

May 15, 1886 — Emily Dickinson dies at the Homestead.

March 4, 1888 — Bronson Alcott dies in Boston.

March 6, 1888 — Louisa May Alcott dies in Boston.

June 8, 1893 — John Muir visits Thoreau's cabin site and leaves a stone on the cairn.

January 3, 1894 — Elizabeth Palmer Peabody dies in Massachusetts.

Notes

Chapter 1

3: Ralph Waldo Emerson quotations on Transcendentalism are from "The Transcendentalist" (a lecture given in 1842 at the Masonic Temple, Boston), in *The Selected Writings of Ralph Waldo Emerson*, ed. Brooks Atkinson (New York: Random House, 1968).

4: "The foregoing generations . . .": Emerson, *Nature*, in *Selected Writings*, 3.

5: "Transcendentalism belongs . . .": Elizabeth Palmer Peabody, "Plan of the West Roxbury Community," *Dial*, January 1842.

5: "seagull with long wings . . .": Edward Thompson Taylor, quoted in Carlos Baker, *Emerson among the Eccentrics* (New York: Penguin, 1996), 78.

5: "The new dialect . . .": Rebecca Harding Davis, *Bits of Gossip* (1904), http://docsouth.unc.edu/davisr/davis.html, 455–456.

6: "The fruits of . . .": Charles Dickens, *American Notes* (1893), 153–154.

Chapter 2

13: "the hub of the solar system": Oliver Wendell Holmes, *Autocrat of the Breakfast Table* (1868), 143.

16–17: Quotations from William Ellery Channing's sermon "Likeness to God" are from Perry Miller, ed., *The Transcendentalists: An Anthology* (Cambridge, MA: Harvard University Press, 1950), 21–25.

18–19: Quotations from Theodore Parker's sermon "Discourses on the Transient and Permanent in Christianity" (1841) are from Miller, *Transcendentalists*, 259–283.

19: "I would rather see . . .": Quoted in L. Annie Foerster's sermon "Theodore Parker: The Best Hated Man in America," January 9, 2000, http://www.uunhf.org/sunday/sermons/text/20000109/.

22: "The great ROMANCER . . .": Oliver Wendell Holmes, "At the Saturday Club" (1884), http://www.ibiblio.org/eldritch/owh/atsat.html.

23: Information on the *Dial* is from Baker, *Emerson*, and Joel Myerson, *Transcendentalism: A Reader* (Oxford: Oxford University Press, 2000), 289–290.

23: Bronson Alcott's "Orphic Sayings" are from http://www.alcott.net/alcott/archive/editions/Orphic_Sayings.html.

23: Information on the rebirth of the *Dial* is from Elisa Kay Sparks, "The Dial Magazine, 1920–1929: A Brief History," http://virtual.clemson.edu/groups/dial/dialhist.htm.

24: "society of liberal . . .": George Ripley, letter to Emerson (1840), in Myerson, *Transcendentalism*, 307.

25: Information on Elizabeth Peabody's bookshop, including Peabody quotation, is from Leslie Perrin Wilson, "Elizabeth Peabody's Foreign Library," http://www.concordma.com/magazine/augsept99/peabody2.html.

27: Ticknor-Alcott anecdote, including quotations, is from Susan Wilson, *Literary Trail of Greater Boston*

(Boston: Houghton Mifflin, 2000), 9.

28: "the shrewdest of publishers . . .": Davis, *Bits of Gossip*, 54.

28: "the hub of the Hub . . .": George Curtis, quoted in Wilson, *Literary Trail*, 8.

28: "In the small . . .": Caroline Ticknor, "Hawthorne and His Friend," in *Glimpses of Authors* (1922), http://www.eldritchpress.org/nh/tick1.html.

28: Information on the Masonic Temple is primarily from Baker, *Emerson*, 45–48.

30: "Mr. Alcott. Yes . . .": Bronson Alcott, *Conversations with Children on the Gospels* (1836), in Miller, *Transcendentalists*, 154.

30: "On this subject . . .": William Lloyd Garrison, "To the Public" (1831), http://www.pbs.org/wgbh/aia/part4/4h2928t.html.

32: Emerson-Whitman anecdote, including journal excerpt, is from Wilson, *Literary Trail*, 34.

35: "Being a ghost, . . .": Hawthorne, "The Ghost of Dr. Harris" (1900), *Miscellaneous Prose and Verse*, vol. 13 of the Centenary Edition of the *Works of Nathaniel Hawthorne*, ed. Thomas Woodson, L. Neal Smith, and Norman H. Pearson (Columbus: Ohio University Press, 1997), 315–387.

36: Description of Emerson's trip is from Baker, *Emerson*, 23.

Chapter 3

40: "Those things . . .": Henry David Thoreau, *Walden: A Fully Annotated Edition*, ed. Jeffrey S. Cramer (New Haven, CT: Yale University Press, 2004), 48.

40: "Yes indeed . . .": John Albee, *Remembrances of Emerson* (1901), quoted in *Walden*, ed. Cramer, 200.

41: Information on Harvard's founding is from the university's website, http://www.news.harvard.edu/guide/intro/index.html.

42: "training of warm . . .": William Ellery Channing, "The Christian Ministry" (1826), http://www.news.harvard.edu/gazette/2000/09.21/divinityhall.html.

42: Information on Phi Beta Kappa is from its website, http://www.pbk.org/about/history.htm.

43: Quotations from "The American Scholar" are from Emerson, *Selected Writings*, 45, 55, 58, 62–63.

44: "intellectual Declaration . . .": Oliver Wendell Holmes, quoted in Myerson, *Transcendentalism*, 195.

44–45: Quotations from the "Divinity School Address" are from Emerson, *Selected Writings*, 64–84.

45: Quotations from Andrews Norton, "The New School in Literature and Religion" (1838), are from Myerson, *Transcendentalism*, 246–249.

46: Quotations from Parker's "Levi Blodgett" letter (1840) are from Myerson, *Transcendentalism*, 260–279.

Chapter 4

54: "dreaming, pastoral . . .": George William Curtis, *Literary and Social Essays* (1895), http://library.beau.org/gutenberg/etext05/8lits10.txt.

54: "There is an inward voice . . .": Ellery Channing, "The River" (1843), http://www.vcu.edu/engweb/transcendentalism/authors/channing/channingpoems.html.

54: "through my rock-like . . .": Emerson, "Musketaquid" (1847), http://www.emersoncentral.com/poems/musketaquid.htm.

54 and 62: Hawthorne quotations are from *Mosses from the Old Manse* (New York: Random House, 2003), 3–27.

54: Information on Concord's history is primarily from "A Brief History of Concord," on the Concord Free Public Library website, http://www.concordnet.org/library/scollect/bhc/bhc.html.

58: Emerson, "The Concord Hymn" (1837), in Emerson, *Selected Writings*, 783.

63: Quotations from *Nature* are from Emerson, *Selected Writings*, 3–42.

64: Information on the Hawthornes' stay at the Manse is from Brenda Wineapple, *Hawthorne: A Life* (New York: Random House, 2004); Baker, *Emerson*; and *Hawthorne, The American Notebooks*, vol. 8 of the Centenary Edition of the *Works of Nathaniel Hawthorne*, ed. Claude M. Simpson (Columbus: Ohio University Press, 1973), 315–387.

66: Hawthorne-Emerson-Thoreau skating anecdote is from Baker, *Emerson*, 216.

67: "Here is a . . .": Emerson, journal entry, May 6, 1842, http://www.concordnet.org/library/scollect/Emerson_Celebration/Em_Con_28.html.

70: "Alcott called it . . .": Hawthorne, letter to Evert Augustus Duyckinck (1852), in *The Letters, 1843–1853*, vol. 16 of the Centenary Edition of the *Works of Nathaniel Hawthorne*, ed. Thomas Woodson, L. Neal Smith, and Norman H. Pearson (Columbus: Ohio State University Press, 1985), 548.

73–74: Information on the Concord School of Philosophy, including Louisa May Alcott quotation, is from Tom Foran Clark, *The Significance of Being Frank: The Life and Times of Franklin Benjamin Sanborn*, chapter 20, http://www.bungalowshop.com/sanborn/chapter20.html; and George B. Bartlett, "A. Bronson Alcott's School of Philosophy," http://www.concordma.com/magazine/marapr01/schoolofphilosophy.html.

74: "his clerical consecration . . .": Hawthorne, in *The American Notebooks*, 343.

75: "We New Englanders . . .": Hawthorne, quoted in Davis, *Bits of Gossip*, 62.

76: Jones Very, "On Visiting the Graves of Hawthorne and Thoreau" (1875), in *Jones Very: The Collected Poems*, ed. Helen Deese (Athens: University of Georgia Press, 1993), 483.

Chapter 5

81: Ellery Channing, "Walden," in *Poems, Second Series* (1847), 157–158.

82–91: Quotations from *Walden* are from *Walden*, ed. Cramer.

83: Hawthorne's descriptions of Thoreau in *Hawthorne, American Notebooks*, 353–356.

85: "a wooden inkstand": Ellery Channing, quoted in Walter Harding, *The Days of Henry Thoreau: A Biography* (Princeton NJ: Princeton University Press, 1992), 182.

86: Information on Thoreau's cabin after he left is from "The Writings of Henry D. Thoreau," http://www.thoreau.niu.edu/thoreau_faq.html.

90: Chair anecdote is from Mary Hosmer Brown, *Memories of Concord* (1926), quoted in *Walden*, ed. Cramer, 135.

91: Descriptions of the ice trade are from *Walden*, ed. Cramer, 284–285.

92: "Thoreau goes to a house . . .": *Walden*, ed. Cramer, 164.

93: Description of the fire in Walden Woods is from *Walden*, ed. Cramer, 241.

93: "I once set fire . . .": Thoreau, *The Journal of Henry D.*

Thoreau, Journal 3: 1848–1851, ed. Robert Sattelmeyer, Mark R. Patterson, and William Rossi (Princeton, NJ: Princeton University Press, 1990), 75–78.

95: Information on Thoreau and Native Americans is from Robert D. Richardson, "Thoreau in Concord," in Joel Myerson, ed., *The Cambridge Companion to Henry David Thoreau* (Cambridge: Cambridge University Press, 1995), 12–24.

95: "seldom walks over . . .": Hawthorne, *American Notebooks*, 354.

95: Louisa May Alcott, "Thoreau's Flute" (1863), http://www.vcu.edu/engweb/transcendentalism/authors/thoreau/flute.html.

96: Information on Thoreau's trip to Katahdin is from Joseph Moldenhauer, "The Maine Woods," in Myerson, *Cambridge Companion*, 124–141. The Thoreau quotation is from Henry David Thoreau, *The Maine Woods*, ed. Joseph Moldenhauer (Princeton, NJ: Princeton University Press, 1974), 70.

97: Information on Walden Grove is from Thomas Blanding, "Historic Walden Woods," file 3, page 3, http://www.walden.org/institute/thoreau/about2/b/thomasblanding/Walden_Woods_3.htm.

99: "All Walden Woods . . .": Thoreau, *The Journal of Henry D. Thoreau*, vol. 12, *March 2, 1859–November 20, 1859*, ed. Bradford Torrey and Francis H. Allen (Boston: Houghton Mifflin, 1949), 382.

100: "The pyramid is . . .": Bronson Alcott, *The Journals of Bronson Alcott*, ed. Odell Shepard (Boston: Little, Brown, 1938), 452.

Chapter 6

105–112: Information on Hawthorne's childhood is primarily from Wineapple, *Hawthorne*; and *Hawthorne in Salem*, http://www.hawthorneinsalem.org.

106: "Here I ran . . .": Hawthorne, quoted in Julian Hawthorne, *Nathaniel Hawthorne and His Wife* (1884), chapter 3, http://www.ibiblio.org/eldritch/nh/nhahw103.html.

107: "It has been . . .": Hawthorne, "On Industry" (1820), http://www.pem.org/homepage/ [select: Hawthorne Interactive].

108: Information on the Salem Athenaeum is from *Salem, Massachusetts: A City Guide*, http://www.salemweb.com/tales/athenm.shtml.

109: "I have not . . .": Hawthorne, letter to Elizabeth Hawthorne (1821), in *Hawthorne: The Letters, 1813–1843*, vol. 15 of the Centenary Edition of the *Works of Nathaniel Hawthorne*, ed. Thomas Woodson, L. Neal Smith, and Norman H. Pearson (Columbus: Ohio State University Press, 1985), 138–139.

109: "It is so long . . .": Hawthorne, letter to Louisa Hawthorne, quoted in Hawthorne, *Nathaniel Hawthorne and His Wife*, chapter 3.

109: "In fact, after freeing . . .": Hawthorne, *Nathaniel Hawthorne and His Wife*, chapter 8.

109: "And year after year . . ." and "My long seclusion . . .": Hawthorne, quoted in Hawthorne, *Nathaniel Hawthorne and His Wife*, chapter 3.

112, 116–117: Quotations about Hawthorne's ancestors, and other passages, are from Hawthorne, *The Scarlet Letter: The Norton Critical Edition*, 3rd edition (New York: Norton, 1988).

113–114: Information on Jones Very, including Very quotation, is from Baker, *Emerson*, 120–128.

115: Jones Very, "The Son" (1838), in *Jones Very*, ed. Deese, 66.

115: "Here I am . . .": Hawthorne, in *Letters, 1843–1853*, vol. 16 of the Centenary Edition of the *Works of Nathaniel Hawthorne*, ed. Thomas Woodson, L. Neal Smith, and Norman H. Pearson (Columbus: Ohio State University Press, 1985), 122.

117: Fields anecdote is from James T. Fields, *Yesterdays with Authors* (1871), http://www.eldritchpress.org/nh/ ywa1.html.

117–118: "I finished . . ." and "It broke . . .": Hawthorne, in *Letters, 1843–1853*, 311–312.

118: "Mrs. Hawthorne published . . .": Hawthorne, in *Letters, 1843–1853*, 462.

118: Information on the House of the Seven Gables is from its website, http://www.7gables.org/.

Chapter 7

123: "Our objects . . ." and "if wisely executed . . .": Ripley, letter to Emerson (1840), in Myerson, *Transcendentalism*, 308.

124: "if the community . . .": Emerson, letter to Ripley (1840), in Myerson, *Transcendentalism*, 312.

124–130: Information on Brook Farm is primarily from Jessica Gordon, "History of Brook Farm," http://www.vcu .edu/engweb/transcendentalism/ideas/brhistory.html; and Baker, *Emerson*.

126: Essay titles from the *Harbinger* are from Sterling F. Delanon, *The Harbinger and New England Transcendentalism* (Cranbury, NJ: Associated University Presses, 1983), 168–204.

126: "The interests of . . .": Ripley, *Harbinger* introductory notice (1845), in Myerson, *Transcendentalism*, 483.

127: "The country members . . .": Emerson, "Historic Notes of Life and Letters in New England" (1880), in Miller, *Transcendentalists*.

128: Quotations from Hawthorne, *The American Note-Books* (1868), 196–222; and *Letters, 1813–1843*.

128: "Ere long . . .": John Thomas Codman, *Brook Farm: Historic and Personal Memoirs* (1894), 191.

130: "It was a . . .": Emerson, "Historic Notes."

131–133: Information on Fruitlands, including quotation, is primarily from Jessica Gordon, "History of Fruitlands," http://www.vcu.edu/engweb/ transcendentalism/ ideas/fruitlands.html; and Baker, *Emerson*.

132: Quotations from Louisa May Alcott, "Transcendental Wild Oats" (1873), http://www.vcu.edu/engweb/ transcendentalism/ideas/wildoats.html.

133: "Fruitlands was . . .": Bronson Alcott, *Concord Days* (1872), 179.

Chapter 8

Dickinson poems quoted in this chapter are from *The Complete Poems of Emily Dickinson*, ed. Thomas H. Johnson (Boston: Back Bay Books, 1976). Dickinson's letters are from *The Letters of Emily Dickinson*, ed. Mabel Loomis Todd (New York: Dover, 2003).

141–143: Information on the Homestead and Dickinson's childhood is primarily from Douglas C. Wilson and Cynthia Dickinson, eds., *Emily Dickinson: The Poet at Home* (Amherst, MA: Dickinson Homestead, 2000).

143–144: Information on Amherst is from Daniel Lombardo, *Amherst and Hadley Massachusetts* (San Francisco: Arcadia Publishing, 1997); and Lombardo, *A Hedge Away: The Other Side of Emily Dickinson's Amherst* (Northampton, MA: Daily Hampshire Gazette, 1997).

146: Robert Frost, "The Road Not Taken" (1916), in *Robert Frost: Collected Poems, Prose and Plays* (New York: Library of America, 1995), 103.

For Further Reading

Writings by the Transcendentalists and Their Contemporaries

Davis, Rebecca Harding. *Bits of Gossip*. Boston: Houghton Mifflin, 1904. The University of North Carolina has produced an electronic edition, http://docsouth.unc.edu/davisr/davis.html.

Dickinson, Emily. *The Complete Poems of Emily Dickinson*. Edited by Thomas H. Johnson. Boston: Back Bay Books, 1976.

———. *The Letters of Emily Dickinson*. Edited by Mabel Loomis Todd. New York: Dover, 2003.

Emerson, Ralph Waldo. *Essays and Journals*. Edited by Lewis Mumford. Garden City, NY: Doubleday, 1968.

_____. *The Selected Writings of Ralph Waldo Emerson*. Edited by Brooks Atkinson. New York: Random House, 1968.

Fields, James T. *Yesterdays with Authors* (1871). Eldritch Press. http://www.eldritchpress.org/nh/ywa1.html.

Hawthorne, Nathaniel. *The American Notebooks*, vol. 8 of the Centenary Edition of the *Works of Nathaniel Hawthorne*. Edited by Thomas Woodson, L. Neal Smith, and Norman H. Pearson. Columbus: Ohio University Press, 1985.

———. *The Blithedale Romance* (1852). New York: Dover, 2003.

———. *Mosses from an Old Manse* (1846). New York: Random House, 2003.

———. *Nathaniel Hawthorne's Tales*. Edited by James McIntosh. New York: Norton, 1987.

———. *The Scarlet Letter* (1850). New York: Norton, 1988.

Howells, William Dean. "Literary Boston as I Knew It." In *Literary Friends and Acquaintance* (1900). Project Gutenberg. http://www.gutenberg.org/etext/3396.

Miller, Perry, ed. *The Transcendentalists: An Anthology*. Cambridge, MA: Harvard University Press, 1950.

Myerson, Joel, ed. *Transcendentalism: A Reader*. Oxford: Oxford University Press, 2000.

Thoreau, Henry David. *Cape Cod* (1865). New York: Penguin, 1987.

———. *Walden: A Fully Annotated Edition*. Edited and annotated by Jeffrey S. Cramer. New Haven, CT: Yale University Press, 2004.

———. *Wild Fruits*. Edited by Bradley Dean. New York: Norton, 2000.

Ticknor, Caroline. *Glimpses of Authors* (1922). Eldritch Press. http://www.eldritchpress.org/nh/tick1.html.

Biographies and Critical Studies

Baker, Carlos. *Emerson among the Eccentrics*. New York: Penguin, 1996.

Clark, Tom Foran. *The Significance of Being Frank: The Life and Times of Franklin Benjamin Sanborn*. http://www.bungalowshop.com/sanborn/.

Delano, Sterling. *Brook Farm: The Dark Side of Utopia*. Cambridge, MA: Harvard University Press, 2004.

Francis, Richard. *Transcendentalist Utopias: Individual and Community at Brook Farm, Fruitlands, and Walden*. Ithaca, NY: Cornell University Press, 1997.

French, Allen. *Hawthorne at the Old Manse*. Eldritch Press. http://www.eldritchpress.org/nh/french.html.

Harding, Walter. *The Days of Henry Thoreau: A Biography*. Princeton, NJ: Princeton University Press, 1982.

Howarth, William. *The Book of Concord: Thoreau's Life as a Writer*. New York: Viking, 1982.

Lombardo, Daniel. *A Hedge Away: The Other Side of Emily Dickinson's Amherst*, Northampton, MA: Daily Hampshire Gazette, 1997.

Richardson, Robert D. Jr. *Henry Thoreau: A Life of the Mind*. Berkeley: University of California Press, 1986.

Wilson, Douglas C., and Cynthia Dickinson, eds. *Emily Dickinson: The Poet at Home*. Amherst, MA: Dickinson Homestead, 2000.

Wilson, Susan. *Literary Trail of Greater Boston*. Boston: Houghton Mifflin, 2000.

Wineapple, Brenda. *Hawthorne: A Life*. New York: Random House, 2004.

Web Resources

American Transcendentalism: An Online Travel Guide. Shepherd University. http://www.shepherd.edu/transweb/travelguide.htm.

American Transcendentalism Web. Virginia Commonwealth University. http://www.vcu.edu/engweb/transcendentalism/.

Eldritch Press. http://www.eldritchpress.org.

Emerson in Concord. Concord Free Public Library (display put together by Leslie Perrin Wilson, Joyce Woodman, and Robert C. W. Hall Jr.). http://www.concordnet.org/library/scollect/Emerson_Celebration/Introduction.html.

Hawthorne in Salem. North Shore Community College (project directors Terri Whitney and Sandra Carriker). http://www.hawthorneinsalem.org.

Thomas Hampson: *I Hear America Singing*. PBS. http://www.pbs.org/wnet/ihas.

Museums of Interest

The following museums and research institutions, all of which were valuable in the research for this book, house fascinating and important collections of material related to the lives and work of the Transcendentalists.

Concord

The Concord Free Public Library
129 Main Street
Concord, MA 01742
(978) 318-3300
http://www.concordnet.org/library/

The Concord Museum
200 Lexington Road
Concord, MA 01742
(978) 369-9763; for taped information, (978) 369-9609
http://www.concordmuseum.org/

The Emerson House
28 Cambridge Turnpike
Concord, MA 01742
(978) 369-2236

The Old Manse
269 Monument Street
Concord, MA 01742
(978) 369-3909
http://www.thetrustees.org/pages/346_old_manse.cfm

The Orchard House
399 Lexington Road
Concord, MA 01742
(978) 369-4118
http://www.louisamayalcott.org/

The Wayside
455 Lexington Road
Concord, MA 01742
(978) 318-7826
http://www.nps.gov/mima/wayside/index1.htm

Walden

The Thoreau Institute at Walden Woods
44 Baker Farm Road
Lincoln, MA 01773
(781) 259-4700
http://www.walden.org/index.htm

Salem

The House of the Seven Gables
54 Turner Street
Salem, MA 01970
(978) 744-0991
http://www.7gables.org/

Peabody Essex Museum
East India Square
Salem, MA 01970
(978) 745-9500
http://www.pem.org/homepage/

Amherst

The Emily Dickinson Museum
280 Main Street
Amherst, MA 01002
(413) 542-8161
http://www.emilydickinsonmuseum.org/index.html

Fruitlands

The Fruitlands Museum
102 Prospect Hill Road
Harvard, MA 0151
(978) 456-3924
http://www.fruitlands.org/

Index

Page numbers in *italics* indicate illustrations or boxed material.

abolitionist movement, 11, 26, 30–31, 90, 92, *92*
Aesthetic Papers, 26–27
African Meeting House (Boston), 30
Agassiz, Elizabeth Cary, 49
Agassiz, Louis, 22, 40, 49
Alcott, Abba, 26, *62*, 71, *132*, 133
Alcott, Bronson, 6, 7, 9, 21, 23, 25, 26, 71, *118*
antislavery activities, 31
Concord School of Philosophy, 29, 73–74, 133
correspondence of, 79
death, 74
England trip, 36, 131
family garden, 67
Fruitlands founding, 122, 131–133, *132*
gravesite, 75
homes of, 35, 37, 53, 61, 68–69, *70*, 72–73, 92
images, *73*, *149*
Temple School, 25, 29–30, 32
Thoreau's rock cairn, *100*
Walden Pond visits, 97
writings, *23*, 30, 132, *132*, 133
See also Fruitlands
Alcott House (England), 36
Alcott, Louisa May, 27, 37, 50, 71
on Concord School of Philosophy, 73–74
death, 74
grave of, 61
gravesite, 75
homes of, 68, 73, *152*
images, *71*
writings, 27, 69, 71, 72, *95*
Alcott, May, 50, *62*, 71
Allen, William, 124, 127
American Anti-Slavery Society, 30
American Renaissance, 4
American Revolution, 56–58, 66
"American Scholar, The" (Emerson), 7, 10, 39, 42–44, 59, 60, 121
American Unitarian Association, 51
Amherst, 7, 9, 135, 143–144, 147
hat industry in, 144
locales
Amherst Academy, 139, *140*
Dickinson home (161 North Pleasant Street), 139, 140
Emily Dickinson Museum (280 Main Street), *134–135*, 136, 139
Emily Dickinson Trail, *138*
Evergreens, 142, 143
Homestead (now Dickinson Museum), 139, 141–143, *143*, *144*
Mount Holyoke College, 139, *140*
Sweetser Park, *146*
West Cemetery, 140–141, *141*
map, *137*
Amherst Academy, 139, *140*
Amherst College, 142
Anderson, Sherwood, 23
Andover Theological Seminary, 41
Anthology Society, 33
Antislavery Women of Concord, 92
Assabet River, 53
"At the Saturday Club" (Holmes), 22

athenaeums, 9, *108*
Atlantic Monthly, 22, 95
Author's Ridge, 75, 76

Baker Farm, 84
Barnum, P. T., 144
Beacon Hill (Boston), *15*, 30, 35, 37
Bell, Alexander Graham, *118*
Blandings, Tom, 99
Blithedale Romance, The (Hawthorne), 118, 130
Blodgett, Levi (pseud.). *See* Parker, Theodore
Boston, *12–13*, 13
  abolitionist movement in, 30–31
  "City on a Hill," 14, 122
  early history, 13–15
  locales
    African Meeting House (8 Smith Court), 30
    Athenaeum (10 1/2 Beacon Street), 33, *34*, 35
    Beacon Hill, *15*, 30, 35, 37
    Boston Common, 32–33
    Boston Garden, *18*
    Charles Street (148), 37
    Church of the Disciples, 29
    Elizabeth Peabody's bookstore, 24–27
    Faneuil Hall, 35
    Federal Street Church (100 Federal Street), 16, *17*
    Freedom Trail, 14, *22*, 28, 35
    Frog Pond, 33
    Immigrant Heritage Trail, 33
    Literary Trail, *22*
    Louisburg Square (10), 37
    Masonic Temple (88 Tremont Street), 28–30, 32
    Mount Vernon Street (83), 37
    Music Hall, 11, 20
    Old Corner Bookstore (3 School Street), 27–28
    Park Street Church (1 Park Street), 30
    Parker House (60 School Street), 22
    Pinckney Street, 37
    Public Garden, 33, 50
    Purchase Street Church, 17
    Quincy Market, 35, *37*
    Temple School, 25, 29–30, 32
  maps, *13*, *15*
  as shipping port, 9
  Transcendentalism in, 7, 9
Boston Athenaeum, 33, *34*, 35
Boston Common, 32–33
Boston-Fitchburg railroad, *151*
Boston Globe, 28
Boston Marathon, 58
Boston Massacre, 14
Boston Tea Party, 14
Boston Vigilance Committee, 31
Bowdoin College, 107, 109
Bowdoin Prize, 113
Bradford, George, 65, 67
Bridge, Horatio, 115, 118
Brisbane, Albert, 123, *126*, 127
Brook Farm Institute of Agriculture and Education, 5, 7, 18, *23*, 64, 118, *123*
  clothing worn at, *127*
  decline, 127–130
  founding, 24, 123–124
  grounds, 124
    the Eyrie, 125
    the Hive, 124–125, *125*, 129
    Margaret Fuller Cottage, 125, 129
    the Nest, 125
    Phalanstery, 127–129
    Pilgrim House, 125
  the *Harbinger*, 125, *126*
  images, *125*, *129*
  life at, 125–127
  map, *122*
  schools at, 126
  as transcendent community, 8–9
  work standards, 127

Brooks, Paul, 99
Brooks, Van Wyck, 23
Brown, John, 31, 127
Brown, Mary Hosmer, 90
Bulkeley, Peter, 55, 59
Bunker Hill, Battle of, 57
Burke, Kenneth, 23
Burns, Anthony, 31
Burroughs, John, 144
Buttrick, John, 57

Cabot, James Elliot, 22
Calvinism, 9, 41
Cambridge, 7, *38–39*, 39
  locales
    Divinity Hall, 44
    Emerson Hall, 47
    Fay House (10 Garden Street), 50–51
    First Parish Church (3 Church Street), 42, *43*
    Harvard College, 39–42
    Harvard Yard, 41, 50
    Houghton Library, 49
    Longfellow home (105 Brattle Street), 50
    Mount Auburn Cemetery, 51
  map, *40*
  modern era, 50
Cape Cod (Thoreau), 97
Carlyle, Thomas, 36
Carson, Rachel, 99
Channing, Ellery, 6, 7, 21, 41, 53, 54, 61, 75
  Cape Cod editing, 97
  home of, 92
  Walden Pond visits, 82, 84, 85, 90, 97
  writings, 81
Channing, Mary, 51
Channing, Rev. William Ellery, 6, 9, 16–17, 35
  as abolitionist, *30*, *31*
  European travel, 36
  Harvard ties, 41–42
  home, 37
  images, *16*
  writings, 4, 16
Child, Lydia Maria, 33, 140
Church, Frederic, 10
Church of the Disciples (Boston), 29
Cilley, Jonathan, *110*
"Civil Disobedience" (Thoreau), 27, 94
Clarke, James Freeman, 21, 25, 29, 30, 42, 129
Cliff Hill, 84
Cole, Thomas, 10
Coleridge, Samuel Taylor, 4, 16, 36
Conant, Roger, 103
Concord, *2–3*, 7–8, 9, 31, *52–53*, 53
  battle of, 56–57, 58, 59
  early history, 54–56
  geography, 53–54
  images, *55*, *61*
  locales
    Concord Bridge, 56
    Concord Free Public Library (129 Main Street), 26, 79
    Concord Museum (200 Lexington Road), 61, 77–79
    Damon Mill, 60–61
    Edward Bulkeley House (92 Sudbury Road), 56
    Emerson home (Coolidge Castle, 28 Cambridge Turnpike), 66–68
    First Parish Church (20 Lexington Road), 63, 77, *78*
    Hillside Chapel, 73
    Hillside/Wayside (455 Lexington Road), 68–72
    Minute Man National Historical Park, *57*
    Old Manse (269 Monument Street), 62–66
    Old North Bridge, 56, *57*, 61
    Orchard House (399 Lexington Road), 62, 72–73
    Parkman Tavern (20 Powder Mill Road), 56
    Sleepy Hollow Cemetery (Bedford Road), 51, 68, 74–77

Thomas Dane house (47 Lexington Road), 56
Wayside/Hillside (455 Lexington Road), 68–72
map, *55*
minute man statue, 50
modern era, 77–79
relationship with Thoreau, 92–94
Revolutionary era, 56–58
"second revolution" in, 58
Concord Academy, 79
Concord Bridge, 56
Concord Freeman, 93
"Concord Hymn" (Emerson), 50, 58–59
Concord River, 53, 54, 63
Concord School of Philosophy, 29, 73–74, 133
Concord Sonata (Ives), 61
Connecticut River, *10*
consociate families, 131, 133
Conversations with Children on the Gospels (B. Alcott), 30
Conway, Moncure, 42
Coolidge Castle (Concord), 61, 66–68
Cousin, Viktor, 4
Cowan, Perez, 138
Cramer, Jeffrey, 99
Cranch, Christopher, 21, *126*
Crane, Hart, 23
Critique of Pure Reason (Kant), 3, 4
Crucible, The (Miller), 104
Cuellar, Guillermo, *136*
Cummings, E. E., 23
Curtis, George, 28, 54
Custom House (Salem), 114, 115, 116–117, *128*
"Custom House, The" (Hawthorne), 112, *116*

Damon Mill (Concord), 60–61, 78
Dana, Charles, 124, *126*
Davis, Cummings, 78
Davis, Rebecca Harding, 5, 28, 75
Dewey, John, 126
Dial, 23, 26, *132*
Dickens, Charles, 5
Dickinson, Austin, 139, 143, *143*, 144, 145
Dickinson, Edward, 139, 140, 141, *143*, 144
Dickinson, Emily, 5, 6, 7, 25, 122, 135
childhood and education, 139–140
death imagery embraced by, 140–141
as gardener, 65, 145
"home is the definition of God," 138
homes of, *134–135*, 139, 140, 141–143, *144*
images, *136*, *146*
as "myth of Amherst," 135–136
reclusiveness of, 138, 140, 143, 144
Transcendentalism in poetry of, 7, 9, 11
writings, 135, 137–139, 141, 145, *146*
Dickinson, Emily Norcross, 139, 141–142
Dickinson, Lavinia, 139, 142
Dickinson, Samuel Fowler, 139, 140
Dickinson, Susan, 143, 145
"Discourse on the Latest Form of Infidelity, A" (Norton), 45–46
"Discourses on the Transient and Permanent in Christianity" (Parker), 18–19
Divinity Hall (Harvard), 42
"Divinity School Address" (Emerson), 7, 11, 18, 39, 44–45, 60, 121, 123
Doughty, Thomas, 10
Douglass, Frederick, *118*
Dred Scott decision, 11
Duveneck, Frank, 47
Dwight, John, 42, *126*

Egg Rock, 53
Emerson Cliffs, 54
Emerson, Ellen, 68
Emerson Hall (Harvard), 47
Emerson, Phebe, 62
Emerson, Ralph Waldo, 3, 4, 5, 6, 9, 144
American vision urged by, 10

antislavery activities, 31
at Boston Athenaeum, 33
Brook Farm involvement, 123–124, 130
conversation with Whitman, 32–33
correspondence of, 79
European travel, 36, 97
favorite walks, 51, 68
Fruitlands involvement, 131
gravesite, 75, *76*, 77
Harvard ties, 40, 42, 46–47, 49, 51
homes of, 25, 53, 61, 61–62, 62–64, 68, 92, 133
images, *3*, *47*, *50*, *60*, *149*
lectures and speeches, 7, 10, 11, 18, 39, 42–44, 44–45, 60, 73, 74
literary collection, 99
on lyceum circuit, 8, 28–29
marriages, 59, 64, 97
as minister of Unitarian Second Church, 20, 42
nature as inspiration, 63–64, 136
philosophical ideals, 63, 136
progressive social ideas, 122
protégés of, 7, 110, 113, 114
publishers for, 28
as Sage of Concord, 36, 59–60
at Salem Lyceum, *118*
symposium participation, 21
theological ideas, *16*
Thoreau and, 83
Thoreau's cairn, *100*
Transcendental Club founding, 21, 122
Walden visits, 84–85, 90, 97
work on the *Dial,* 23, 24, 26
writings, 4–5, 10, 39, 42–44, 50, 54, 58, 59, 60, 63–64, 121, 123, 127
Emerson, Rev. William, 56, 58, 59, 62, 63, *78*
Emerton, Caroline, 118
Emily Dickinson Museum (Amherst), *134–135*, 136, 139, 142–143
Emily Dickinson Trail, *138*
Evergreens (Amherst), 142, 143, *143*, 145
Eyrie, the (Brook Farm), 125

Fair Haven Bay, *93*
Fair Haven Cliff, 54, 68, 84, *93*
Faneuil Hall (Boston), 35
Farley, Francis, 127
Fay House (Radcliffe), 50–51
Federal Street Church (Boston), 16, *17*
Fenn School (Concord), 79
Fields, James T., 27, 28, 35, 37, 117, *117*, *118*
First Parish Church (Boston), 20, 58, 59
First Parish Church (Cambridge), 42, *43*
First Parish Church (Concord), 63, 77, *78*
Flat Hat Club, 42
Flower Fables (L. M. Alcott), 69
Fourier, Charles, 123, *124*, 127
Francis, Convers, 18
Freedom Trail (Boston), 14, *22*, 28, 35
Freeman, Brister, 90
French, Daniel Chester, 50, *57*, 75
Frog Pond (Boston), 33
Frost, Robert, *146*, 147
Fruitlands, 9, 26, 36, *120–121*
as consociate family, 131
founding, 122, 131–132
images, *131*
social and moral philosophy, 132–133
Fruitlands Museum, 133
Fugitive Slave Law, 31
Fuller, Margaret, 6, 7, 21, 125, *128*
cenotaph, *51*
death of, 36
discussion groups led by, 25
as editor of the *Dial,* 23, 24, 123
as foreign correspondent, 26, 36
Harvard ties, 41, 49
homes of, 61, 67
images, *25*

literary works, 26
as Transcendental leader, 26

gardens, Transcendentalists', 56, 145
Garrison, William Lloyd, 30, 31
Gatlin, George, 10
George Robert White Memorial, 50
Gethsemane Jewish Cemetery (West Roxbury), 130
"Ghost of Dr. Harris, The" (Hawthorne), 35
Gibran, Kahlil, 23
Gleason, Herbert Wendell, 79
Glimpses of Authors (Ticknor), 28
Gospel Covenant, The (Bulkeley), 59
Graves, William, *110*
"Gray Champion, The" (Hawthorne), 111
Greeley, Horace, 26, 123, *126*
Grimshawe House (Salem), 111–112
Growing Ground, 65

Harbinger, 125, *126*
Harpers Ferry, 11, 31
Harris, William Torey, *74*
Harvard College, 7, 11, 20, 26, 113
bicentenary, 42
Concord year, 58
early history, 41
gates to, *43*
Hyde Collection of Dr. Samuel Johnson, 49
modern era, 47, 49
relationship with Transcendentalists, 39, 41
shield, *39*, 42
Society for the Collegiate Instruction of Women, 49
Theodore Roosevelt Collection, 49
Unitarianism embraced by, 39, 42, 144
Harvard Divinity School, 16, 18, 20, 21, 25, 41–42, 44, 49, 59, 114, 123
Harvard, John, *41*
Harvard (Massachusetts), 131
Harvard Yard, 41, 50
Hathorne, John, 112
Hathorne, William, 112
Hawthorne, Julian, 109, *110*
Hawthorne Memorial Association, *105*
Hawthorne, Nathaniel, 5, 6, 7, 8, 21, 22, 67
Athenaeum membership, 33, 35, *108*
at Brook Farm, 124, *128*, 130
children, 109, *110*, 115, 118
consulship, 70–71
development as writer, 107, 109
early years, 105–107
education, 106–107, 109
European travel, 36
garden of, 65
gravesite, 75
homes of, 25, 35, 53, *57*, 61, 64–66, 105–106, 107, 115–116, 133
images, *105*, *110*, *119*
lyceum activities, *118*
marriage, 25, 66, 111–112
as publisher of *Spectator*, 107
publishers for, 26, 28
as recluse, 109–110
at Salem Custom House, 115, 116–117, *128*
on Thoreau, *83*
Walden visits, 85
writer's block, 117
writings, 8, 35, 54, 63, 66, 70, 104, 110–111, 112, 115, 117–118, *128*, 130
Hawthorne, Sophia, 66, 70, 75
Hedge, Frederic Francis, 6, 23, 36, 67
as founder of Transcendental Club, 21, 123
Harvard ties, 40, 41, 42
Henley, Don, 99
Henley Library, 99, *100*
Henry D. Fearing Hat Factory (Amherst), 144
Higginson, Thomas Wentworth, 6, 25, 31, 40, 41, 73, *126*
Hills Hat Factory (Amherst), 144

Hillside Chapel (Concord), 73
Hillside (Concord), 68–69, *70*, 92, 133
  See also Wayside (Concord)
Historic Boston, 28
"Historic Notes of Life and Letters in New England" (Emerson), 127, 130
Hive, the (Brook Farm), 124–125, *125*, 129
Hoar, Edward, 93
Hoar, Elizabeth, 64
Holbrook, Josiah, 8
Hollis Chair of Divinity, 16, 41
Hollis Hall (Harvard), 40
Holmes, Oliver Wendell, 13, 22, 28, 44, 59, *118*
Homestead (Amherst), *134–135*, 139, 141–143, *143*, *144*
Hosmer, Joseph, 56, 90
Houghton Library (Harvard), 49
Houghton Mifflin, 28
House of the Seven Gables (Salem), 118, *119*
House of the Seven Gables, The (Hawthorne), 70, 118
Howard, John, 50
Hudson River School, 10
"Hymn of Humanity" (Higginson), *126*

Ice King. *See* Tudor, Frederic
Idealists, 4
  See also Transcendentalism
Immigrant Heritage Trail (Boston), 33
industrial revolution, 9
Ingersoll, Susannah, 118
Ives, Charles, 61

Jackson, Helen Hunt, *138*
Jackson, Lidian, 64, 97
Johnson, Dr. Samuel, 49

Kansas-Nebraska Act, 31
Kant, Immanuel, 3, 4
Keats, John, 16
Keller, Helen, *49*
Kesselring, Marion, *108*

Lane, Charles, 9, 36, 122, 131–133, *132*
Larned, Samuel, 131–132
"Latest Form of Infidelity Examined, The" (Ripley), 46
Lathrop, Harriet, 72
Lenox, 118
Letters from New York (Child), 140
Lexington, 56, 58
Liberator, The, 30
Liberty Pole, 56
"Likeness to God" (Channing), 4, 16
Lincoln Memorial, 50
literacy, 11
Literary Trail (Boston), *22*
Little Men (L. M. Alcott), 71
Little Women (L. M. Alcott), 27, 69, 71, 72
Locke, John, 4
Longfellow, Henry Wadsworth, 28, 33, 50, 117, 141
Lowell, Amy, 23, 33
Lowell, James Russell, 28
Lyceum Bar & Grill (Salem), *118*
lyceum movement, 8, 9, 60
Lyceum (Salem), *118*
Lyrical Ballads (Wordsworth and Coleridge), 16

Mack, David, 139, *143*
Make Way for Ducklings (McCloskey), 33
Mann, Horace, 61, *118*
Mann, Mary Peabody, 61
Manning, Mary, 107
Manning, William, *108*
maps
  Amherst, *137*
  Boston, *13*, *15*
  Brook Farm, *122*, *125*
  Cambridge, *40*
  Concord, *55*

Fruitlands, *122*
Salem, *104*, *105*
Walden Pond, *84*, 88
West Roxbury, *122*, *125*
Margaret Fuller Cottage (Brook Farm), 125, 129
Martin Luther House (West Roxbury), 129
Masonic Temple (Boston), 28–30, 32
Materialists, 4
Melville, Herman, 118
Merrimack River, 53
Metcalf, Keyes, 49
Millennium Park (West Roxbury), 130
Miller, Arthur, 104
"Minister's Black Veil, The" (Hawthorne), 111
Minute Man National Historic Park, *57*, 72
minute man statue (Concord), 50, *57*
minute men, 56
Moore, Marianne, 23
Morton, Ichabod, 125
Mosses from an Old Manse (Hawthorne), 54, 62, 64, 70
Mount Auburn Cemetery (Cambridge), 51
Mount Holyoke, *10*, 142
Mount Holyoke College, 139, *140*
Mount Katahdin, 96
Mount Monadnock, 54
Muir, John, *100*
"Musketaquid" (Emerson), 54
Musketaquid people, 55

Native Americans, Transcendentalists and, 26, 60, 95
"Natural History of Massachusetts, A" (Thoreau), 23
nature, in Transcendentalism, 4–5, 9, 63–64, 65, 88–90, 96, 110, 118
Nature (Emerson), 4–5, 42, 60, 63–64, 121
Nearing, Helen and Scott, 99
Nest, the (Brook Farm), 125
New England
as geographic center of Transcendentalism, 7–9
manufacturing in, 9
Unitarianism in, 4, 9
New England Anti-Slavery Society, 30
"New School in Literature and Religion, The" (Norton), 45–46
"new times," 3–4
New York, 9
New York Tribune, 26, 123
Newcomb, Charles, 67
Norton, Andrews, 18, 123
at Harvard, 41–42, 45–46
writings, 45–46

Old Burying Point, 112
Old Corner Bookstore (Boston), 27–28
Old Corner Bookstore (Salem), *118*
Old Manse, 25, *52–53*, 54, 58, 61, 62–66, 115
Old North Bridge (Concord), 56, *57*, 58
Old Sturbridge Village, 65
"On Visiting the Graves of Hawthorne and Thoreau" (Very), 76
Orchard House (Concord), 62, 72–73
"Orphic Sayings" (B. Alcott), *23*
Orvis, John, 127
Osgood, Charles, *110*
Ossoli, Marquis, 36
O'Sullivan, John, *110*
Oversoul, concept of, 4, 30, *132*

Park Street Church (Boston), 30
Parker House (Boston), *22*
Parker, Theodore, 6, 7, 11, 18–20, 30, 31
"Discourses on the Transient and Permanent in Christianity" (1841), 18–19
European travel, 36
ties to Harvard, 41, 42
work on the *Dial*, 23
writings, 46
Partisans, The (Pitynski), *33*
Patriots' Day, 58

Peabody, Elizabeth Palmer, 6, 7, 8, 64
  Aesthetic Papers published by, 26–27
  "conversations" held by, 25, 26
  gravesite, 75
  Hawthorne and, 111
  images, *19*, *74*
  kindergarten founded by, 26, 29, 37, 61
  relationship with Channing, 17
  in Transcendental Club, 21
  Very and, 113–114
  work on the *Dial*, 23, 26
  writings, 5, 20, *29*
Peabody Essex Museum (Salem), *108*, 119
Peabody home (Salem), 111–112
Peabody, Sophia, 24–25, 64, 111–112, 118
Peabody's bookstore (Boston), 24–27, 136
Phalanstery (Brook Farm), 127–129
phalanx, 123, *124*, 127, 131
Phi Beta Kappa Society, 42, 60, 121
Philosophical Library (Salem), *108*
Pierce, Franklin, 70
Pilgrim House (Brook Farm), 125
Pinckney Street (Boston), 37
Pioneer Valley, *10*, 142
Plato, 73
"Plea for Captain John Brown, A" (Thoreau), 31
Plummer, Caroline, *108*
Plummer Hall (Salem), *108*
Plummer, John, 129
Polk, James, 117
Pound, Ezra, 23
Pratt, Bela Lyon, *105*
Pratt, Maria, 124
Pratt, Minot, 124
Prescott, Dr. Samuel, 56
Public Garden (Boston), 33, 50
Purchase Street Church (Boston), 17, 123
Putnam, George, 41
Putnam's Monthly, *97*

Quincy, 9
Quincy, Josiah Sr., 42
Quincy Market (Boston), 35, *37*
Quoil, Hugh, 90

Radcliffe College, 49, 50
Rationalism, 4
Records of a School (Peabody), *29*, 30
"Resistance to Civil Government" (Thoreau), 27, 94
Revere, Paul, 14, 56
"Rhyme of the Ancient Mariner, The" (Coleridge), 16
Ripley, Ezra, 58, 62–63, *78*
Ripley, George, 6, 7, 25, 64, 67
  as editor of the *Harbinger*, 125, *126*
  founding of Brook Farm, 9, 121–122, 123–124, 129
  founding of Transcendental Club, 18, 21, 123
  Harvard ties, 41, 42, 46
  images, *123*
  as minister of Purchase Street Church, 17–18
  at *New York Tribune*, 130
  work on the *Dial*, 23, 24, 123
  writings, 123–124
  See also Brook Farm Institute of Agriculture and Education
Ripley, Marianne, 124, 126
Ripley, Samuel, 25, 66
Ripley, Sophia, 121, 124, 126
Robert Frost Trail, *138*
"Roger Malvin's Burial" (Hawthorne), 111
Romantic movement, 16, 36
Roosevelt, Theodore, 49
Root, Abiah, 139
Rousseau, Jean-Jacques, 4
Russell and Russell, publishers, 23

Safdie, Moshe, 119
Salem, 7, 8, 9, 13, *102–103*
  decline, 105
  early history, 103

Hawthorne in, 105–111, 115–117
locales
Athenaeum (337 Essex Street), *108*
Custom House (174 Derby Street), 114, 115, 116–117
Grimshaw House (53 Charter Street), 111–112
Hawthorne home (10½ Herbert Street), 106, 107, 115
Hawthorne home (14 Mall Street), 115
Hawthorne home (18 Chestnut Street), 115
Hawthorne home (27 Union Street), 105–106, *106*
House of the Seven Gables (54 Turner Street), 118, *119*
Lyceum (43 Church Street), 113, *118*
Old Burying Point, 112
Peabody Essex Museum, *108*, 119
maps, *104*, *105*
Very in, 113–115
witch trials, 104
Salem Gazette, 107
Salisbury, Charles, 127
Sanborn, Franklin, 6, *7*, 29, 31, 41
at Concord School of Philosophy, 73
homes of, 53
preparatory school opened by, 61, 79
Sandburg, Carl, 23
Saturday Club, 22
Scarlet Letter, The (Hawthorne), 1–4, 8, 66, 70, 105, 110, 112, 115, 117–118, *117*
School for Human Culture. *See* Temple School
Seaman's Bethel (Boston), 5
Sears, Clare Endicott, *131*, 133
Second Massachusetts Regiment, 129
Shelley, Percy Bysshe, 16
Sherwood, Mary, 99
Sidney, Margaret (pseud.). *See* Lathrop, Harriet
Silsbee, Mary, *110*
Sims, Thomas, 31
slavery, abolition sentiment in New England, 11
"Slavery in Massachusetts" (Thoreau), 31
Sleepy Hollow Cemetery (Concord), 51, 68, 74–77
Social Destiny of Man, The (Fourier, tr. Brisbane), 123
Social Library (Salem), *108*
Society for the Collegiate Instruction of Women (Harvard), 49
Southey, Robert, 16
Spectator, 107
Springfield Republican, 144
Staël, Madame de, 4
Staples, Sam, 94
Stearns, Sarah, 124
Still River, 133
Stowe, Harriet Beecher, 144
Sudbury River, 53

Taylor, Edward Thompson, 5
Taylor, Zachary, 117
Temple School (Boston), 25, 29–30, 32
Thayer, Scofield, 23
theology, Transcendentalists' effect on, 16
Thoreau, Cynthia, 64
Thoreau, Henry David, 5, *6*, *7*, 21, 27, 51, 54, 61, 122
accidental fire started by, 93
antislavery activities, 31, 90, 92
correspondence of, 79
desire to be a writer, 82
Emerson as mentor, 83
garden of, 65
gravesite, 75, *76*
as Harvard alumnus, 40
homes of, 35, 37, 53, *152*
images, 83, 94
as influence on progressive thinkers, 94
jailed for not paying taxes, 93–94
on lakes, 88
on lyceum circuit, 8, *118*
Native Americans and, 95, 96

relationship with Concord, 92–94
rock cairn dedicated to, *100*
self-reliance of, 121
as surveyor, *75*
travel by, 96, *97*
views on humanity, 83
Walden Pond stay, 82, 83–94, 96
pond survey, 87–88
visitors, 90, 92
work on the *Dial*, 23, 24
writings, 81, 94, *97*
See also Walden; or, Life in the Woods
Thoreau Institute at Walden Woods, 99, *100*
Thoreau Society, 99
"Thoreau's Flute" (L. M. Alcott), 95
Ticknor and Fields, 26, *27*, 28
Ticknor, Carolyn, 28
Ticknor, William, 28
Todd, Mabel Loomis, 136
Transcendental Club, 7, 18, 21, 24, 25, 26, 42, 51, 59, 121, 123, 136
"Transcendental Wild Oats" (L. M. Alcott), 132, *132*
Transcendentalism, 3–4
abolitionist movement and, 30–31
Boston as home of, 14–15
defined, 4–7
educational reforms, 29–30
effect of on theology, 16
geography of, 7–9
historical context, 9–11
influence of Unitarianism on, 16–20, 21, 39, 121
meeting places, 20–32
nature in, 4–5, 9, 65
original relation to the universe in, 4–5
Romanticism's influence on, 36
self-reliance and, 121
symposiums, 21
tenets of, 110
travel abroad, 36
women's involvement in, 26
Trustees of Reservations, 66
Tucker, Ellen (Mrs. Ralph Waldo Emerson), 59
Tudor, Frederic, *91*
Twenty-eighth Congregational Society, 20
Twice-Told Tales (Hawthorne), 70, 105, 111

Underground Railroad, 11, 31
Unitarian Second Church (Boston), 20, 59, *150*
Unitarian Universalist church, 21
Unitarianism, 4, 7, 9, 16–20, 21, 121, 144
Upham, Rev. Charles Wentworth, 114
USS *Friendship*, 119
utopian communities, 121–123, 133
Brook Farm, 5, 7, 18, 23, 24, 25, 64, 118, 121–122, 123–130, *123*
Fruitlands, 122, 131–133

Very, Jones, 6, 7, 8, 21, 41, 76, *118*
at Harvard, 113
images, *113*
mental illness, 113–114
writings, 113, *115*
Virzi, Michael J., *146*

Walden; or, Life in the Woods (Thoreau), 8, 61, 82, 83, 84, 85–86, 87–90, 92–94, 97
inconsistencies in, 92–94
Walden Grove, 97–98
Walden House, 84, 85–86
Walden Pond, 5, 7, 8, *11*, 61, 79, 81–82
images, *80–81*, *83*, *85*, *87*, *89*, *98*, *101*
later history, 97–98
locales
house replica, 86
Main Beach, 98
Thoreau Institute (44 Baker Farm Road), 99, *100*
Walden Grove, 97–98
Walden House, 84, 85–86

Walden Pond State Reservation (915 Walden Street), 99
map, 85, 88
water source, 86–88
woods surrounding, 88–90
Walden Pond State Reservation, 99
Walden Woods, 100
Walden Woods Project, 99, 101
Ware, Henry Jr., 113
Ware, Henry Sr., 16, 41
Wayside (Concord), 54, *57*, 61, 69, 70–72
See also Hillside (Concord)
Webster, Daniel, *118*
Webster, Noah, *138*
Weeks, Jordan, and Company, publishers, *23*
West Cemetery (Amherst), 140–141, *141*
West Roxbury, 9, 18, 121, 131
Brook Farm (679 Baker Street), *122*, 123–130
Gardner Street Landfill, 130
Gethsemane Jewish Cemetery, 130
map, 122, *125*
Millennium Park, 130
West Street Grille (Boston), 26
White, Zilpha, 90
Whitman, Walt, 7, 33
in Concord, 61
conversation with Emerson, 32–33
image, *151*
Thoreau's cairn, *100*
Whitmore, Charles, 124
Whitney, Samuel, 56
Willard, Simon, 55
Wineapple, Brenda, *110*
Winthrop, John, 14, 122
witch attractions (Salem), 119
Woman in the Nineteenth Century (Fuller), 26
women
discussion groups for, 25
at Harvard, 49
involvement in Transcendentalist movement, 26
Transcendentalist views on, 60
Wordsworth, William, 16, 36
Wyeth, Nathaniel, *91*
Wyman Farm (Harvard, MA), 131

Yale University, 144
Yeats, William Butler, 23
Yesterdays with Authors (Fields), *117*
"Young Goodman Brown" (Hawthorne), 110

Credits

The cover image, Josiah Wolcott's *Brook Farm* (1844), is courtesy of the Massachusetts Historical Society.

Images on pages 2, 3, 8, 19 (portrait of Elizabeth Palmer Peabody), 23, 24 (foreign library advertisement), 46, 50 (French's bust of Emerson), 55, 60, 62, 63, 68, 70, 71 (Louisa May Alcott), 73 (Bronson Alcott), 74, 82, 83 (daguerreotype), 88, 89, 92, 96, 98, 126, 149 (Emerson), and back cover (Emerson) are courtesy Concord Free Public Library.

Image on page 10, James Hamilton's *Scene on the Hudson (Rip van Winkle)* (1845), is courtesy Smithsonian American Art Museum, Washington, DC/Art Resource, NY.

Images on pages 12, 17, 22, 27 (Ticknor and Fields), 29 (Masonic Temple), 32, 34, and 37 are courtesy of the Bostonian Society/Old State House. Image on page 91 (ice harvesting) is courtesy of the Bostonian Society/Old State House: Arthur Hansen Photograph Collection.

Image on page 18 is courtesy Chris Wiener.

Image on page 29 (record of Temple School) is courtesy University of Michigan, Making of America.

Image on page 31 (John Brown), John Steuart Curry's *The Tragic Prelude* (1932), is a mural in the Kansas State Capitol.

Image on page 36, Robert Salmon's *Boston Harbor as Seen from Constitution Wharf*, is courtesy the U.S. Naval Academy Museum.

Image on page 38, George G. Smith, after Eliza S. Quincy, *Harvard University with the Procession of the Alumni from the Church to the Pavilion* (engraving,

1840), is courtesy the I. N. Phelps Stokes Collection, Miriam and Ira D. Wallach Division of Art, Prints and Photographs, The New York Public Library, Astor, Lenox and Tilden Foundations.

Image on page 41 is from the Harvard Club of New Mexico website.

Image on page 50 (Longfellow house) is courtesy Alexey Sergeev.

Image on page 56, Alonzo Chappel's *Battle of Concord*, is courtesy Line of Battle and Naval Heritage Museum.

Image on page 57 (statue) is courtesy http://philip.greenspun.com.

Image on page 75 is courtesy the Henry W. and Albert B. Berg Collection of English and American Literature, The New York Public Library, Astor, Lenox and Tilden Foundations.

Image on page 91 (Frederic Tudor) is from the Library of Congress, LC-USZ62-64264.

Images on pages 102, 106 (postcard), 107, 108 (library card), 110, and 117 are courtesy Peabody Essex Museum.

Image on page 106 (house being moved) is courtesy the House of the Seven Gables.

Image on page 114 is from Gleason's Pictorial Drawing-Room Companion, Vol. IV, No. 20—Whole No. 98, Boston, Saturday, May 14, 1853, used courtesy of McLean Hopsital/Harvard University.

Images on pages 120, 131, and back cover (Fruitlands) are used courtesy Fruitlands Museum.

Image on page 125 (map) is from Donald Mitchell's *American Lands and Letters* (New York: Scribner's, 1904).

Image on page 125 (the Hive) is from Mary Caroline Crawford's *Romance of Old New England Rooftrees* (Boston: L. C. Page & Co., 1902).

Image on page 136 and back cover (portrait of Emily Dickinson) is by and used courtesy of Guillermo Cuellar.

Image on page 138 is courtesy Yan Mei.

Images on pages 139, 144 (Amherst College Fields), and 147 are courtesy Jones Library Collection.

Image on page 145 is courtesy Marta McDowell.

Image on page 175 is courtesy Betsy Archer.

All other images are in the author's collection or in the public domain.

About the Author

R. Todd Felton is a writer and photographer based in Amherst, Massachusetts. The breadth of his interests and accomplishments would do justice to a Transcendentalist. He is a former English department chair and the founding director of a writing center. He has directed plays and appeared on stage for the Hampshire Shakespeare Company. His articles have appeared in the *Massachusetts Sierran*, the *Wesleyan*, and *WMA Responds*, while his poetry has been published in *Our Turn*. He has contributed commentary to the local NPR affiliate and covered Major League Soccer for www.realtfs.com. He is also the author of two other books in the ArtPlace series, one focusing on the Irish literary revival, the other on Britain's Romantic poets and Lake District. His prize-winning photographs have appeared in a number of exhibitions and publications. Todd lives in Amherst with his wife and two young sons.

About the ArtPlace Series

This book is part of the ArtPlace series published by Roaring Forties Press. The series explores how renowned artists, writers, and thinkers and world-famous cities and regions helped to define and inspire each other. ArtPlace volumes are intended to stimulate both eye and mind, offering a rich mix of art and photography, history and biography, ideas and information. While the books can be used by tourists to navigate and illuminate their way through cityscapes and landscapes, the volumes can also be read by armchair travelers in search of an engrossing and revealing story.

Other titles include *A Journey into Dorothy Parker's New York*, *A Journey into Steinbeck's California*, *A Journey into Georgia O'Keeffe's New Mexico*, *A Journey into Flaubert's Normandy*, *A Journey into Lichtenstein's New York*, *A Journey into Matisse's South of France*, and *A Journey into Ireland's Literary Revival*.

Visit Roaring Forties Press's website, www.roaringfortiespress.com, for details of these and other forthcoming titles, as well as to learn about upcoming author tours, readings, media appearances, and all kinds of special events and offers. Visitors to the website may also send comments and questions to the authors of the ArtPlace series books.

A Journey into the Transcendentalists' New England

This book is set in Goudy and Futura; the display type is Futura Condensed. The interior and cover of the book were designed by Jeff Urbancic, who also made up the pages. Sherri Schultz and Nigel Quinney edited the text, which was proofread by Karen Mead and indexed by Sonsie Conroy.

A Journey into the

Transcendentalists' New England

From picturesque towns around the bustling city of Boston, Henry David Thoreau, Ralph Waldo Emerson, Emily Dickinson, and the other Transcendentalists revolutionized American ideas about the artistic, spiritual, and natural worlds. This fascinating and beautiful volume examines the intertwined lives of these remarkable men and women and explores the places that inspired them. Lavishly illustrated with photos, paintings, and maps, the book vividly recaptures 19th-century New England while discovering the Transcendentalists' enduring legacy in Walden, Cambridge, Concord, Salem, Amherst, and Boston.

R. Todd Felton is a professional writer and prize-winning photographer based in Amherst, Massachusetts.

With a foreword by Jeffrey S. Cramer.

ARTPLACE SERIES

ROARING FORTIES PRESS

$19.95 U.S. / $26.95
ISBN 09766

www.roaringfortiesp